THE EAST
COAST
See pp76–

0 kilometres   20

0 miles

CENTRAL
SARDINIA AND
BARBAGIA

THE
EASTERN
COAST

THE
WESTERN
COAST

Oristano

Cagliari

CAGLIARI
AND THE
SOUTH

Isola di
Mal di Ventre

Isola
San Pietro

Isola di
Sant'Antioco

CAGLIARI AND
THE SOUTH
See pp50–75

EYEWITNESS TRAVEL GUIDES

SARDINIA

Main contributor: FABRIZIO ARDITO

LONDON, NEW YORK,
MELBOURNE, MUNICH AND DELHI
www.dk.com

Produced by Fabio Ratti
Editoria Libraria e Multimediale, Milano, Italy

PROJECT EDITOR Diana Georgiacodis
EDITORS Anna Lia Deffenu, Giovanni Francesio,
Renata Perego, Laura Recordati
DESIGNERS Paolo Gonzato, Stefania Testa, Studio Matra
MAPS Paul Stafford
PICTURE RESEARCH Fabio De Angelis, Riccardo Villarosa

Dorling Kindersley Ltd
PROJECT EDITOR Fiona Wild
EDITOR Francesca Machiavelli
DTP Cooling Brown
DTP DESIGNER Ingrid Vienings

MAIN CONTRIBUTOR Fabrizio Ardito
ADDITIONAL CONTRIBUTORS Patrizia Giovannetti, Raffaella Rizzo

ILLUSTRATORS Giorgia Boli, Alberto Ipsilanti,
Daniela Veluti, Nadia Viganò

ENGLISH TRANSLATION Richard Pierce

Reproduced by FGV (Milano), Lineatre Service (Milano)
Printed and bound by Mondadori (Italy)

First published in Great Britain in 1998
by Dorling Kindersley Ltd, 80 Strand, London WC2R 0RL
Reprinted with revisions 2000, 2001, 2002, 2003

Copyright 1998, 2003 © Dorling Kindersley Limited, London
A Penguin Company

A CIP CATALOGUE RECORD IS AVAILABLE FROM THE BRITISH LIBRARY.

ISBN 0 7513 4814 7

FLOORS ARE REFERRED TO THROUGHOUT IN ACCORDANCE WITH BRITISH
USAGE; IE THE "FIRST FLOOR" IS THE FLOOR ABOVE GROUND LEVEL.

**The information in this
Dorling Kindersley Travel Guide is checked regularly.**
Every effort has been made to ensure that this book is as up-to-date
as possible at the time of going to press. Some details, however,
such as telephone numbers, opening hours, prices, gallery hanging
arrangements and travel information are liable to change. The
publishers cannot accept responsibility for any consequences
arising from the use of this book, nor for any material on third party
websites, and cannot guarantee that any website address in this
book will be a suitable source of travel information. We value the
views and suggestions of our readers very highly. Please write to:
Publisher, DK Eyewitness Travel Guides,
Dorling Kindersley, 80 Strand, London WC2R 0RL, Great Britain.

◁ **The promontory of Castelsardo on the northern coast**

CONTENTS

**Sheep grazing in pastures filled
with spring flowers**

INTRODUCING
SARDINIA

**A prehistoric tower of the Santu
Antine nuraghe at Torralba**

The beach at Stintino on the tip of the northwestern coast

Flamingoes wintering in the ponds and marshes of Sardinia

Knight on horseback during the Sa Sartiglia festival at Oristano

A bird's-eye view of the city of Alghero

How to Use this Guide

This guide helps you get the most from your visit to Sardinia, providing expert recommendations as well as detailed practical information. *Introducing Sardinia* sets the island in its geographical, historical and cultural context. The five area chapters in *Sardinia Area by Area* describe the main sights and monuments in detail, with maps, pictures and illustrations. *Travellers' Needs* offers recommendations on hotels, restaurants and bars, as well as features on what to eat, drink and where to shop. The *Survival Guide* contains practical information on everything from transport to safety.

Sardinia Area by Area

Sardinia has been divided into five main sightseeing areas, each coded with a coloured thumb tab for quick reference. A map illustrating how the island has been divided can be found on the inside front cover of this guide. The sights covered within the individual areas have been plotted and numbered on a *Pictorial Map*.

Each area can be identified quickly by its colour coding.

1 Introduction
The landscape, history and character of each region is described here, showing how the area has developed over the centuries and what it has to offer visitors today.

A locator map shows the region in relation to the other areas of Sardinia.

2 Pictorial Map
This gives an illustrated overview of the whole area. All the sights covered in the chapter are numbered and there are useful tips on getting around by car and public transport.

Features and story boxes highlight special or unique aspects of an area or sight.

3 Detailed Information
All the important towns and other places of interest are described individually. They are listed in order, following the numbering on the Pictorial Map. Within each entry there are details on the important buildings and other major sights.

4 Major Towns
All the important towns are described individually. Within each entry there is further detailed information on important buildings and other sites. The Town Map shows the location of the main sights.

A Visitors' Checklist gives you the practical details to plan your visit, including transport information, the address of the tourist office, market days and festivals.

The Town Map shows all major and minor roads. The key sights are plotted, along with train and bus stations, parking areas, churches and tourist information offices.

5 Street-by-Street Map
Towns or districts of special interest to the visitor are given a bird's-eye view in detailed 3D with photographs and descriptions of the most important sights.

A suggested route for a walk covers the most interesting streets in the area.

Opening hours, telephone number and transport details for the sight are given in the Visitors' Checklist.

6 The Top Sights
These are given two or more pages. Historic buildings are dissected to reveal their interiors, while the photographs highlight the most interesting features.

Stars indicate sights that visitors should not miss.

INTRODUCING
SARDINIA

Putting Sardinia on the Map

SARDINIA LIES WEST of mainland Italy, surrounded by the Mediterranean Sea. Flanked by the Tyrrhenian Sea to the east and by the Sardinian Sea to the west, to the north it is separated from Corsica by the Straits of Bonifacio. A population of 1,700,000 lives in an area of 24,000 sq km (9,300 sq miles) divided into the provinces of Cagliari, Nuoro, Oristano and Sassari.

SWITZERLAND

Bolzano

Lago di Como

Tre

Lago di Garda

Bergamo

Brescia

Vice.

Milan

Mantova

Vero

Turin

Po

Parma

Fer

Valence

Genoa

Bologn

La Spezia

Lucca

Nice

FLORENCE

San Remo

Pisa

MONACO

Livorno

Siena

Marseille

Piombino

Bastia

Elba

Ligurian Sea

CORSICA

Ajaccio

Tyrrhen

Sea

EUROPE

NORWAY   FINLAND

SWEDEN   ESTONIA

FED. RUSS.

DENMARK   LATVIA

LITHUANIA

REP OF IRELAND   UNITED KINGDOM   NETHERLANDS

BELORUSSIA

BELGIUM   GERMANY   POLAND

LUXEMBOURG   CZECH REP.   UKRAINE

FRANCE   SLOVAKIA

SWITZERLAND   AUSTRIA   HUNGARY

ITALY   ROMANIA

PORTUGAL   SPAIN   Rome   BULGARIA

ALBANIA   GREECE

Cagliari

ALGERIA   TUNISIA

Porto Torres   Olbia

Sassari

Nuoro

S A R D I N I A

Oristano

Cagliari

See inside back cover

M E D I T E R R A N E A

| 0 kilometres | 125 |
| 0 miles | 125 |

TUNISIA   TUNIS

The imposing castle at Castelsardo in northern Sardinia

AUSTRIA
Graz
Klagenfurt
Cortina d'Ampezzo
Villach
Dráva
Belluno
Udine
SLOVENIA
Gorizia
LJUBLJANA
Treviso
Trieste
VENICE
Rijeka
Krk
Pula
Cres
Rab
Lošinj
Pag
Ravenna
Rimini
Pèsaro
Dugi Otok
Zadar
SAN MARINO
Kornat
Ancona
Zirje
Gubbio
Perugia
Ascoli Piceno
Korcula
Peljesac
Niksic
Orvieto
Lastovo
Mljet
Dubrovnik
Viterbo
Pescara
itavecchia
L'Aquila
Isole Tremiti
ROME
Sulmona
Anzio
Foggia
Bari
Benevento
Greece Turkey Egypt
Naples
Pompei
Greece
Isola d'Ischia
Amalfi
Brindisi
Isola di Capri
Agri
Lecce
Taranto
I o n i a n
Cosenza
S e a
Catanzaro
Isole Eólie or Lípari
KEY
Trapani
Palermo
Reggio di Calabria
SICILY
Catania
Siracusa
Malta
Isola di Pantelleria

A d r i a t i c   S e a

Satellite view over Northern Italy and Sardinia

KEY

☐	Area covered by this guide
⚓	Ferry port
✈	Airport
═	Motorway
▬	Major road
- -	Ferry routes
-·-	International boundaries

A PORTRAIT OF SARDINIA

THE VERY ISOLATION OF THIS LARGE ISLAND *set in the middle of the Mediterranean has shaped its unique character. For thousands of years Sardinia has stood on the sidelines of mainstream Mediterranean historical events, remaining a singular world to itself. Even the Romans found it a difficult place to subdue.*

The experience of invasion from across the water over the centuries has left a legacy which is still evident today. The roads tend to follow valleys inland rather than tracing a scenic path along the beautiful coastline. There are yachting marinas and harbours, but fishing is not a mainstay of the economy and, even in peacetime, Sardinia has never really become a seafaring nation. Over the years Sardinia's shores have seen the arrival of Phoenicians, Romans, Genoans battling for supremacy with Pisans and Arabs, the Spanish, and finally the House of Savoy. The different cultures have all contributed to the art, architecture and cultural life of Sardinia and evidence is scattered throughout the island: prehistoric

Detail of a mural at Orgosolo

dwellings and fortresses from the earliest known inhabitants, ancient rock-cut tombs, and Romanesque churches which resemble those of Pisa or Lucca. Introduced artistic styles were often taken up and developed with distinctive Sardinian character – the altar paintings in the Spanish *retablo* tradition, for instance. In 1848 this untamed island became part of the newly created nation of Italy.

The 20th century brought with it dreams of industrialization and new-found prosperity, as well as the beginnings of a tourist industry.

However, the Sardinia that brings the visitors is a land of white beaches and deep blue sea, which does not really represent the essence of the place. The coastline is certainly beautiful, apart from some stretches

The stately procession of Sant'Efisio passing through Pula

◁ The rugged cliffs of Punta Cristallo

where random building has spoilt the views. But the interior is stunningly beautiful too, and deserves further exploration. The natural scenery is extremely varied, providing totally different environments and habitats for plants, animals and birds. In some areas there are fertile alluvial plains, in others steep mountains of granite and limestone where panoramas change from horizontal to vertical in the space of a few kilometres.

PEOPLE, LANGUAGE AND MUSIC

Human settlements have existed in the interior for thousands of years, and Sardinia is studded with the traces of ancient pastoral civilizations, further proof that the people have always tended to prefer to live in the comparative safety of the mountainous interior rather than along the coasts. The passing of the seasons is still marked by the stages in the agricultural year, and by celebrations of successful harvests. Ancient traditions – now deeply rooted in Catholicism

Hand loom at the Museo Etnografico in Nuoro

Fishermen at work on Isola Rossa

but showing traces of far older religions – are manifested in numerous festivals, which are often based on the very close relationship between the people of the island and their natural environment.

A number of very different dialects can be heard in the interior of the island, and the Sardinian language still has a clear Latin base – the word *domus* is used to mean a house, for instance, instead of the Italian *casa*. Years of Spanish rule mean that in Alghero, on the west coast, you can still hear Catalan spoken on the streets, and, on the island of Sant'Antioco in the southwest, the traditions and the cooking reflect a Ligurian heritage.

Music features strongly in Sardinian life, at feast days and weddings and even everyday events, especially in the interior, are always celebrated with music. Musicologists and musicians – such as Peter Gabriel, who recorded the music of the Tenores de Bitti group in his world music series – have described traditional Sardinian music as unique in Europe. Today it is undergoing something of a revival. There is a great deal of vocal and instrumental variety; based on the sound of the *launeddas*, a cane wind instrument, and polyphonic music for

Decanting ewes' milk after the morning milking

four voices. The most well-known exponents of the art are the Canto a Tenores, who perform regularly to growing numbers.

ECONOMIC DEVELOPMENT

In an uneasy position between the past and the future, the economy of Sardinia is complex. Agriculture and shepherding used to be the key factors in the economy, and there was also a mining boom in certain areas after unification, particularly around Sulcis, an abundant source of both coal and metals. But the Sardinian mining industry declined, especially after World War II, and is unlikely to recover. Other schemes for promoting industry have badly affected the environment, and have been abandoned. However, attempts in the 1950s to eradicate malaria, by treating marshy areas with pesticides, produced impressive results: in a short space of time the coast became habitable.

TOURISM IN SARDINIA TODAY

Interest in creating the facilities needed for tourism in Sardinia was initially subdued, and services were slow to take off. The gradual development of

Traditional bread from the Sulcis region

tourism has, however, made the island famous, opening up Sardinia to the outside world, as well as increasing awareness of its history, local culture, arts and handicrafts.

The island's varied wildlife was perhaps bound to be affected by increasing numbers of visitors, and wildlife and marine reserves have now been established to protect unique habitats and their flora and fauna. The vast, wild Gennargentu range is also now a protected National Park. In recent years, the rare monk seal, thought to be extinct, has been sighted once again off the western coast, an indication that it is possible for tourism and ecology to co-exist in comfort. Sardinia possesses some of the most unspoilt scenery in Europe which, like its other special qualities, can only be fully appreciated by visiting the island.

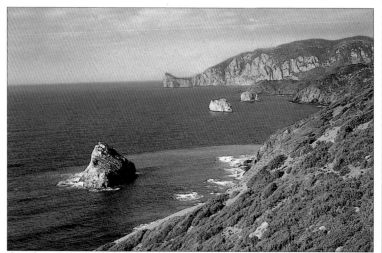

The stacks on the Masua and Nebida coastlines

Marine Life of Sardinia

Prawn

THE WATERS around Sardinia are considered to be the cleanest in Italy and are rich in flora and fauna. The generally healthy sea beds are havens for both scuba divers and naturalists. The sheer cliffs along the coast are home to dozens of species of nesting birds and birds of prey. Years of marine research in the Golfo di Orosei, on the eastern coast, have finally confirmed the return of the fabled monk seal, once so widespread in the area that caves and inlets were named after it. Dolphins and other large sea mammals, such as small whales, can occasionally be seen in the northwestern waters and the Straits of Bonifacio. In recent years the area has been declared an international marine reserve.

Neptune grass (Posidonia oceanica) *is a sea plant with shaggy leaves that grows down to a depth of 30–35 m (100–115 ft). Sea grass, as it is also known, has flowers, which is unusual for a marine plant.*

Rocks of volcanic origin

The striped sarago, *quite a common fish in the Mediterranean, combs the sea bed in search of prey.*

Rocks are covered with seaweed such as *Cystoseira.*

Sardinian coral *can be various shades of red or white and lives on the rocky sea bed, between 15–100 m (50–330ft) below sea level.*

The lobster *is a crustacean that lives mostly along the rocky shores, but can also be found at depths of up to 100 m (328 ft). The meat is a local delicacy.*

The sea anemone *attaches itself to rocks in shallow water. Its deceptively delicate tentacles contain stinging cells, enabling it to capture small fish and crustaceans.*

Gorgonian coral *survives because the water is so clean. The flexible branches may be white, yellow or red, and can grow to be 1m (3 ft) tall.*

BIRDS OF THE COASTLINE

The cliffs along the Sardinian coastline provide an ideal habitat for birds. Wild pigeons build safe nests here and raise their young without being disturbed. Herring gulls, Audouin's gulls and cormorants perch on the rocks between bouts of fishing. Further up the cliff edge, birds of prey such as the peregrine falcon, the red kite and the rare griffon vulture, build their nests.

Cormorants on the cliff ledges

Audouin's gull

Herring gull

Peregrine falcon

Red kite

UNDERWATER MEDITERRANEAN

The Mediterranean Sea has a rich and varied ecosystem, sustained by warm currents and clean waters. There is coral and myriad species of seaweed, a wide variety of fish, crustaceans and molluscs and marvellous rock formations for snorkellers and scuba divers to enjoy.

Cracks and crevices in the rocks make an ideal habitat for the moray eel.

Fronds

Brown meagres move in schools to defend themselves from predators by day. At night they hunt molluscs, small fish and prawns.

Dolphins are frequently seen riding the waves at the bow of a boat in the warm waters around Sardinia, particularly in the clear seas around Maddalena along the northern shore.

The moray eel has powerful teeth and poisonous mucus. It also has an excellent ability to camouflage itself, making it one of the most dangerous creatures in the Mediterranean Sea.

Monk seals, once thought to be extinct, have returned to the Golfo di Orosei where they live in grottoes and solitary caves.

The Sardinian Coastline

Grains of quartz on Is Arutas

WASHED BY THE CLEAR blue waters of the Mediterranean, Sardinia offers a varied coastline of sculpted cliffs and coves. Secluded inlets alternate with golden sand dunes, where wild lilies and cistus bloom, or rugged cliffs that plummet into the sea. The most well-known resort is the world-famous Costa Smeralda where visitors come to enjoy luxury villas and pretty, sandy beaches. Other popular areas are the coast south of Olbia, including the sheltered Cala Gonone, and the southeastern tip of the island, near Villasimius (easily accessible from Cagliari). Several stretches of coastline have remained untouched, such as the isolated coves between Orosei and Arbatax, and the southwestern area between Baia Chia and Oristano.

At Capo Caccia, sheer limestone cliffs, 168 m (551 ft) high, jut out from the sea

Between Bosa and Alghero *the spectacular coastline is punctuated by cliffs of volcanic origin, covered with mastic trees.*

Around Piscinas *the coast is known for its impressive wind-carved sand dunes. The sand is an ideal habitat for juniper and tamarisk.*

The cliffs on the island of San Pietro, *eroded by sea and wind, are of pink and grey trachyte. Crevices and ledges offer useful shelter to rare birds like Eleonora's falcon.*

Isola dell'Asinara

GOLFO DELL'ASINARA

Porto Torres

THE NORTH
THE COST
SMERALD

Alghero

MAR DI SARDEGNA

THE WESTERN COAST

⑤ Bosa Marina

④ Is Arutas
• Oristano

③
Piscinas Dunes
② Cala Domestica

Cagliari

Isola di San Pietro

CAGLIARI AND THE SOUTH

Isola di Sant'Antioco

G
C

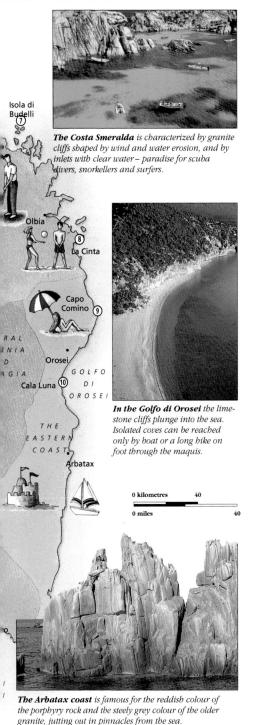

The Costa Smeralda *is characterized by granite cliffs shaped by wind and water erosion, and by inlets with clear water – paradise for scuba divers, snorkellers and surfers.*

Isola di Budelli (7)

Olbia

La Cinta (8)

Capo Comino (9)

Orosei

GOLFO DI OROSEI

Cala Luna (10)

In the Golfo di Orosei *the limestone cliffs plunge into the sea. Isolated coves can be reached only by boat or a long hike on foot through the maquis.*

THE EASTERN COAST

Arbatax

RAL NIA
D
AGIA

0 kilometres   40

0 miles   40

The Arbatax coast *is famous for the reddish colour of the porphyry rock and the steely grey colour of the older granite, jutting out in pinnacles from the sea.*

SARDINIA'S TEN BEST BEACHES

Most lively (1)
Il Poetto, just outside Cagliari, is the largest and liveliest beach on the island. Locals throng here at weekends and through the summer.

Most hidden beach (2)
Cala Domestica, protected by a Saracen tower, is invisible from the sea. In World War II it was used as a German military base.

Best dunes (3)
At Piscinas there are 9 km (5 miles) of sand dunes covered with maquis vegetation. Some are as high as 50 m (164 ft), the highest found in Europe.

Most tropical (4)
The beach at Is Arutas is made of tiny "grains" of quartz. A forest of pine trees forms a green backdrop to the sand.

Cleanest sea (5)
Bosa Marina, unchanged since the 1950s, has won medals for being the cleanest beach in Italy.

Best windsurfing (6)
A strong and constant breeze from the mouth of the Liscia river makes Porto Pollo (*Porto Puddu* in Sardinian dialect) perfect for windsurfing.

Best coral beach (7)
The beach on the island of Budelli consists of pieces of shells, coral and marine micro-organisms. Now, however, landing on the island is forbidden.

Best beach for young people (8)
La Cinta, 1 km (half a mile) long, is a favourite with the trendy younger set. It is ideal for soaking up the sun and for windsurfing.

Most remote beach (9)
Berchida, with its white beach and red rocks, can only be reached via a long sandy track through the shrubby maquis.

Most inaccessible beach (10)
The secluded Cala Luna, with its white sand, pink oleanders and green mastic trees, is only accessible by boat or on foot.

The Flora and Fauna of Sardinia

FROM THE RUGGED GENNARGENTU massif to the Campidano plains, and from the Nurra hills to the wind-eroded rocks of the Gallura area, Sardinia offers a great variety of natural habitats for wildlife. The forests, especially in the north, are dominated by cork oaks, for centuries a useful source of raw material. The Mediterranean maquis is permeated with the scents of lentiscus, cistus, myrtle and strawberry trees. Despite decades of farming, the fauna is still varied and interesting. Deer and wild boar abound in the scrub and forests and the rocks are home to the moufflon. The small Monte Arcosu reserve retains a tiny population of rare Sardinian deer, and the island of Asinara is the home of wild donkeys. In the spectacular Giara di Gesturi plateau, unbroken horses graze freely. Assorted reptiles can also be found, but no vipers.

Donkey at Gesturi

The moufflon *is an ancient inhabitant of the island. It has a thick coat and impressive curving horns.*

Sardinian deer *are stocky, with smaller horns than their mainland counterparts.*

Foxes *can still be seen on Monte Limbara and Gennargentu.*

Mountain

Woods

M

The Sardinian horse *is a compact animal native to the island. The horses roam on the Giara di Gesturi plateau and on the Capo Caccia headland.*

The Kermes oak (Quercus coccifera) *thrives mostly on the southern coastline.*

The cork oak (Quercus suber), *important to the economy, dominates the forest of Gallura (see p151).*

Sardinian boar *live in various parts of the island. They are smaller and stouter than species on mainland Italy.*

e holm oak (Quercus ilex) *predominates in almost all medium-altitude woods.*

THE MEDITERRANEAN MAQUIS

This thick, often impenetrable, shrubby vegetation (*macchia* in Italian) thrives in the coastal and mountainous regions of Sardinia. The shrubs – including myrtle, arbutus (strawberry tree) and blackthorn – flower in spring, rest in summer and revive again in autumn. Even in winter the island looks green, with splashes of colour from berries. In recent years the area of maquis has increased, as a result of forest fires which encourage plenty of new growth.

Myrtle in flower

Strawberry tree

White cistus flowers

The kite's *habitat is the wooded upland valleys.*

THE SARDINIAN TERRAIN

The southwestern corner of Sardinia began to emerge from the sea over 500 million years ago.

Turtles, which may grow up to as much as 1 m (3 ft) in length, are dying out because their eggs are highly prized.

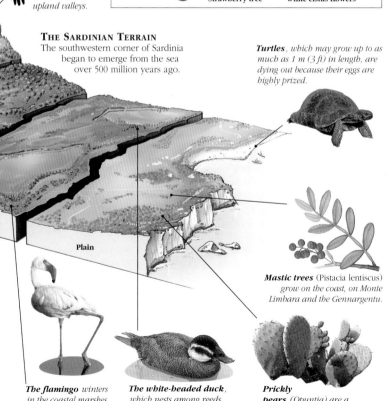

Plain

Mastic trees (Pistacia lentiscus) *grow on the coast, on Monte Limbara and the Gennargentu.*

The flamingo winters in the coastal marshes and lagoons, and now nests on Sardinia.

The white-beaded duck, which nests among reeds, is quite a rare sight on Sardinian marshland.

Prickly pears (Opuntia) *are a characteristic feature everywhere along the coastline.*

The Nuraghi

THERE ARE OVER 7,000 NURAGHI in Sardinia, their distinctive truncated cones a familiar part of the landscape. Little is known about their builders, a civilization that flourished on the island from 1800 to 500 BC (in some areas the nuraghic peoples resisted the Romans long after this date). Initially a nuraghe con-sisted of a single tower made of huge blocks of stone laid without mortar. Later, more towers were added, with connecting ramparts, resulting in more complex structures such as the Losa nuraghe at Abbasanta, the Santu Antine at Torralba and the Su Nuraxi at Barùmini. Nuraghi served as both dwelling and fortress, and the towers were often surrounded by a village and wall. There is no trace of any written language, but over 1,500 bronze figures have been found in tombs and near holy wells. The figures, and other finds, are now on display in Sardinia's archaeological museums.

Bronze quiver

Tribal chief
This bronze figure comes from the nuraghic village of Santa Vittoria, at Serri, one of the largest in Sardinia. It is a portrait of a prince at prayer.

Simple nuraghe
This is the most commonly seen and simplest form of nuraghe, consisting of a single tower with a chamber made of inwardly stepped circular tiers of stones. At times these nuraghi had more than one storey.

The central tower is in the shape of a truncated cone.

The rampart incorporates three defence towers.

Outer defence wall

• Sassari

Nuoro

• Oristano

Cagliari

• Principal Nuraghic Sites

The Losa Nuraghe at Abbasanta
This nuraghe is in three parts and is surrounded by a rampart with small towers. The oldest tower dates from before 1500 BC. There is a fine panoramic view of the Gennargentu mountains from the terrace.

Maiori Nuraghe at Tempio Pausania
This ground-floor room of the Maiori nuraghe in northern Sardinia could only be illuminated by light filtering in from the outside.

NURAGHIC BURIALS

The nuraghic peoples built monumental tombs known as Tombe dei Giganti (Tombs of Giants) to bury their dead. Each tomb consisted of a long covered corridor constructed with huge slabs of stone. The shape represented the horn of the Bull God. A monolithic oval stele, with an opening at the base, formed the front face. Two rows of stones on either side, forming an arch, completed the burial chamber. The central, arched stele could sometimes be as much as 3 m (10 ft) tall. The area around a typical Tomba dei Giganti was often surrounded by long rows of menhirs.

The Tomb of Giants at Li Lolghi is one of the most famous prehistoric sites in Sardinia

The central tower had three superimposed chambers.

The side towers were built at a later stage, in the early Iron Age.

The rampart created a solid defence system.

SANTU ANTINE NURAGHE
The central tower of this roughly triangular nuraghe is surrounded by a three-sided rampart with three towers. It was built in different stages in the 9th–8th centuries BC. The huge complex was later dedicated to the Roman emperor Constantine.

This reconstruction shows the original layout of Santu Antine. The central tower was the main fortress and dwelling, protected by the external towers.

Arrubiu Nuraghe
This consists of a massive fortress built in red stone covering an area of about 3 hectares (7 acres) at the edge of a plateau dominating the Flumendosa valley. Imposing external ramparts with five towers protected the inner courtyard and the central nuraghic construction, which was 16 m (52 ft) high.

Music and Dance in Sardinia

A nuraghic bronze statuette of a flute player shows the musician playing reed pipes, the instrument that later became known as the launeddas.

Sardinian bells

THE MUSIC of Sardinia ranks among the oldest in the Mediterranean. This is demonstrated by the nuraghic bronze figure (8th–7th centuries BC) from Ittiri, now in the Museo Archeologico in Cagliari *(see p58)*. The bronze represents a musician playing the *launeddas*, a three-piped Sardinian wind instrument still used in processions and dances. It is a difficult instrument to play and requires a special breathing technique. It consists of three flutes of varying length: *su tumbu* (the longest), *sa mancosa* and *sa mancosedda*. The *Canto a Tenores* is unaccompanied four-part polyphonic music for male voices: *sa boghe* (the soloist, who also directs the group); *sa contra* and *su basso* (accompanying voices with guttural sound); and *sa mesa boghe* (a soft, low voice that serves to blend the different sounds). Dance has always been a fundamental part of religious feasts and festivals linked with the stages in the farming year. The dancers move in short steps, their heads high, backs straight and bodies rigid.

Canto a Tenores is unaccompanied four-part singing.

The singers wear typical Nuoro costume.

Organittu, *together with the guitar and accordion, are the main instruments used to accompany the popular Sardinian round dances.*

The four voices are: *sa boghe, sa contra, sa basso* and *sa mesa boghe.*

MUSICAL INFLUENCES

For years Sardinian musicians have used their folk tradition and instruments to create experimental music. The most famous are the Tenores di Bitti, who have recorded with a number of highly successful bands, including Peter Gabriel's Real World, plus the famous jazz artist Ornette Coleman. The *launeddas* player Luigi Lai has worked together with Angelo Branduardi. Paolo Fresu, one of Italy's top jazz musicians, is Sardinian, and often draws inspiration from the music of his native land. Fresu was the driving force behind *Sonos 'e memoria*, an interesting project that brought together the leading island musicians to perform live for the soundtrack of a black-and-white film on Sardinian life in the first half of the 20th century.

Cover for the Tenores di Bitti's album *Intonos*

Paolo Fresu

Sardinian rock groups often adapt traditional music and instruments to a modern style, as well as developing new ideas.

THE MUSIC MUSEUM

Tadasuni, a village on the shores of Lake Omodeo, near Ghilarza, has a jewel in store for music-lovers. The **Museo degli Strumenti della Musica Popolare della Sardegna** (Museum of Sardinian Folk Music Instruments) houses over 300 instruments collected by the local parish priest, Don Giovanni Dore. He spent decades travelling around the island to gather the instruments, which for the most part feature typical island wind and reed instruments,

The *solittos*, a wind instrument

such as the *launeddas*. This ancient three-pipe wind instrument, made from seasoned cane, emits an uninterrupted sound (similar to the bagpipes). Other wind instruments on display in the museum include the *cornetts*, the *solittos*, the *bena doppia* and *bena semplice*, all flute-like instruments made of cane. There are also drums, such as the *tumbarinu 'e gavoi*, the *moggiu* and the *tumbarineddu* made of cork, tin or wood. The drum skin is traditionally made of stretched dog, donkey or goat skin. Of these, the *trimpanu* was used to frighten horses and unseat the Carabinieri riders in times of civil unrest. There are also barrel organs, introduced in Sardinia in the mid-19th century.

🏛 **Museo degli Strumenti della Musica Popolare della Sardegna**
Via Adua 7, Tadasuni. 📞 0785-501 13.
🕐 *by appt only.*

THE TENORES DI BITTI

The Tenores from Bitti are the most famous Canto a Tenores group. They have appeared with Peter Gabriel and Ornette Coleman, increasing awareness of Sardinian folk music.

The dance's name derives from the position of the dancers, who form a circle.

The dance takes place outside, during feasts and festivals.

Men and women hold hands.

Traditional costumes are still worn.

The Round Dance
This 19th-century print depicts a Sardinian round dance. The dance is now only found in Sardinia and there are numerous local variations.

SARDINIA
THROUGH THE YEAR

PRING IS BY FAR the best season to visit Sardinia. Perfumed flowers are in bloom in the maquis thickets, the woods and meadows are still green and, although the weather is warm enough for swimming as early as May, it has not reached the scorching temperatures of summer. Easter, with its colourful processions, marks the religious high point of the island. During the rest of the year, towns and villages organize festivals to commemorate the feast day of the local patron saint and sanctuaries are enlivened by

celebrations and banquets. The summer months are dedicated to activities along the island's stunning coast, such as bathing, sailing and windsurfing. Inland, it can get stiflingly hot in summer, but the higher mountainous areas provide a cool retreat from the crowds and an ideal place for walking. Grape harvesting begins in the autumn, and in early winter there is heavy snowfall on the Mount Gennargentu massif. At times snow can even fall on the lower areas covering the rocky landscape of the Supramonte.

Mask from Mamoiada

Narcissus in bloom, a typical flower of the Mediterranean

SPRING

ONCE THE WARM spring weather sets in, the sheep and goats grazing on the hillsides will be moved to higher pastures. The aromatic plants and strongly scented flowers of the maquis are in full bloom, and bees abound. They produce the rather bitter honey used in many traditional Sardinian cakes.

In the flatlands and on the hills of the Anglona and Montiferru regions the fruit trees are in blossom, while in the countryside young artichokes are almost ready to be picked. These are shipped to vegetable markets on mainland Italy and are traditionally the first on the market.

MARCH AND APRIL

Holy Week and **Easter** *(Mar or Apr)* are a time of great religious celebrations, with colourful processions taking place throughout the island.

In Cagliari there is an important procession through the streets on Good Friday. A representation of the *Iscravamentu* and *Incontru* mystery plays is performed at Iglesias. At Oliena the costume procession known as *S'Incontru* takes place on Easter Sunday. *Su Concordu* in the town of Santu Lussurgiu features 15th-century psalms sung in Gregorian chant. On Holy Monday at Castelsardo, there is the *Luni Santu*, a religious feast of Spanish origin. The **Livestock Festival** *(25 Mar)*, at Ollastra Simaxis, is in honour of St Mark.
Sagra del Riccio di Mare *(early Mar)*. A festival of the sea urchin in Alghero.
Festa Patronale *(2nd Sat after Easter)*. The island of Sant'Antioco celebrates its patron saint's feast day.

MAY

Sant'Efisio *(1–4 May)*, in Cagliari, offers a grand procession commemorating the end of the plague in 1656. The saint's statue is carried through the city and is then taken to Nora on an ox-drawn cart. During this splendid display of religious feeling the faithful cast flowers onto the street as the statue passes by.
San Francesco's feast day *(second Sun)*. Held at Lula, this is one of the most popular celebrations in the Baronie and Nuoro areas.
Festa dell'Annunziata *(third Sun)*, at Bitti. A pastoral celebration of the Annunciation.
San Bachisio *(29 May)*. This feast day consists of three days of *Ballu Tundu* (round dance) in the squares of Onani.

The *S'Incontru* procession in the streets of Oliena on Easter Day

AVERAGE DAILY HOURS OF SUNSHINE

hours

Jan Feb Mar Apr May Jun Jul Aug Sep Oct Nov Dec

Sunshine Chart
Summer is the sunniest, as well as the hottest time, and June has the maximum hours of sunshine daily. The least sunny month is January, but the weather varies a great deal between inland and coastal regions, and in general, coastal areas will be brighter.

The Ardia horse race in front of the Sant'Antine sanctuary at Sedilo

Cavalcata Sarda *(Ascension Day)*. Although this is a fairly new tradition, the "Sardinian Horseride" has become one of the island's major folk festivals. Handicraft stalls and general festivities fill the streets of Sassari's old town centre. People from all over the island crowd into the town on horseback or dressed in colourful costumes to hear traditional songs and poetry from the different towns and regions of the island.

SUMMER

THE HIGH TEMPERATURES and stunning coastline draw locals and visitors alike to the seashore during the summer months. The coastline is filled with bathers and windsurfers, and yachts and sailboats from all over Europe dock at the small, pretty harbours. For snorkellers and scuba divers there are underwater beds of posidonia to explore. Sailing, windsurf and scuba diving clubs organize lessons throughout the summer months *(see pp198–9)*.

The cooler temperatures on the slopes of Gennargentu make it excellent for hikers, and the climb down the gorges of Su Gorroppu is also popular.

This is the period of rural festivals, when small religious sanctuaries hidden among the valleys and hills come to life with pilgrimages and feasting. **Pani, Pisci, Pezza e Piricchittus** *(Jun–Sep)*, meaning bread, fish, pizza and almond pastry, is a food festival held in the restaurants of Quartu. Cagliari offers a programme of music, theatre and cinema. At San Gavino Monreale there are concerts and other cultural events as well as sports activities at night.

JUNE

Horse Festival *(2 & 3 Jun)*. Santu Lussurgiu holds an important agricultural festival with a handicrafts exhibition. **Sagra delle Ciliegie** *(first Sun of month)*. Festival celebrating the cherry harvest at Villacidro, Bonarcado and Burcei. **Handicrafts Fair** *(11 Jun)*. The streets of Villanova Monteleone teem with stalls.

JULY

Ardia *(5–8 Jul)*. This characteristic rural festival is held at San Costantino a Sedilo in front of the Santu Antine sanctuary. A lively horse race accompanies celebrations honouring the saint. **Sagra del Torrone** *(second Sun of month)*. At Tonara, at the foot of the Gennargentu mountains, the festivities end with the preparation of the famous nougat *(torrone)*. **Sagra delle Pesche** *(17 Jul)*, is a peach festival held at San Sperate on the feast day of the town's patron saint. **Estate Musicale** *(Jul–Aug)*, at Alghero, with concerts in the Chiostro di San Francesco. **International Folklore Festival** *(end of Jul)*, held in Tempio Pausania, during the summer Carnival. **Carpet Fair** *(two weeks in Jul or Aug)* at Mogoro. This is one of the leading displays of Sardinian handicrafts, in particular carpets, tapestry and hand-made furniture. **Music in Antas Valley** *(Jul– Aug)*. Classical music concerts held in the splendid setting of the Temple of Antas at Fluminimaggiore *(see p68)*.

Advanced sailing lessons off the Costa Smeralda

AVERAGE MONTHLY RAINFALL

Rainfall Chart
In Sardinia most of the rainfall occurs in the autumn and winter. The rainfall is heavier in the mountainous regions of the interior, with precipitation as high as 1,000 mm (39 inches) per year. The driest season is during the summer months, particularly in the coastal regions.

AUGUST

Mauretanian Wedding
(1–15 Aug) at Santadi. A ceremony dating back to the ancient traditions of the North Africans who inhabited the Sulcis region in Roman times.

Dieci Giorni Sulcitani
(1–15 Aug) in Sant'Antioco. This consists of ten evenings of traditional local entertainment, including plays in dialect, recitals of Sardinian poetry, traditional folk dances and local choral music.

Carpet Show *(first Sun of month)*. Traditional hand-made carpets and blankets are exhibited at Aggius.

Madonna della Neve feast day *(first Sun of Aug)*. The hardships of winter are exorcised in the Tascusì sanctuary at Desulo.

Sagra del Vino *(4 Aug)*. Wine festival at Jerzu with costume parades, dances, traditional songs and Cannonau wine.

Vernaccia Wine Festival *(6 Aug)*. Festival of the local wine at Baratili San Pietro, near Oristano.

Sagra del Pomodoro *(11 Aug)*. The tomato festival offers tomato-based dishes

A drummer playing at the Time in Jazz festival at Berchidda

served outdoors at Zeddiano. There is also an exhibition of local farm produce.

Faradda de li Candelieri *(14 Aug)*. Candles *(candelieri)*, weighing between 200–300 kg (440–660 lbs) are carried by members of the ancient guilds in Sassari. Each candle is decorated with the coat of arms of the guild and its patron saint.

Time in Jazz *(the week incorporating Ferragosto)*. Berchidda hosts an annual jazz festival.

Processione del Redentore *(29 Aug)*. Nuoro hosts one of Sardinia's most popular celebrations with a procession through the streets of honour

of Christ the Redeemer, and performances of local folklore.

Launeddas Festival *(fourth Sun)* at San Vito. This festival features performances by leading musicians of the traditional triple-piped wind instrument *(see p90)*. The music is accompanied by the *Ballu Tundu*, a circular dance.

Rassegna di Musica Leggera *(Aug–Sep)*. Performances of popular music and theatre in Piazza Peglia, Carloforte.

Regata Vela Latina *(end of Aug)*. A regatta for traditional Sardinian fishing boats held in Stintino *(see p120)*.

Mostra del Tappeto *(mid-Aug–late Sep)*. A carpet fair held at Nule.

AUTUMN

IT IS STILL POSSIBLE to swim in the sea well into September, but the air becomes cooler in the evening. October is grape harvest time and autumn marks the beginning of the hunting season. The favourite game is wild boar, a tasty meat used in the strongly-flavoured Sardinian cuisine. The chestnut harvest in the mountains often ends with lively festivals.

SEPTEMBER

Pilgrimage to the Madonna di Gonare Sanctuary *(8 and 16 Sep)*. Departures to this hilltop church alternate between the centres of Sarule *(see p103)* and Orani.

Fiera del Bestiame *(third Sun of month)* at Serri. A livestock fair on the day of Santa Lucia.

Santa Cosma *(27 Sep)*. The *Mamuthones (see p102)* parade through the streets of Mamoiada in sheepskins.

Traditional costumes worn for the Madonna della Neve festival at Desulo

AVERAGE MONTHLY TEMPERATURE

Temperature Chart
The summer months between June and September are hot and dry, with temperatures above 20° C (68° F), and at times reaching 30° C (86° F). In winter the temperatures are mild, rarely dipping below 5° C (41° F). January generally has sunny days and cold nights.

Masked figures (Boes) with cowbells during carnival at Ottana

OCTOBER

Santa Vitalia Festival *(first Mon of month)*. A festival dedicated to agriculture held at Serrenti, with stalls selling local handicrafts.
Sagra delle Castagne e delle Nocciole *(fourth Sun)*. Festival to celebrate the ripening and the harvest of chestnuts and hazelnuts at Aritzo. There is also a handicrafts fair.

NOVEMBER

Festa della Madonna dello Schiavo *(15 Nov)*. A statue of the Madonna is worshipped as it passes through the town of Carloforte. The statue is said to have been sculpted by citizens from Carloforte, who had been kidnapped by pirates and held in Tunis.
Santa Caterina *(25 Nov)*. The saint's feast day is celebrated in Abbasanta.

WINTER

WINTER IS A FAIRLY cold season throughout the island and snow covers the mountainous interior. Livestock is returned to its lower winter pastures and pens, and the chill wind puts an end to fishing activity along the coast. As well as **Christmas**, which is very important in Sardinia, there are many other feast days and local festivals in the Carnival period before Lent.

DECEMBER

Sagra delle Salsicce *(first Sun of month)* held at Siligo. After the pig slaughter, preparation and curing of the meat, the sausage festival is an opportunity to taste the year's new delicacies.
Christmas is celebrated at home with presents and by preparing traditional sweets.

JANUARY AND FEBRUARY

Feast of Sant'Antonio Abate *(16–17 Jan)* is celebrated at Fluminimaggiore *(see p68)* with huge bonfires in the various quarters of the town.
Carnival *(the ten days before Shrove Tuesday)*, is extremely popular in Sardinia, especially in the small villages of the Barbagia region. Masked and costumed figures parade on Shrove Tuesday and the last Sunday of Lent. At Mamoiada, the *Mamuthones*, men dressed in sheepskins with heavy bells around their necks, are run out of town by the *Issocadores (see p102)*. Similar festivals during carnival are the *Thurpos* at Orotelli, and the *Merdules* and *Boes* at Ottana *(see p101)*. At *Sa Sartiglia* in Oristano, masked horsemen spear a silver star hanging from a tree. There are cakes and free wine at Iglesias *(see p68)* and food is served in the main square at Perfugas. At Tempio Pausania an effigy of "King George" is burned and at Santu Lussurgiu *(see p128)* there is the *Sa Carrela 'e Nanti* horse race.
Processo a Su Conte *(Ash Wednesday)*. At Ovodda the stuffed figure of "Su Conte" is tried in the main square and burned at the stake.

PUBLIC HOLIDAYS

New Year's Day (1 Jan)
Epiphany (6 Jan)
Easter Sunday and Monday (Mar or Apr)
Liberation Day (25 Apr)
Labour Day (1 May)
Ferragosto (Assumption Day, 15 Aug)
All Saints' Day (1 Nov)
Immaculate Conception (8 Dec)
Christmas Day (25 Dec)
Santo Stefano (26 Dec)

Snow-covered mountains of the Gennargentu in winter

THE HISTORY OF SARDINIA

THE ORIGINS of Sardinian history go back thousands of years. The first people to settle are thought to have reached the island by crossing over a natural causeway which once linked Tuscany and Sardinia, perhaps between 450,000 and 150,000 years ago. A succession of different cultures led up to the rise of the nuraghic civilization. These tribes of shepherds and warriors lived in round stone dwellings called nuraghi, defended by walled fortresses, and their occupation left exceptional megalithic ruins across the island. Of the 7,000 nuraghi left in Sardinia, some are in an excellent state of preservation: the Su Nuraxi settlement at Barùmini, the Santu Antine complex and the nuraghi at Losa.

The Macomer Venus in the Museo Archeologico in Cagliari

The Phoenicians arrived in 1000 BC, settling along the coastline at Tharros, Nora, Bithia and Cagliari and, after winning the Punic Wars, the Romans occupied the island. Roman dominion lasted 700 years despite strong resistance from Sardinians, and evidence can still be seen in the many ruins. When the Roman Empire fell, Sardinia again fell prey to various conquerors. For centuries the Vandals, Byzantines and Arabs fought for possession of the strategic harbours, until the maritime republics of Pisa and Genoa made their appearance on Sardinian waters. A golden age of Sardinian Romanesque architecture was introduced, which gave way to Gothic when the House of Aragon conquered the island. After 400 years of Spanish rule, control of the island passed to Austria, which ceded it to the House of Savoy in 1718. The Kingdom of Sardinia survived up to the unification of Italy. A long period of neglect was ended only after World War II, with the reclamation of the malarial marshes. The scheme's success opened up possibilities for a tourist industry and the development of an autonomous, modern Sardinia.

Calaris, **modern-day Cagliari, in a print dating from 1590**

◁ **The Roman Temple of Antas at Fluminimaggiore, built over a 6th–5th century BC Phoenician temple**

Prehistoric Sardinia

Bronze figure from Teti-Abini

ALTHOUGH SOME stone tools found at Perfugas show that Sardinia was inhabited from the Paleolithic period (150,000 years ago), it was only around 9000 BC that the island began to be settled by populations from Asia Minor, the African coasts, the Iberian peninsula and Liguria. The fertile, mineral-rich land and the obsidian mines at Monte Arci were a major factor in the island's prosperity. By around 3000 BC the Sardinians had grouped into tribes. They lived in villages with thatched-roof huts and buried their dead in rock-cut tombs called *domus de janas* (house of fairies). By about 1800 BC this rural society had evolved into the warrior nuraghic civilization, who built thousands of circular stone towers *(nuraghi)* across the island. Many of these remarkable prehistoric constructions are still visible.

Necklace with Tusk
This ornament was found in a tomb dating from 2000–1800 BC, the bell-shaped pottery era.

Earthenware
These jugs and vases were everyday objects used to store water and grain.

The motifs on the prow have more to do with the land than the sea.

Monte d'Accoddi ruins
These traces reveal the ruins of a tiered, terraced construction, probably a temple, dating from the 3rd millennium BC. It looked remarkably similar to the famous ziggurat temples of Mesopotamia and the Aztec pyramids.

TIMELINE

6000 BC Sardinian peoples make tools and weapons from the obsidian found at Monte Arci

Obsidian arrowhead

A typical example of domus de janas

6000 BC	4000 BC

Boar tusk, an ornament from the early Neolithic period

4000–3000 BC The age of the Bonu Ighinu culture – small communities living by raising sheep and goats. Distinctive, high quality grey pottery with incised decoration is produced

Bronze Artifacts from Abini
These spears were part of a hoard of 100 kg (220 lb) of objects hidden in large clay vessels, perhaps to conceal them from the Roman invaders.

Candelabrum

These bronze figurines were made using the melted wax technique.

EX VOTO WITH DEER MOTIF
This ex voto lamp in the shape of a ship was one of 70 or so found at Is Argiolas near Bultei. It dates from the 8th–7th centuries BC, and is now in the Museo Archeologico Nazionale in Cagliari. In the nuraghic age, Sardinians had a love-hate relationship with the sea, which ended with the arrival of the Carthaginians, Romans and later conquerors, who forced the local inhabitants to live in the interior.

WHERE TO SEE PREHISTORIC SARDINIA

Pre-nuraghic ruins include a ziggurat at Monte d'Accoddi and rock-cut tombs *(domus de janas)* at Pranu Muteddu (Goni). Nuraghic villages survive at Su Nuraxi *(see pp64–5)*, Serra Òrrios *(see p84)*, Tiscali *(see pp104–5)* and Abini. Burial chambers, or "Tombs of Giants", can be seen at places such as Sa Ena 'e Thomes, and holy wells can be visited at Santa Cristina (Paulilàtino) and Santa Vittoria (Serri).

The nuraghic village of Serra Òrrios *is one of the best preserved in Sardinia. It consisted of about 70 dwellings* (see p84).

The Montessu necropolis *houses domus de janas of the Ozieri pre-nuraghic era.*

3000 BC Era of Ozieri or San Michele culture. Villages are established throughout the island and the dead are buried in the *domus de janas*

Replica of the goddess Mater Mediterranea of Senorbi

1800 BC Rise of nuraghic civilization, characterized by truncated cone-shaped buildings erected at the edges of upland plateaus

1000 BC Phoenician ships moor along coast

3000 BC | **2000 BC** | **1000 BC**

2000–1800 BC Civilization known for its bell-shaped pottery. Rectangular or round dwellings constructed

Dolmen at Luras

1500 BC The first simple forms of nuraghe appear

The Santa Barbara nuraghe at Macomer

The Phoenicians, Carthaginians and Romans

AROUND 1000 BC Phoenician ships began to use the inlets of the Sardinian coasts as harbours. When commerce intensified about 200 years later, they founded the cities of Nora, Sulcis, Tharros, Olbia and, later on, Bithia and Karalis (today's Cagliari). But good relationships with the local chiefs soon waned. After a brief period of peace, the nuraghic populations attacked the Phoenician settlements which, in 509 BC, asked Carthage for help. In 238 BC the Carthaginians, defeated in the first Punic War, ceded Sardinia to the Romans, who made it their province. For over a century the Sardinians put up fierce resistance, a situation which ended in 215 BC with the battle of Cornus *(see p129)*. The Romans never succeeded in subduing the entire island and rebellion in the interior continued for years. However, Roman civilization gave the island a network of roads, as well as baths, temples, aqueducts and amphitheatres.

Oil jar, 2nd century BC

Gold Bracelet
Decorated with palmettes, lotus flowers and a scarab beetle, this bracelet came from Tharros (pp132–3).

This shape of nose is typical of the Phoenicians.

Glass Vase and Perfume Bottle
In Roman times glass was used to make ornamental vessels as well as practical objects like cups, bowls and bottles. Numerous glass pieces have been found in burial grounds and examples can be seen in the Museo Archeologico Nazionale in Cagliari (p58).

Lines on the face imitate tattoos.

Carthaginian Necklace
Carthaginian jewellery was often quite elaborate, as shown by this necklace with pendants carrying human and animal symbols.

GRINNING MASK
This mask dates from the 4th century BC, when the island was under Carthaginian rule. Masks like these were used to ward off evil, to protect children or ensure the sleep of the dead. This mask was found in the settlement beneath the town of San Sperate *(see p62)*.

TIMELINE

900 BC Nuraghic villages, bronze figures and stone sculptures

Phoenician ship

500–400 BC Sardinians flee to Barbagia after losing battles against Carthaginians

900 BC	750 BC	500 BC

730–700 BC First Phoenician harbours built: the future Nora, Tharros, Bithia and Karalis

ca. 550 BC The Carthaginians arrive and found the first Punic cities

509 BC The nuraghic peoples attack the coastal cities, who ask Carthage for help

Statue of Drusus Junior (13 BC–AD 23)

The portrait of the Roman consul, son of the emperor Tiberius, was found at Sant'Antioco (see p72), together with other busts from the early Empire.

The incisions show lotuses and rosettes.

The nose-ring is shaped like a leech.

WHERE TO SEE PUNIC–ROMAN SARDINIA

The best preserved Punic-Roman cities are Nora *(see pp74–5)* and Tharros *(see pp132–3)*. The ruins at Sulki, present-day Sant'Antioco *(see p72)*, are wholly Punic. Roman ruins include the amphitheatre in Cagliari *(see p54)*, near the Villa of Tigellio *(see p59)*, and baths at Fordongianus *(see p136–7)*.

Roman amphitheatre at Cagliari, *2nd century AD.*

The Roman theatre at Nora *is still used for summer cultural events.*

Punic Inscription
This inscription was engraved on the base of the pedestal of a 4th-century BC statuette, found in the Temple of Antas.

Glass Bowl with the Figure of Christ
This beautiful early Christian piece was found inside a tomb near Ittiri. Christ is depicted in the role of both legislator and emperor.

238 BC The Carthaginians lose the first Punic War

227 BC Sardinia, together with Corsica, becomes Roman province

Mosaic found at Nora

AD 200–300 Full of disease, Sardinia becomes a deportation site

250 BC	0	AD 250

Temple of Antas dedicated to Sardus Pater

27 BC Sardinia is divided from Corsica and becomes a senatorial province

AD 66 Roman Sardinia becomes an imperial province and is occupied by legions

The Middle Ages, from the Vandals to the Aragonese

Arborea's coat of arms

I N AD 456 the Vandals conquered Sardinia. Shortly afterwards, liberated by Byzantium, the island became one of the seven African provinces of the Eastern Roman Empire. The subsequent power vacuum, aggravated by Arab invasions, gave rise to the four autonomous *giudicati*, or principalities, of Torres, Gallura, Arborea and Cagliari. Around AD 1000 the Pisans and Genoese, after fierce campaigns against the Arabs, took over parts of the island. The long relationship with Aragon was formalized in 1295, when Pope Boniface VIII signed the papal bull naming James II of Aragon as King of Corsica and Sardinia. On 12 June 1323 the Infante Alfonso landed in Sardinia with his army.

The Castello quarter, Cagliari
Built during the era of Pisan rule, the fortified Castello quarter in Cagliari was the heart of the city until the 1800s.

Eleonora of Arborea

This remarkable woman inherited Arborea from her father Mariano IV in 1383. After two wars against the Aragonese, Eleonora gained control of most of Sardinia in 1394. Known as the Giudica, she remains a symbol of Sardinian independence.

Papal coat of arms

Benedetto Caetani was the real name of Pope Boniface.

66,
de
elet
pol

Barison I's seal

In 1038 the Pisans, after wresting Sardinia from the Arabs, helped Barison I of Arborea to take possession of its four giudicati *(principalities).*

BONIFACE VIII

In 1295, Pope Boniface VIII (depicted here while celebrating the Jubilee of 1300) signed the papal bull giving control of the *Regnum Sardiniae et Corsicae* to James II of Aragon, in exchange for relinquishing Sicily. The Aragonese continued to annexe Sicily, ignoring the agreement.

TIMELINE

534 Byzantium liberates Sardinia which, together with Corsica, becomes one of its seven African provinces

Pope Gregory the Great

AD 500	600	700	800

Earthenware from Vandal tombs

600 Pope Gregory the Great sets out to convert Sardinia to Christianity

711 Arab invasions begin

815 Sardinian diplomats ask France for aid in war against Arabs

Capo Falcone
This tower was part of a defence system which finally put an end to barbarian raids on Sardinia in the 16th century.

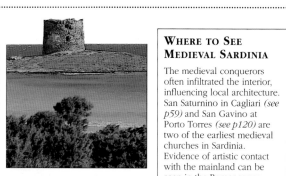

Pope Boniface VIII

WHERE TO SEE MEDIEVAL SARDINIA

The medieval conquerors often infiltrated the interior, influencing local architecture. San Saturnino in Cagliari *(see p59)* and San Gavino at Porto Torres *(see p120)* are two of the earliest medieval churches in Sardinia. Evidence of artistic contact with the mainland can be seen in the Romanesque churches of Logudoro *(see pp156–7)*, the cathedral of Oristano *(see pp134–5)* and the cathedral of Santa Maria in Cagliari *(see p55)*. Some castles remain: the Rocca at Castelsardo *(see p164)* and the Castello complex in Cagliari *(see pp56–7)*.

Santissima Trinità di Saccargia *is Pisan Romanesque (see pp158–9).*

The Castello Malaspina *dominates the town of Bosa (see pp126–7).*

Boniface VIII, despite this serene pose, was a highly controversial pope.

Alghero city walls
The massive walls and their towers date from the 14th-century period of Catalan rule.

1016 Pope Benedict VIII asks Pisa and Genoa to intervene in Sardinia	1087 Guglielmo di Massa, in Cagliari, becomes the first non-Sardinian ruler	1164 Frederick Barbarossa makes Sardinia a kingdom	1257–9 Last years of the Cagliari and Torres principalities	*James II of Aragon*
1000	**1100**	**1200**		**1300**
	Frederick I Barbarossa		1243 Frederick II crowns his son Enzo King of Sardinia	1323 12 June: Alfonso of Aragon lands in Sardinia

Spanish Rule

Aragonese coat of arms

THE SPANISH CONQUEST of Sardinia was slow: the rulers of Arborea waged a lengthy war against the invaders, there were determined revolts in Alghero and, in 1355, the Spanish crown was forced to grant a form of parliament to the six largest cities. The Aragonese took power definitively only in 1409, when the principality of Arborea was eliminated after the bloody battle of Sanluri and replaced by the marquisate of Oristano. Spanish domination of Sardinia was strengthened in 1479, with the marriage of Ferdinand of Aragon and Isabella I of Castile and Leon. The Spanish era also saw the founding of the first universities: Sassari in 1562 and Cagliari in 1620. Following the Peace of Utrecht in 1714, the island was ceded to Austria who then, in the Treaty of London, passed it over to King Vittorio Amedeo II of the House of Savoy.

Vittorio Amedeo II of Savoy
Vittorio Amedeo became king in 1718 when Austria gave Sardinia to him in exchange for Sicily. The Cagliari parliament swore allegiance to the new king on 2 August 1720.

VICTOR AMÉDÉE.

Four Moors Coat of Arms
Of Catalan origin, the coat of arms with four Moors first appeared in Sardinia after the arrival of Alfonso of Aragon in 1323. It has become one of the symbols of the island.

The upper part shows scenes from the life of St Peter; below are the saints with St Peter in the centre.

Decorated border

The Four Evangelists are depicted in the elaborately bordered predella. Sardinian artists put their own stamp on the Catalan *retablo* style.

TIMELINE

1355 Sardinian parliament established	**1409** Battle of Sanluri; end of Arborea as a principality	**1541** On his way to Tunis, Charles V stops at Alghero
1350	**1400**	**1500**
1402 *Anno de Sa Mortagia Manna*, the year of the great plague	*Ferdinand of Aragon and Isabella of Castile*	**1509–1520** Repeated Arab pirate raids on Sardinia

Alghero Cathedral
The interior of the cathedral of Santa Maria, begun in the 16th century, is a splendid example of the Catalan Gothic style in Sardinia.

THE ST PETER *RETABLO*

The *retablo* is a religious panel painting that was quite often used as an altarpiece. It was one of the most important artistic genres in 16th-century Sardinia under Spanish rule. This work, *Madonna and Child with Saints Peter, Paul and George of Suelli*, is by Pietro and Michele Cavaro (1533–5). It is now in the church of San Giorgio at Suelli (Cagliari). The elaborate frame and wealth of decorative elements reveal its Flemish derivation.

Retablos often combined painting, sculpture and carved decoration.

Philip V (1683–1746)
Forced to relinquish France and Sardinia, Philip tried to reconquer Sardinia in 1717 with the help of his chief minister Alberoni.

WHERE TO SEE SPANISH SARDINIA

The first Spanish building in Sardinia was the Gothic-Aragonese chapel in the cathedral in Cagliari *(see p55)*, followed by San Francesco in Iglesias, San Giorgio in Perfugas, and San Francesco and the cathedral in Alghero *(see p118)*. The cathedral in Sassari was built in the style known as "Colonial Baroque". Baroque influence is also evident in Àles cathedral. A notable school of *retablo* painting developed. There are 15th- and 16th-century paintings in the Art Gallery in Cagliari.

***This Aragonese house** at Fordongianus was built in the 15th–16th centuries.*

***San Francesco** in Alghero (14th century) was rebuilt in the Gothic-Aragonese style.*

Charles V

1620 Under Philip III the University of Cagliari is founded

1688 Discontent and uprisings: the Spanish viceroy is assassinated

1600	1700

1718 Treaty of London: Sardinia ceded to the House of Savoy

Cardinal Alberoni, Philip V's chief minister

1717 Philip V of Spain tries to reconquer Sardinia and Naples

The Kingdom of Sardinia

O NE OF THE FIRST acts of the Savoyard government
was to reinstate the island's universities. However,
a serious economic and social crisis led to unrest and
the spread of banditry. After the Revolution of 1789,
France made vain attempts to conquer Sardinia, but,
by 1795, the island was overwhelmed by revolutionary
fervour of its own and a "Sardinian revolution" broke
out in Cagliari. In 1799 the Savoys took refuge on the
island after losing their other territories to Napoleon. In
1847, in Cagliari and Sassari, huge crowds persuaded
the Savoys to link the kingdom of Sardinia with
Piedmont in *"fusione perfetta"*. In 1861 both became
part of the Kingdom of Italy.

The Harbour at Cagliari
*The port was developed
after the arrival of the Savoy
rulers. Together with Porto
Torres it became the island's
principal harbour.*

The University of Cagliari
*The university was founded as part of a
cultural reorganization and development
policy adopted by Carlo Emanuele III
(1730–73), who set up a committee for
Sardinian affairs in Turin.*

Carlo Emanuele IV
*King of Sardinia
from 1796 to
1802, Carlo
Emanuele took
refuge here after
losing his main-
land territories to
Napoleon in 1798.
His brother Vittorio
Emanuele I became
King of Savoy.*

THE ABSOLUTIST VICEROY

Carlo Felice, seen here receiving the keys
of Cagliari, was viceroy of Sardinia from
1799 to 1821, when he became king.
Unchallenged, he nonetheless governed
the island as an absolute monarch.

TIMELINE

1720 Filippo
Pallavicino becomes
the first Savoyard
viceroy of Sardinia

*Throne of the
Kingdom of Sardinia
in Turin*

1793 Anti-Savoy
rebellion

1720	1740	1760	1780

1764–5
Re-establishment of
Cagliari and Sassari
universities

1788 The court of the
House of Savoy flees
Turin and remains in
Cagliari until 1815

Memorial Tablet
This tablet, embedded in Palazzo Viceregio in Cagliari, was dedicated to Carlo Felice by Vittorio Emanuele I, his brother, who abdicated in his favour in 1821.

Giuseppe Garibaldi
After years in exile because of his republican ideas, Garibaldi came to Caprera in 1857. He settled here permanently after conquering the Kingdom of Two Sicilies for the House of Savoy with his army of 1,000 volunteer soldiers, the Redshirts (see p148).

House of Savoy Coat of Arms
Dating back to the 11th century, the dynasty first ruled Savoy and Piedmont, then the Kingdom of Sardinia and finally the Kingdom of Italy.

WHERE TO SEE SAVOYARD SARDINIA

Important Savoy buildings are the theatres in Cagliari, Sassari and Alghero, the provincial administration buildings and Cagliari Town Hall *(see p58)*. Many of Sardinia's railway lines were laid down in this era. Statues of prominent Savoy figures, like the one of Garibaldi at Caprera, were put up everywhere. The Villa Aymerich at Làconi was one of many country houses to be rebuilt.

The Galleria Comunale d'Arte di Cagliari, *the capital's art gallery.*

Monument to Carlo Emanuele III *at Carloforte, the town he founded.*

Vittorio Amedeo III, king of Sardinia (1773– 89)

1847 Sardinia and Piedmont join forces

1857 Garibaldi settles on Caprera and then buys part of the island

1820	1840	1860

Tomb of Carlo Emanuele IV of Savoy, Cagliari

1826 Alberto La Marmora's *Voyage to Sardinia* published

Alberto La Marmora

1861 Sardinia, together with Piedmont, becomes part of Kingdom of Italy

Sardinia and a United Italy

Ashes, by Grazia Deledda

INDUSTRIALIZATION in Sardinia began to make progress after unification: in 1871 the first railway line was built and the mines in Sulcis and Iglesiente became fully operational. The first daily newspapers were founded and Nuoro became the centre of a cultural movement that included the Nobel Prize-winning novelist Grazia Deledda. In World War I the heroism of the Brigata Sassari brigade emerged as a symbol of the island's new confidence, and led to the foundation of the Partito Sardo d'Azione political party in 1921. Between the wars the mining industry continued to develop, and the town of Carbonia was founded in 1938. A wide-ranging programme of land reclamation and artificial lakes – such as Lake Omodeo, created by a dam on the Tirso river – was carried out, significantly altering the health of previously malarial areas. On 31 January 1948 the island became an autonomous region of Italy.

The Monteponi mine
A 19th-century print shows the huge plant at this important Sardinian lead and zinc mine.

The crowd consisted of the social groups suffering most from the high cost of living.

Carbonia
In 1938 Mussolini himself inaugurated the newly-built town of Carbonia (see p71). The town was meant to become the leading mining centre in Sardinia.

Brigata Sassari
The brigade consisted entirely of Sardinians. They distinguished themselves in World War I by their heroism, winning two gold medals of honour.

Emilio Lussu (1890–1975) *This author recorded his World War I experiences in the Brigata Sassari in Un anno sull'altopiano (One Year on the Plateau).*

TIMELINE

1871 Writer Grazia Deledda is born

1889–1899 Arrival of army task force to combat rampant banditry in Sardinia

1897 First ever special restrictive laws passed in Sardinia

1870	1880	1890	1900

Quintino Sella, Minister of Finance in 1862, 1865, 1869–73

1889 The first daily newspaper in Sardinia, *Unione Sarda*, is founded

1891 Political writer Antonio Gramsci born in Ales

Antonio Gramsci

The Cagliari-Arbatax Railway
As part of a unified Italy, Sardinia embarked on a programme of modernization. The first railway lines were laid in 1871; by 1881 Cagliari and Sassari were linked by rail. The line connecting Cagliari and Arbatax passes through lovely scenery and is now an attractive tourist route (see pp92–3).

The strikers attacking the customs and excise office to protest against the bread tax.

The Dam on the Tirso River
This dam, 70 m (230 ft) high, with a 40-m (130-ft) drop, was begun in 1918, creating Lake Omodeo. At 20 km (12 miles) long, it was the largest artificial lake in Europe of its time.

THE STRIKE IN CAGLIARI
At the turn of the century, social conflict and tensions were so strong in Sardinia that the first special restrictive laws were enacted. The unrest of miners at the Buggerru mine on 3 September 1904 led to the first general strike in Italy. In 1906, distress at the high cost of living led to a wave of riots in Cagliari which were brutally repressed; ten people died and many others were injured.

The Cabras Marsh
The marsh, extending over 20 hectares (49 acres), is one example of the wide-ranging land reclamation schemes carried out in Sardinia. These public works freed the island from malaria, paving the way for the development of a tourist industry.

1915–18 The Sardinians make a significant contribution to the war effort

1924 The "billion lira law" finances vast public works programme in Sardinia

Flag of the Region of Sardinia

1943 Allied bombings seriously damage Cagliari

0	1920	1930	1940

1921 Partito Sardo d'Azione founded

1926 The Sardinian writer Grazia Deledda wins Nobel Prize

1938 Mussolini founds mining town of Carbonia

1948 Sardinia declared an Autonomous Region

Modern Sardinia

Burgee of the Costa Smeralda Yacht Club

THE RECLAMATION OF Sardinia's coastal marshes was crucial to the modern development of the island. Sardinia's lovely coastline, abandoned and shunned for millennia, could now be developed and seaside resorts built. New luxury villas and holiday villages sprang up, and the Costa Smeralda, or Emerald Coast, became world-famous as an exclusive holiday area. Reclaimed land could also be used for agriculture for the first time, and market gardens and orchards could be planted. The economy has started to shift as a result. Sheep-rearing is on the decline, while industry and services are developing, sometimes adversely affecting the environment. Sardinia today appears to be at a crossroads: modern life competing with the most precious resource: unspoilt nature and habitat diversity.

1971 The Cagliari football team of star striker Gigi Riva wins the Italian championship for the first time

1962 Antonio Segni, a Christian Democrat from Sassari, is elected President of the Italian Republic

1972 The first mines are abandoned, signalling the decline of the Sardinian mining industry

1979 Revolt of terrorists in maximum security prison on island of Asinara

1950	1960	1970

1950	1960	1970

1956 Sardinia starts receiving television broadcasts from RAI, the Italian state TV

1953 First island kidnapping at Orgósolo, marking the beginning of one of Sardinia's most serious postwar problems, one which has fortunately decreased in recent years. Vittorio de Seta's film on Sardinian banditry was awarded a prize at the 1961 Venice Film Festival

1950 No Sardinian cases of malaria, for the first time. The American Rockefeller Foundation's public health programme eliminates the *Anopheles maculipennis* mosquito, which transmits the disease

1970 Pope Paul VI visits Sardinia

1971 Industrial workers outnumber farmers for the first time

1962 Creation of the Costa Smeralda syndicate, promoted by Karim Aga Khan (left), which triggers development in the Costa Smeralda and a consequent tourist boom in north-eastern Sardinia. That same year a law is passed with the aim of stimulating all business sectors

1974 The oil crisis in the Middle East damages the Sardinian petrochemical industry

1979 Cases of kidnapping increase: well-known Italian singer/ songwriter Fabrizio De André and his wife Dori Ghezzi kidnapped

1972 Enrico Berlinguer from Sassari (centre) elected secretary of the Italian Communist Party, a post he holds until his death (1983), promoting a "third way to socialism" and the "historic compromise" between Communists and Christian Democrats

1989 Fires, mostly cases of arson, kill ten tourists on the northeastern coast

1980 The Caprera National Park is founded

Today Together with tourism, the livestock industry (cattle breeding, dairies, tanning) is the leading force in the island's present-day economy

1990 Sardinia struck by a terrible drought

1990	2000
1990	2000

1995 The mining industry crisis worsens; the Sulcis coal mines are put up for sale

2002 The Euro replaces the Lira, becoming Italy's new currency

2001 Gold Mines of Sardinia and the Homestake Mining Company of California agree to open up Sardinia's gold deposits. The metal was first detected in the 1980s, when traces were discovered in streams

1985 Francesco Cossiga from Sassari, former Prime Minister and Home Secretary, is elected President of the Italian Republic

2000 The island's marinas, especially those at Porto Cervo, are rated among the best in the entire Mediterranean

SFIDA ITALIANA AMERICA'S CUP 1983

1983 The first Italian participation in the America's Cup, with the yacht *Azzurra*, is promoted by the Costa Smeralda Yacht Club

SARDINIA
AREA BY AREA

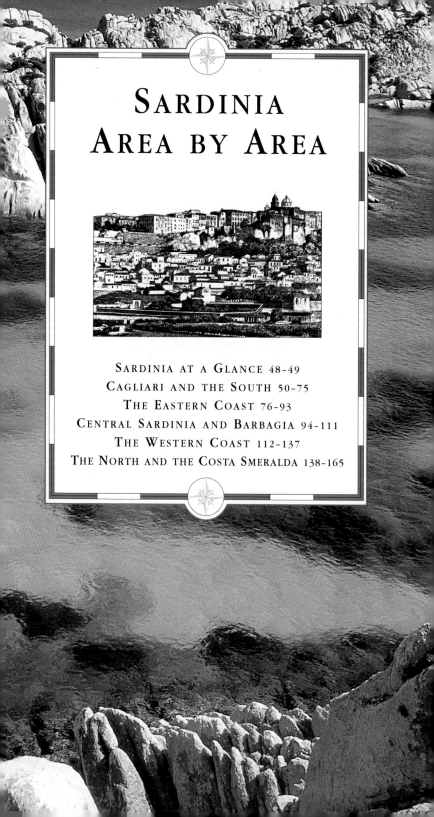

Sardinia at a Glance

Famous mostly for its sea and coastline, Sardinia also abounds in spectacular natural scenery and numerous archaeological ruins. Prehistoric nuraghi are scattered throughout the island, from Su Nuraxi to Orroli, Santu Antine and Silanus. Besides the Costa Smeralda, northern Sardinia is dotted with Romanesque churches in the Logudoro and Gallura countryside. In the Barbagia region and the eastern coast, which are dominated by the large Gennargentu National Park *(see pp82–3)*, the maquis vegetation reigns in the isolated valleys and on inaccessible hilltops. The south and west have interesting Punic ruins (Nora, Sant'Antioco, Tharros), as well as a relatively wild and undiscovered western coastline.

Ardara's Romanesque church, Santa Maria del Regno *(see p156)*

Flamingoes wintering in the marshes around Oristano *(see pp134–5)*

The impressive ruins of Tharros *(see pp132–3)*

THE WESTERN COAST

• Oristano

0 km   20

0 miles   20

CAGLIARI AND THE SOUTH

The rugged coast near Buggerru *(see p68)*

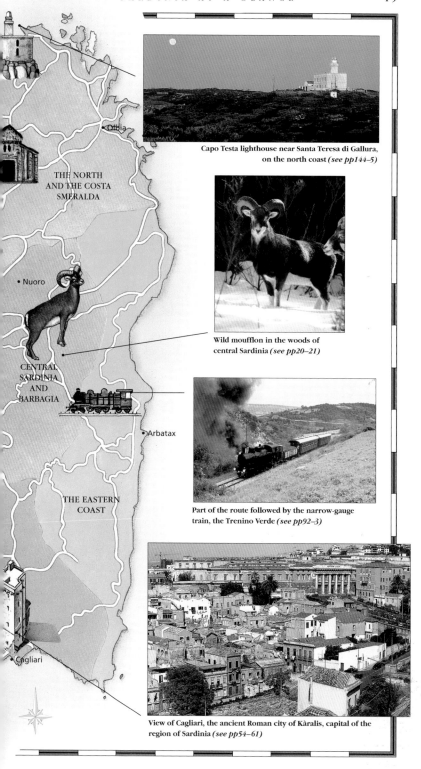

Capo Testa lighthouse near Santa Teresa di Gallura, on the north coast *(see pp144–5)*

Wild moufflon in the woods of central Sardinia *(see pp20–21)*

Part of the route followed by the narrow-gauge train, the Trenino Verde *(see pp92–3)*

View of Cagliari, the ancient Roman city of Kàralis, capital of the region of Sardinia *(see pp54–61)*

CAGLIARI AND THE SOUTH

*S*OUTHERN SARDINIA *has a varied landscape with tall sand dunes along the coast, marshland where pink flamingoes build their nests and abundant maquis where the rare Sardinian deer still survive. It is also an area of interesting prehistoric sites, such as Nora and Su Nuraxi, and it was once the mining heartland of the island.*

The mining history of the area dates back to 5000 BC, when the island's inhabitants discovered how to extract and smelt copper and silver. The Phoenicians used the area as a base for trade and shipped local ores across the Mediterranean. In the Middle Ages the Pisans brought new wealth to the region with expansion of the silver mines. During the Fascist era, Mussolini exploited the island's coal in an attempt to make Italy self-sufficient.

Today, after years of decline, the industrial buildings of the Sulcis and Iglesiente areas are being converted into tourist attractions with mines and museums to visit. The area's natural beauty merges with the 19th-century mining buildings, which look like Gothic castles among the maquis.

The island's capital, Cagliari, was founded by Phoenician sailors, but it was the Aragonese who left the most enduring mark. The Spanish fortification, or Castello district, still dominates today's city.

North of Cagliari lies the Campidano plain, bordered by prickly pears and eucalyptus. This has long been Sardinia's "bread-basket", but farm labour now combines with factory work, especially around Cagliari.

In the uplands to the east are the ruins of Sardinia's largest prehistoric site, Su Nuraxi, chosen for its vantage point over the surrounding plains.

The islands of San Pietro and Sant'Antioco are separate from the mainland culturally as well as geographically: the towns of Calasetta and Carloforte are inhabited by the descendants of Ligurian coral fishermen who were held hostage in North Africa by Muslim pirates and, once freed, were offered a home on the islands. Today, their dialect, cuisine and traditions remain little changed.

Volcanic rock framing Goloritzé bay

◁ **Cagliari's seafront with the arcaded Via Roma and the Castello district extending along the skyline**

Exploring Cagliari and the South

THE SOUTHWESTERN COAST is one of the most
unspoiled on the island, with undisturbed
coves and beaches. Few roads run along the
coast, so the best way to explore is by sea or
on foot. Inland, the wild maquis of the rugged
Iglesiente and Sulcis terrain contrasts with the
derelict 19th-century industrial buildings of this
former mining area. In the north, excavations
at Su Nuraxi have revealed a complex nuraghic
settlement. Cagliari offers the city's sights and
a wildlife sanctuary in the salt flats, and is
also a good base for the ancient site of Nora.

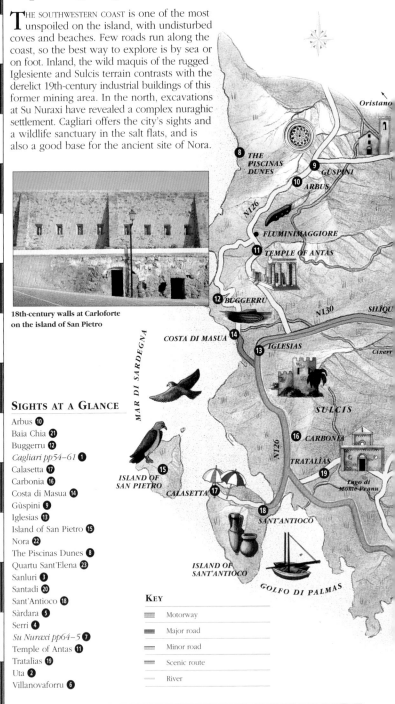

18th-century walls at Carloforte
on the island of San Pietro

SIGHTS AT A GLANCE

KEY

▬▬	Motorway
▬▬	Major road
▬▬	Minor road
▬▬	Scenic route
──	River

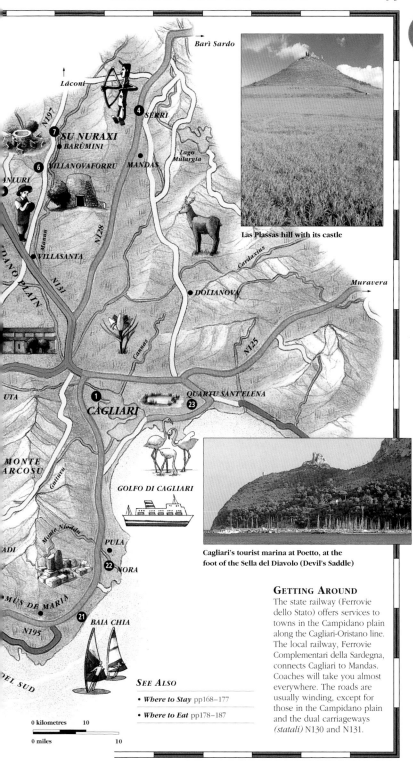

Las Plassas hill with its castle

Cagliari's tourist marina at Poetto, at the
foot of the Sella del Diavolo (Devil's Saddle)

GETTING AROUND

The state railway (Ferrovie
dello Stato) offers services to
towns in the Campidano plain
along the Cagliari-Oristano line.
The local railway, Ferrovie
Complementari della Sardegna,
connects Cagliari to Mandas.
Coaches will take you almost
everywhere. The roads are
usually winding, except for
those in the Campidano plain
and the dual carriageways
(statali) N130 and N131.

SEE ALSO

0 kilometres   10

0 miles   10

Cagliari ❶

Lion on a pulpit in the Cathedral

THE CITY'S SHELTERED position, tucked into the Golfo di Cagliari, has long made Cagliari an important harbour. The Phoenicians chose the eastern shore of Santa Gilla lagoon in the 8th–6th centuries BC, as a stopover for trade ships en route between the Lebanon and the Iberian peninsula. Kàralis ("rocky city") soon became one of the leading Mediterranean centres of trade. The city's present appearance was the work of the Pisans, who developed the Aragonese Castello district. Local inhabitants, who could only enter the city during the day, lived in the walled villages of Stampace and Villanova. These fortifications were demolished in 1862 and the areas are now part of the city. Modern-day Cagliari, capital of the region, is flanked on three sides by sea and marshes and has only expanded northwards.

Sala della Giunta, Palazzo Comunale

Arcaded 19th-century buildings on Via Roma

Exploring Cagliari

For those arriving by sea, the elegant boulevard of Via Roma, parallel to the quay and lined with 19th-century buildings and long arcades, is the first view of the city. During the day crowds throng along this busy shopping street, stopping at the cafés to relax and chat. Stretching out behind are the narrow streets and run-down alleys of the old Marina district. Formerly inhabited by fishermen and merchants, this area is now filled with traditional trattorias and rustic taverns as well as shops selling antiques and local handicrafts. Heading northeast from Via Roma, Largo Carlo Felice is a wide, tree-lined avenue dating from the mid-1800s, with a statue of Carlo Felice, the viceroy of Sardinia (see pp40–41).

City's coat of arms

🏛 Palazzo Comunale

Via Roma. **☎** 070 67 71.
✉ Call 070 67 78 80 12.
At the corner of Via Roma and Largo Carlo Felice is the Palazzo Comunale (town hall). Built in the early 20th century in Neo-Gothic style, the building was restored after World War II. Its façade is decorated with double lancet windows and turrets. Paintings by Filippo Figari and Giovanni Marghinotti hang in the Sala della Rappresentanza, and in the Sala della Giunta there is an interesting triptych of I Consiglieri (Councillors).

🏛 Bastione San Remy

Terrazza Umberto I.
Built in the late 19th century over the Spanish ramparts, the bastions can be reached from Piazza Costituzione up a stairway that leads to a wide terrace, Terrazza Umberto I. From here, there is a magnificent view over the seafront to the surrounding marshes. Every Sunday morning a lively flea market fills the terrace. The covered passageway on the middle level is used for exhibits and cultural events.

♪ Roman Amphitheatre

Viale Fra Ignazio. **☎** 070 65 29 56.
◌ May–Sep: 9am–1pm, 5–7pm daily; Oct–Apr: 9am–1pm, 2:30–5pm daily.
Northwest of the city centre is the most significant evidence of Roman Cagliari. The 2nd-century AD amphitheatre was entirely hewn out of the rock, in the style of Greek theatres. Circus acts with wild beasts were performed here, as well as naumachiae, popular recreations of famous naval battles. A canal system made it possible to fill the arena with water. Much of the brick masonry collapsed during the Middle Ages and quantities of stone were taken from the tiers to build the Castello district. Still visible are the cavea, the pit that held the wild beasts, the corridors behind the tiers and underground passageways, as well as some of the tiers where the spectators sat.

The ruins of the 2nd-century AD Roman amphitheatre

♣ Orto Botanico

Viale Fra Ignazio 13. 🎧 *070 67 53 501.* 🕓 *8am–1:30pm daily; 3pm–6:30pm Mar–May; 3pm–8pm June–Sept.* 🌙 *pm Nov–Mar.* 📷 ♿

South of the amphitheatre, the Botanic Gardens extend over an area of about 5 hectares (12 acres). Founded in 1865, the gardens contain over 500 species of tropical plants from America, Africa, Asia and the Pacific, as well as from the Mediterranean region.

The Orto Botanico is full of small caves such as the Grotta Gennari, used to cultivate ferns because of its ideal temperature and high levels of humidity. There are also remains of Roman tunnels, constructed to improve the water supply to the gardens, a Roman gallery and a well.

♙ Cathedral

Piazza Palazzo. 🕓 *8am–noon, 4–7pm daily.* **Museo Capitolare** 🎧 *070 66 38 37.* 🕓 *by appt.*

Cagliari's Cathedral of Santa Maria was built by the Pisans in the 11th and 12th centuries. Gradually transformed over the centuries, particularly with 17th-century additions, today's façade is the result of radical restoration

The Baroque marble interior of the Cathedral of Santa Maria

Holy water basin detail

in the 1930s, which reinstated the original Romanesque style. Four lions guarding the entrance date from this period. Inside, Santa Maria retains much Baroque decoration, as well as some original detail. Near the entrance are two pulpits by Mastro Guglielmo, sculpted in 1162 for the cathedral of Pisa and donated to Cagliari by the Tuscan city. A marble basin for holy water is decorated with the image of an angel. A crypt under the altar houses the tombs of the princes of the House of Savoy.

In the chapterhouse a collection of paintings includes a *Flagellation of Christ* attributed to Guido Reni. The **Museo Capitolare** (Treasury) displays precious church items such as chalices and amphoras, as well as a large gilded silver cross.

VISITORS' CHECKLIST

Road map C6. 🏘 *177,000.*
ℹ *Piazza Matteotti 9 (070 66 92 55); Piazza Deffenu 9 (070 60 42 41).* 🚢 *Sun, Terrazza Umberto I (antiques); Sun, Sant' Elia district (general).* 🎭 *1 May: Sant'Efisio Feast Day.*
🌐 *www.comunedicagliari.it*

CAGLIARI TOWN CENTRE

Bastione San Remy ④
Cathedral ⑤
Cittadella dei Musei ⑥
Exma ⑧
Orto Botanico ②
Roman Amphitheatre ①
San Saturnino ⑨
Torre dell'Elefante ⑦
Villa di Tigellio ③

KEY

▮ Street-by-Street *see pp56–7*
🚉 Railway station
⛴ Ferry boarding point
🅿 Parking
ℹ Tourist information
✚ Hospital
✝ Church

0 metres 350
0 yards 350

Street-by-Street: Castello

Torre dell'Elefante detail

THE CASTELLO DISTRICT, the oldest part of Cagliari, was built by the Pisans and Aragonese. Positioned at the top of a hill, and protected by ancient city walls, it consisted of aristocratic mansions and the city's Cathedral. With time its function as a centre of power waned, and the elegant buildings gradually deteriorated. At the centre of the district is Piazza Palazzo with the Palazzo Arcivescovile (Archbishop's Palace) and the Cathedral. Surrounding the ancient citadel, imposing watchtowers dominate the entrance gates, and parts of the fortifications have been transformed into a museum complex and an esplanade.

★ Cathedral
Santa Maria Cathedral, re-built several times, combines Pisan, Aragonese and Baroque features. The multi-coloured marble interior has fine sculptures. (See p55).

★ Cittadella dei Musei
This modern complex, converted from the former Savoyard arsenal, houses the city's most important museums. (See p58).

Palazzo Arcivescovile

Torre di San Pancrazio
The northern gate of the Castello district was built in 1305 by Giovanni Capula. It is dressed on three sides with limestone ashlar, while the inner face is open, exposing the stairs and wooden balconies of the interior.

Via La Marmora
A number of craft workshops and antique shops line the characteristic Via La Marmora.

★ Bastione San Remy
In the early 1900s the Spanish defensive walls were transformed into the bastions of San Remy, opening out onto a wide esplanade with spectacular views.

Porta dei Leoni
The gate that leads into the lower Marina district owes its name to the two Romanesque lions' heads (leoni) above the arch.

BASTIONE SAN REMY

VIA CANNELLE

VIA LA MARMORA

PIAZZA CARLO ALBERTO

VIA VIVALDI

SI

VIA UNIVERSITA

Palazzo Boyl
Overlooking the bastions of San Remy, this palazzo was built in 1840. It incorporates the remains of the Torre dell'Aquila (Eagle's Tower), one of the large Pisan towers that stood over the entrance gates of the ancient city.

Torre dell'Elefante
The "Elephant's Tower" was built by local architect Giovanni Capula in 1307. The mechanism for opening the gates is still visible and an elephant statue, after which the tower was named, can be seen on the façade.

KEY

--- Suggested route

0 metres   50
0 yards   50

STAR SIGHTS

★ Cittadella dei Musei

★ Cathedral

★ Bastione San Remy

Cittadella dei Musei, the modern complex in the Castello district

Cittadella dei Musei

Piazza Arsenale.

At the northern end of the Castello district is the modern museum complex, the Cittadella dei Musei. Fashioned from the former royal arsenal which had been built on the site of the Spanish citadel, the complex houses the Museo Archeologico Nazionale, the Museo Civico d'Arte Orientale Stefano Cardu and the Pinacoteca Nazionale. A terrace offers fine views of the city.

🏛 Museo Archeologico Nazionale

Cittadella dei Musei, Piazza Arsenale. **(** 070 65 59 11. **◯** 9am–8pm Thur–Sun. 📷 📹 ♿
The National Archaeological Museum is devoted to the history of Sardinia. The ground floor exhibits are arranged in chronological order, from the Neolithic era to the Middle Ages. In the Neolithic hall are fine alabaster statues of female divinities, including one in the shape of a cross from Senorbi. Objects from the late Bronze Age include axes with raised edges. There is an interesting collection of nuraghic bronze figurines *(see pp32–3)*, found in the Tempio di Teti at Abini. Some of these hold votive swords decorated with the head of a deer, a tribal chief or a warrior. In the third hall is a statuette of a musician playing the Sardinian flute, the *launeddas (see p90)*.

The Phoenician and Roman periods are represented by objects found mostly at sites around Cagliari, Tharros and Nora. These include jewellery and amulets, small coloured glass heads and terracotta votive statuettes. Among the loveliest pieces of jewellery are an embossed golden bracelet and gold earrings from Tharros.

The Early Christian pieces, such as jugs, lamps and gold jewellery, give an insight into the island's medieval culture, and influences from Byzantine, Vandal and Moorish invaders.

🏛 Museo Civico d'Arte Orientale Stefano Cardu

Cittadella dei Musei. **(** 070 65 18 88. **◯** 9am–7:30pm Tue–Sun. 📹
The Museum of Oriental Art, reopened in late 1996, has on exhibition most of the 1,300 objects donated to the city in 1917 by Stefano Cardu, a Sardinian who served at the court of the King of Siam. The collection includes imperial gold and silver objects, ivory statues and vases, mostly dating from the 11th century.

🏛 Pinacoteca Nazionale

Cittadella dei Musei. **(** 070 67 40 54. **◯** 9am–7pm Tue–Sun. 📷 📹 ♿
The entrance to the three-storey National Gallery is on the upper floor. Here, 15th- and 16th-century paintings include a collection of Catalan and Sardinian altarpieces, such as the *Annunciation* by Juan Mates (1391–1431), *Sant'Eligio* by the Master of Sanluri (early 16th century), and *Nostra Signora della Neve* (1568) by Michele Cavaro.

The middle floor houses a collection of 17th- and 18th-century paintings as well as a display of typical Sardinian costumes and objects. The lower floor features a painting by the Stampace school, *Chiesa di San Francesco*, which was damaged by fire in 1871.

🏛 Galleria Comunale d'Arte

Giardini Pubblici, Viale Regina Elena.
(070 49 07 27. **◯** 9am–1pm, 5–9pm (Oct–Apr: 3:30–7pm) Tue–Sun. 📹 📷 ♿
The Municipal Art Gallery has a collection of significant works by Sardinian artists from the late 19th century to the 1970s. On the ground floor are works by Francesco Ciusa. The first floor features contemporary art.

⌂ Necropoli Tuvixeddu

Via Falzarego. **◯** Mar–Sep: 8am–sunset.
The hundreds of underground burial chambers of the Punic necropolis, west of the Botanical Gardens, are overgrown with brambles. The funerary paintings on the tombs, however, are worth a visit, especially the *Tomba del Guerriero* (Warrior's Tomb) and the *Tomba dell'Ureo*.

⌂ Grotta della Vipera

Viale Sant'Avendrace. **(** 070 41 108. **◯** 9am–5pm Tue–Sun.
One of the tombs in the necropolis is that of Atilia Pomptilla, wife of Cassius Philippus, exiled here in the 1st century AD. Two snakes adorn the façade of the "viper's cave" and on the walls are inscriptions in Greek and Latin.

Marble sarcophagus (4th century AD) from the Archaeological Museum

The early Christian church dedicated to San Saturnino, patron saint of Cagliari

⋔ Subterranean Cagliari

Viale Fra Ignazio. 070 66 30 52. to the public.

Northeast of the city centre, in the area below the Roman amphitheatre, the hospital and the Orto Botanico, there are underground chambers and passageways cut out of the rock by the Phoenicians. The most spectacular of these is the vast chamber named after King Vittorio Emanuele II. From the Casa di Riposo in Viale Fra Ignazio, it is accessed via a dingy stairway which leads into the eerie chamber. The walls, around 2,500 sq m (26,900 sq ft), are covered with thick facing to protect them from the humidity.

The Phoenician underground chamber, "Vittorio Emanuele II"

⌂ Villa di Tigellio

Via Tigellio. to the public.

Situated southeast of the Botanical Gardens, Villa di Tigellio is a group of three aristocratic Roman villas and baths dating from the Imperial era. The *tablinum*, the room used to receive guests, opens onto the central atrium.

⌂ Exma

Via San Lucifero. 070 66 63 99. 9am–1pm, 5pm–midnight (Oct–Apr: 9am–8pm). Mon.

On the eastern side of the Castello district stands the former municipal slaughterhouse, built in the mid-19th century and closed in 1964. The dark red building, decorated with sculpted heads of cows, has been restructured to house the city's arts centre.

The centre's cultural calendar offers temporary exhibitions of photography, painting and sculpture, as well as courses for children and adults. Classical music concerts are held in the courtyard in the summer and in the auditorium in the winter.

A cow's head on the Exma building

There are plans to make this the permanent home of the graphic arts section of the Galleria Comunale d'Arte.

⌂ San Saturnino

Piazza San Cosimo. 070 201 01. 9am–1pm Mon–Sat. public hols.

East of the Exma building is the church of San Saturnino, also known as Santi Cosma e Damiano. Reopened after 18 years of restoration, and still not completely refurbished, this simple church is one of the oldest Christian buildings on the island. It was begun in the 5th century to commemorate the martyrdom of Saturno, the city's patron saint.

In the Middle Ages, San Saturnino, together with its adjacent monastery, became an important religious and cultural centre. The Greek cross plan of the church was enlarged in the 11th century by French Victorine friars from Marseille, who built three aisles with barrel vaults. Inside, a marble ex voto holds the oldest representation of San Saturno.

Glass windows have been placed in the sturdy tufa construction to prevent further damage and decay from humidity and air, and this has given the church a rather modern appearance. Nonetheless, it is still a fascinating place to visit.

The Marshes and Salt Flats

A yellow-bellied toad from the marshes

A NETWORK OF MARSHES and lakes extends around the outskirts of Cagliari, particularly along the western shore of the bay. The vast lagoon of the Santa Gilla marsh stretches over 4,000 hectares (9,800 acres), including the ancient Macchiareddu salt flats. These saltworks are now the only ones in operation in the area. After years of neglect and environmental deterioration, the marshy areas around Cagliari have finally become reserves, and the area once again has a rich and varied fauna. To the east of the city, the Molentargius marsh is a favourite refuge for migratory birds. At least 170 species have been identified here, which is one-third of the entire bird population of Europe. Between August and March, flamingoes attract dozens of naturalists. Since 1993 these creatures have begun once again to nest along the banks of the Molentargius marsh.

A Naturalist's Paradise
In autumn the marshes are filled with migratory birds and are a favourite with bird-watchers.

The Saltworks
Of the numerous saltworks that once operated around Cagliari, only those in the Macchiareddu industrial area are still active.

Macchiareddu Salt Flat

N130

Fishing port of Giorgino

GOLFO D
CAGLIAR

Stagno di
Santa Gilla

N195

Nesting Grounds
In recent years, flamingoes have begun to use the marshes as a nesting ground again.

VISITORS' CHECKLIST

Road map C6. 🚗 *P from Via Roma for Poetto; 8 for Santa Gilla.* 🛈 *EPT Piazza Deffenu 9, Cagliari (070-60 42 41). The best period for bird-watching is August–March.*

WILDLIFE OF THE MARSHLANDS

Many migratory and endemic bird species populate the marshes around Cagliari. These feed upon the small creatures, such as the brine shrimp *Artemia salina*, which thrive in the salt-rich water. As well as the colony of flamingoes, which sometimes exceeds 10,000, you will also see many other species of water birds such as blackwinged stilts, avocets, cormorants and teals. The waters of Macchiareddu salt flats, on the other hand, are populated by mallards, coots and pintail ducks, which hunt peacefully among the islets and inlets.

Flamingo

Blackwinged Stilt

Avocet

Cormorant

Teal

Cat's-tail flowers

D

N554

Torre dell'Elefante, Cagliari

Stagno di Molentargius

Stagno di Simbirizzi

N125

CAGLIARI
(see pp.54–9)

Stagno di Quartu

Quartu Salt Flat

Il Poetto beach

GOLFO DI CAGLIARI

0 kilometres   2

0 miles   2

Golfo degli Angeli

Capo Sant'Elia

KEY

▭	Motorway
▭	Major road
▦	Salt flat
▦	Marsh

Molentargius Marsh

This is an ideal stopping place for migratory birds from Africa.

The Romanesque church of Santa Maria at Uta

Uta ❷

Road map C6. 👥 7,000. 🚌 🚊
ℹ️ Via Umberto I (070 96 66 02 01).
🎭 26–31 Aug: Santa Lucia.

THE FLOURISHING agricultural town of Uta is situated at the edge of the Campidano plain, a vast fertile corridor that stretches northwards from Cagliari to Oristano. On the outskirts of town is the simple church of **Santa Maria**, built in 1140 by French Victorine friars from Marseille. The church façade is made of light-coloured stone, with blocks of a darker hue, and is decorated with blind arches and a small bell gable. Sculptures of human heads, deer, calves and geometric patterns adorn the arches.

ENVIRONS: The village of **San Sperate**, 8 km (5 miles) north-east of Uta, is a living museum with murals, and sculptures by local artist Pinuccio Sciola.

🏛 **Santa Maria**
Via Santa Maria. 📞 070 96 81 57.
🕐 by appt only.

Sanluri ❸

Road map C5. 👥 9,000. 🚌 🚊
ℹ️ Piazza Mazzini 4 (070 937 05 05).
🎭 10 Aug: San Lorenzo.

AN IMPORTANT TOWN in the Campidano plain, Sanluri developed around the 14th-century castle of Eleonora d'Arborea (see p36). This stronghold changed hands several times before it was taken by the Aragonese in 1709. The massive square structure has towers on its four corners and an ornate wrought-iron gate.

Today the castle is owned by the Villasanta family and houses the **Museo Risorgimentale Duca d'Aosta**. The historical exhibits include fine furniture such as a 16th-century bed. A sculpture of San Michele (St Michael) stands in the entrance hall. On the upper floor is the **Museo della Ceroplastiche** in which there are 343 pieces of wax from 1500 to 1800.

In the restored 16th-century Convento dei Cappuccini, on a hill overlooking the town, the **Museo Storico Etnografico** displays a collection of tools and archaeological finds.

Wax statue in Sanluri's Museo della Ceroplastica

🏛 **Museo Risorgimentale Duca d'Aosta**
Castello di Eleonora d'Arborea.
📞 070 930 71 05. 🕐 Jul–Sep: 4:30–8:30pm Tue, Wed, Fri; Oct–Dec & Mar–Jun: 9:30am–1pm, 3pm–sunset first & third Sun of month, Easter Mon, 25 Apr, 1 May. 🚫 📷

🏛 **Museo Storico Etnografico**
Via San Rocco 6. 📞 070 930 71 07.
🕐 8am–noon, 3pm–7pm daily.
📷 🚻 ♿

Serri ❹

Road map C4. 👥 810. 🚌 🚊
ℹ️ Via Municipio 1 (0782 80 60 81).
🎭 Third Sun of Sep: Santa Lucia.

THIS SHEEP-FARMING centre lies on the edge of a rocky plateau dominating the Trexenta hills. Right on the spur of the promontory is the **Santuario Nuragico di Santa Vittoria**, one of Sardinia's most fascinating nuraghic sites. The archaeological ruins here have yielded some important bronze votive statuettes, now housed in the Museo Archeologico Nazionale in Cagliari (see p58). Pilgrims came here to worship the God of Water at the sacred well. The temple well, which is in an excellent state of preservation, is reached via 13 amazingly precise basalt steps. A short five-minute walk from the entrance takes you to the Recinto delle Feste (festivities area). This elliptical building has a porticoed courtyard surrounded by rooms for the pilgrims. This is possibly a predecessor of the many rural sanctuaries (cumbessias or muristeni) found today in Sardinia's country churches.

🏠 **Santuario Nuragico di Santa Vittoria**
7 km (4 miles) NW. 📞 0782 80 62 37. 🕐 by appt only.

A modern mural in the village of San Sperate

The 16th-century parish church of the Beata Vergine Assunta at Sàrdara

Sàrdara 5

Road map C5. 🏛 5,000. 🚌
🎉 22 Sep: Santa Maria is Acquas.

SITUATED AT the northern edge of the Campidano plain, the town of Sàrdara lay on the border between the medieval principalities of Arborea and Cagliari (see pp36–7). Stone houses from this period, with large arched doorways, have been preserved in the district around **San Gregorio**. This Romanesque church was built in the 6th century. Its tall, narrow façade, however, shows the initial influence of Gothic architecture. On the western outskirts of town is the 16th-century parish church of **Beata Vergine Assunta**, interesting for its sculpted columns and arches, and vault patterned with stars.

Near the Assunta church are the remains of a nuraghic well-temple. This underground chamber, from the 9th–10th centuries BC, has walls of basalt and limestone and an domed ceiling. Also known as the *Funtana de is Dolus* (fountain of pain), it is where worshippers came to take the curative spring waters. The source of the temple water was an ancient underground well, and a stone canal carried the mineral water from the sacred spring to the temple. Decorated earthenware votive objects found in the temple are now kept in the Museo Archeologico Nazionale in Cagliari (see p58).

Sàrdara is also famous for its carpet-weaving and woollen and cotton tapestries. These are colourfully embroidered with traditional animal and floral decorative motifs.

ENVIRONS: Ruins of the medieval **Castello di Monreale**, a fortification of the principality of Arborea, stand on a hill 1 km (half a mile) southwest of town. A little further west are the remains of the **Aquae Neapolitanae**, Roman baths, and nearby is the Gothic church of **Santa Maria is Acquas**, where a festival takes place in September.

Villanovaforru 6

Road map C5. 🏛 730. 🚌
ℹ Piazza Costituzione (070 930 00 00). 🎉 15 Jul: Santa Marina.

THIS SMALL agricultural centre was founded in the 17th century by the Spanish and has retained much of its original layout. Many houses have kept their decorative features and character. Today, the Monte Granatico building (formerly a grain store), in the town's central square, houses a small but well-run **Museo Archeologico**. Finds from the nearby nuraghic site of Genna Maria are on display here, including bronze, iron and ceramic objects from the 9th century BC on the ground floor. On the first floor are votive objects dedicated to Demeter and Persephone from the Roman era.

ENVIRONS: On the road to Collinas, 1 km (half a mile) west of the town, is the nuraghic village of **Genna Maria**. Discovered in 1977, the site, which is still being excavated, is on a prominent hilltop. This nuraghe has a typical design (see pp36–7). Thick walls with three towers form a triangle which encloses a central tower and courtyard with a well. Another wall with six corner towers surrounds the entire village area.

🏛 **Museo Archeologico**
Piazza Costituzione. 📞 070 930 00 50.
🕐 9:30am–1pm, 3–6pm (May–Sep: 7pm) Tue–Sun. 📷 🎫 combined ticket with Genna Maria. ♿
⛰ **Genna Maria**
1 km (half a mile) W. 📞 070 930 00 48. 🕐 9:30am–1pm, 3:30–7pm (Oct–Mar: 6pm) Tue–Sun.

THE SAFFRON OF SARDINIA

Stigma

The production of Sardinian saffron, prized throughout Europe, is based around San Gavino in the Campidano plain. Saffron is obtained by drying the dark red stigma of *Crocus sativus*, a purple flower that carpets the barren fields in autumn. The harvest, however, is very brief as the stigmas must be collected the day the flower comes into bloom. Saffron, once considered as precious as gold, was used to make dyestuff for fabrics and rugs, as a colouring agent for sweets and as a spice for savoury dishes. It is still used in today's cooking (see p180).

Crocus flowers

Su Nuraxi ❼

E XCAVATIONS EAST OF BARÙMINI have brought to light the largest nuraghic fortress in Sardinia, Su Nuraxi. The original settlement dates from 1500 BC, during the Middle Bronze Age. Built on a hill, the 19 m (62 ft) high fortress occupied an excellent vantage point, with clear views over the surrounding plains. In the 7th century BC, with the threat of Phoenician invasion, the central section of the fortress, consisting of a tower connected to four external nuraghi, was further protected by a thick outer wall with turrets and a sentinel's walkway. The village gradually developed outside the main fortifications with single- and multi-room dwellings, including a flour mill and bakery. The area was inhabited for almost 2,000 years although, after the Carthaginian conquest, the upper parts of the fort were demolished and the site lost its strategic importance.

Single Dwellings
The oldest living quarters were circular with a single room.

Defences
In order to defend themselves from Carthaginian invasions, the Nuraghic inhabitants built an outer bulwark. This consisted of seven towers connected by a wall with a walkway for sentinel patrols.

The circular assembly hall was built against the outer wall. During meetings the elders sat on a long stone bench that ran along the inside of the wall. Objects found here are held in Cagliari's archaeological museum (see p58).

Multi-room Dwellings
These living areas were made up of seven or eight square or trapezoidal rooms which opened onto a courtyard or vestibule, often with a well.

Northeastern Tower
The outer corner towers of the fortress were pierced by a double row of radially arranged fissures through which light could penetrate.

VISITORS' CHECKLIST

Road map C4. 1 km (half a mile) E of Barùmini. ◼ to Barùmini then 1 km (half a mile) on foot. ☎ 070 936 81 28. ◯ 9am – sunset daily. ◎ ☑ ☑

Building Techniques
Huge irregular blocks of stone, laid in "dovetail" fashion without mortar, were used to build the nuraghi. The inner walls of the towers were often reinforced by another wall of stone.

The outer wall was added in the 7th century BC.

The "keep", or central section, was the highest part and the centre of military operations.

The four main towers were connected by a central courtyard.

Sentinel's walkway

The Village
The dwellings were built outside the fortress walls between the 8th–6th centuries BC. There were about 200 circular houses with roofs made from wooden beams and branches.

The Piscinas Dunes ❽

THE HILLS OF SAND at Piscinas and Is Arenas ("the sands" in Sardinian) are "moving" dunes, sometimes as much as 50 m (164 ft) high, that rise up around the estuary of the River Piscinas. Wind erosion by the mistral, the cold north wind that blows in from France, continually changes the landscape, while strongly rooted pioneer plants work their way across the sand. The robust roots of marram grass *(Ammophila arenaria)* gradually stabilize the dune slopes, which are then covered by other salt-resistant plants such as juniper and lentiscus. This unique ecological niche is also the habitat for many animals, and footprints of foxes, wild cats, partridges and rabbits are a common sight on the sand. Remains of the 19th-century mines that were once the mainstay of the Sulcis regional economy are also still visible.

Piscinas beach
The sandy beach at Piscinas is 9 km (5 miles) long. Exposed to the strong mistral wind in winter, the shape of the beach is continually changing.

Marine turtles
The isolated position of Piscinas makes it an ideal spot for loggerhead turtles to lay their eggs.

The Sardinian partridge
favours sunny habitats. It was introduced from North Africa by the Romans.

The sand, shaped by the wind, is an ever-changing landscape.

Tracks of wild animals can often be seen in the sand, particularly in the morning.

Le Dune Hotel
This hotel overlooking the sea shore occupies an old restructured mine building (see p174).

The wild lily, though slim and delicate, manages to bloom and survive even in arid environments.

Mine railway
A section of the 19th-century narrow-gauge railway, once used to transport material from the mines to the sea, has been reopened near the beach.

Marram grass
This strongly rooted, perennial plant, Ammophila arenaria, *is typical of sandy environments.*

Wild rabbits are a common sight on the dunes. You may also come across other small animals such as foxes and lizards.

The sand dunes
Areas of the dunes are covered in thick maquis vegetation.

San Nicola di Mira, at Gùspini

Gùspini ❾

Road map B5. 👥 14,000. 🚗 ℹ City Hall, Via Don Minzoni 10 (070 97 09 09). 🎭 15–31 Aug: Santa Maria.

OVERLOOKING the flat and fertile Campidano plain, Gùspini is surrounded by olive groves and backed by the gradually rising foothills of Monte Arcuentu. The town's lovely 16th-century church of **San Nicola di Mira**, in the main square, boasts a large rose window and is the hub of local life. The feast day of Santa Maria is celebrated with a procession and a horse race.

The **Montevecchio mine**, 8 km (5 miles) west, was one of the largest in Europe until the 1950s. Despite the state of abandon, the miners' houses, headquarters, church, school and hospital are worth a visit. In the summer there are guided tours of the mine and the office building as well as an exhibition on the life of the miners in the past.

The rose window of San Nicola di Mira

🏭 Montevecchio mine
8 km (5 miles) W of Gùspini. 🏨 368 53 89 97. 🕐 Jun–Oct: daily. 🚫 compulsory: 9:30, 10am; 5, 6pm.

Arbus ❿

Road map B5. 👥 8,000. 🚗 ℹ City Hall, Via XX Setiembre (070 975 94 44). 🎭 13 Jun: Sant'Antonio; 21 Aug: Santo Lussorio Palio (horse race).

GRANITE HOUSES characterize the village of Arbus, set on the slopes of Monte Linas. Arbus is known for the production of traditional knives with curved blades, *arrasoias,* made by local craftsmen.

Southwest down the N126 for 7 km (4 miles), then due west across a winding mountain road, is the mining village of **Ingurtosu**, built by the French firm Pertusola. Once home to over 1,000 mine workers, the houses, office building and church are now abandoned. The pine forest surrounding the dilapidated buildings was planted by the mine workers.

A dirt road runs among the old mines, abandoned buildings and former dumping area as far as Naracauli, where there are ruins of a more modern mine complex built shortly after World War I. A train once transported the extracted lead and zinc to the sea, where it was loaded onto ships. Certain sections of the narrow-gauge track and some carriages can be seen on the Piscinas beach.

Stretching northwards from the dune beach of Piscinas is a maquis-covered coast aptly called the Costa Verde. A quiet, scenic road follows the coastline, offering spectacular views of the sea. The road goes as far as the resort of Marina di Arbus, with easy access to sandy beaches.

The large tanks at the Montevecchio mine

Temple of Antas **⓫**

Road map B5. 🚌 *to Fluminimaggiore.*
ℹ️ *Via Cavour 17, Fluminimaggiore
(0781 58 09 90).* 🌐 *www.tiscalinet.
it/tartuao*

FIRST DISCOVERED in 1966, the
ancient Temple of Antas is
believed to have been a sacred
nuraghic site. It was adopted
by the Carthaginians in the
4th century BC and dedicated
to Sid Addir Babài. A century
later the Carthaginians restructured the temple with an
atrium and a central chamber.
Egyptian and Ionic decoration
adorned the temple.

In the 3rd century AD, the
Romans rebuilt the temple
using some of the existing
material, such as the Ionic
capitals of the columns. This
temple was dedicated to the
god and "creator of Sardinians",
Sardus Pater. Although only
six of the columns remain
standing today, the temple's
isolated position amid the
wild maquis makes it an
enchanting place to visit.

ENVIRONS: Set in the fertile
valley of the River Mannu,
9 km (5 miles) north, is the
small agricultural village of
Fluminimaggiore, founded
in the 18th century. Turning
west towards the sea for 9 km
(5 miles), the road proceeds to
Portixeddu beach, protected
by sand dunes. The headland
of Capo Pecora offers stunning
views of the sea and coast.

The old mining community of Buggerru, now a tourist resort

Buggerru **⓬**

Road map B5. 🚶 *1,500.* 🚌
ℹ️ *Via Roma 41 (0781 544 04).*

SITUATED IN A VALLEY opening
out onto the sea, Buggerru
was founded in the mid-18th
century in an area rich in
mineral deposits. It soon
became a flourishing mining
town with a small theatre
where opera singers used to
perform, and the headquarters
of the French *Société Anonyme
des Mines de Malfidano.* The
mines have now closed and
the town is surrounded by
slag heaps. In the lower part
of the town, sculpture by
Pinuccio Sciola *(see p62)* is
dedicated to the miners who
died in the strikes of 1904.

Today, the town has been
reclaimed as a harbour for
pleasure boats, the only one
between Carloforte and
Oristano. The docks, where

boats were once loaded with
local minerals for export, now
serve as a port for visitors to
the wild western coast of the
island and its long stretches
of sandy, sheltered beaches.
To the south is the long and
secluded **Cala Domestica**, a
rocky bay overlooked by a
Spanish watchtower.

Iglesias **⓭**

Road map B5. 🚶 *30,000.* 🚌 🚃
ℹ️ *Biblioteca Comunale, Via Gramsci
(0781 417 95).* 🎭 *Easter Week.*

IGLESIAS, or Villa Ecclesiae,
was founded in the 13th
century by Count Ugolino
della Gherardesca (mentioned
in Dante's *Inferno* XXXIII).
The Pisans had conquered
the area in 1257 and reopened
mines abandoned in Roman
times. Silver was extracted, and
the city had the right to mint

TEMPLE OF ANTAS

This plan shows how the later
Roman temple incorporated the
3rd-century BC Carthaginian
temple. The rectangular plan
and six columns of the pronaos,
the enclosed portico leading to
the temple chamber, are still
visible. An architrave above the
entrance supported a triangular
pediment and
steps led up
to the temple.

The columns, 8 m
(26 ft) high, were made
of smooth limestone
blocks placed on bases
about 1 m (3 ft) wide.

The capitals were
in the Ionic style
but are atypical,
lacking the abacus
and volutes.

Pronaos

Columns

Steps

The Roman temple
was built over the
Carthaginian temple.

The Easter procession during Holy Week at Iglesias

its own coins. In the mid-19th century more mines were opened and Iglesias grew into an important mining centre.

Today, the ruins of the mine buildings, most of which have been abandoned, create a striking contrast with the well-preserved historic centre. The elegant pedestrian shopping street, Corso Matteotti, leads to Piazza del Municipio and the Palazzo Vescovile (Bishop's Palace), built in 1785. On the west side is the 19th-century Palazzo del Comune (Town Hall) and opposite is the cathedral of **Santa Chiara**. Completed in the late 17th century, the cathedral has a Romanesque façade dating from 1288.

The narrow, winding streets around the cathedral are lined with two-storey buildings adorned with wrought-iron balconies. **San Francesco** on Via Don Minzoni was built between the 14th and 16th centuries and has side chapels dedicated to noble families. Half an hour's walk from Piazza Sella is the **Castello di Salvaterra**, built in 1284 as part of the city's medieval defensive walls. A part of these walls is also visible in Via Eleonora d'Arborea.

During Easter week, holy processions and performances of mystery plays take place in the town (see p26).

THE SULCIS MINES

The history of Sardinia's mines is inextricably linked with the island's economic development. Ancient rock formations, particularly in the southwestern region of the island known as Sulcis, have left rich mineral deposits of silver, copper, lead, iron and zinc. Nuraghic people are known to have had metalworking skills and there is evidence of Phoenician and Roman mines. In the short-lived boom of 19th-century industrialization, the mines stood like citadels in a predominantly agricultural country. Today, the dream of prosperity through mining is vanishing, and all that remains is a rich heritage of mining architecture and culture.

Entrance to an abandoned mine

The area around Iglesias is the mining heart of Sardinia, and the landscape descending to the sea has been deeply scarred by mine working. At Monteponi the industrial plants, mine shafts and miners' houses look as though they were only recently abandoned, while at Masua, tunnels and railways are still visible. At Buggerru, the Malfidano mine, exploited for eight centuries, opens onto the sea front.

ENVIRONS: At Case Marganai, 10 km (6 miles) northeast of Iglesias, the **Linasia Botanical Gardens** extend over an area of 9 sq km (3 sq miles) with examples of plants from the maquis. The **Museo Casa Natura** here has a collection of local plants and pieces from mine shafts.

Guided tours of local mines are organized by the **Associazione Minatori** (Miners' Association). One tour takes in the lead and zinc Monteponi mine, with the elegant Bellavista building and Sella shaft. Another tour begins at the San Giovanni mine and ends at the abandoned village of Seddas Moddizzis. This includes the Santa Barbara mine shaft whose crenellated walls make it look like a medieval castle.

Romanesque portal of Santa Chiara, Iglesias

🍁 **Linasia Botanical Gardens**
Località Marganai. 📞 0781 200 61.
🕐 Oct–Apr: 9am–1pm Sat & Sun; May–Sep: 9am–noon, 4–7:30pm Tue, Thu, Sat & Sun. 🎟 **Museo Casa Natura** phone in advance.
🏭 **Associazione Minatori**
Località Nicolay, Monteponi.
📞 0781 49 14 10. 🔲

Costa di Masua ⑭

Road map B5. ℹ (0781 261 21).

THE CORNICHE ROAD between Fontanamare and Masua, 12 km (7 miles) north, follows a wild and splendid coastline. At Masua, the little beach of Porto Flavia is overlooked by pillars of eroded limestone and, offshore, the unmistakable profile of Pan di Zucchero ("sugarloaf") island. This sheer rock rises 132 m (433 ft) from the sea. At Nebida you can see the abandoned mines of the industrial archaeological area.

A panoramic path along the coast leads to the abandoned remains of La Marmora mine buildings and shafts.

The island of Pan di Zucchero jutting out from the sea

Island of San Pietro ⑮

NAMED AFTER THE APOSTLE PETER, who is said to have taken refuge here during a storm, the island of San Pietro was virtually uninhabited until 1736, when Carlo Emanuele III offered it to a community of Ligurian coral fishermen whose ancestors had been exiled to the island of Tabarca, off the Tunisian coast. San Pietro's Ligurian origins can be seen in the architecture, dialect and cuisine, which also bears traces of North African influences. The rugged coast, inhabited by the rare Eleonora's falcon, has spectacular coves that can be reached only by sea. The island is covered in thick maquis vegetation.

La Punta
Houses which once belonged to the tuna fishermen are being converted into holiday homes.

Cala Fico
Walls of silver rock on one side and brown rock on the other enclose this sheltered inlet.

Cala Vinagra

Montagna di Ravenna

Carloforte •

Capo Sandalo
The westernmost point of the island, dominated by a lighthouse, is frequently exposed to the mistral wind.

Eleonora's falcon, so named because Eleonora d'Arborea *(see p36)* was the only one allowed to hunt it, is protected in this reserve. The conservation area has observation points and marked footpaths.

Monte di Gasparro

La Caletta

Stagno della Vinagra

0 kilometres   2

0 miles   2

Salt flats on the outskirts of Carloforte attract a large number of migratory birds.

La Caletta
Protected from rough seas by Punta Spalmatore, the sheltered bay of La Caletta has a white, sandy beach.

KEY

▬▬	Major road
═	Minor road
▩	Salt flat
━	River

VISITORS' CHECKLIST

Road map B6. 🏠 *7,000.*
ℹ️ *Corso Tagliafico 1, Carloforte
(0781 85 40 09).* ⛴ *Saremar
(0781 85 40 05) from Calasetta
or Portovesme. In August the
ferries can get busy and it is
advisable to book. The Laguna
and Sir Lawrence motor boats at
Carloforte offer trips around the
island.* 🎉 *29 Jun: San Pietro.*

Isola
Piana

Carloforte
*The only town on the island,
Carloforte overlooks the port,
with alleys and stairways
descending to the water.
The centre of social life is
Piazza Carlo Emanuele III.
The San Pietro feast day
procession of boats is also
worth watching.*

Punta delle Colonne
*The name, Cape of Columns,
refers to the trachytic stacks
that jut out from the sea.*

Carbonia's Piazza Roma, a typical example of Fascist architecture

Carbonia 🔟

Road map B6. 🏠 *34,000.* 🚌
ℹ️ *Piazza Marmilla (0781 67 16 27).*
@ *carbonia@sardinia.net*
W *www.sardinia.net/carbonia/*

Carbonia, LOCATED in the
mining region of Sulcis,
was founded by Mussolini in
1936, during the international
embargo imposed against
Italy because of the Abyssinian
campaign. The town, which
only took two years to build,
has retained its Fascist town
planning and architectural
conception, with imposing
buildings and broad streets
that converge at the central
Piazza Roma. The town's most
important public buildings are
found here, including the
Town Hall, the Torre Civica
tower and the parish church
of San Ponziano, with its
trachyte bell tower.

Villa Sulcis, the former
residence of the director of
the mines, has become the
Museo Archeologico. On
display are earthenware and
bronze statuettes and jewels
from local *domus de janas*,
and finds from the archaeological sites at Monte Sirai.

ENVIRONS: West of Carbonia
along the N126, a signposted
road leads to the imposing
hill occupied by the Monte
Sirai archaeological site. The
stunning view alone is worth
the visit, as you can see the
islands of Sant'Antioco and
San Pietro. The fortified
Acropolis of Monte Sirai
was built by the Phoenicians
in the 4th century BC to
defend Sulki (present-day
Sant'Antioco). The thick outer
wall protected the acropolis
and the surrounding garrison
town, which could house 500
foot soldiers and 100 mounted
soldiers. The ruins of this
ancient military camp were

discovered in 1963 and excavations are still under way.

The necropolis, northwest
of the main citadel, has a Phoenician section with common
graves, as well as an area of
Punic tombs with underground
burial chambers.

🏛 Museo Archeologico
Villa Sulcis, Via Napoli 4. 📞 *0781
640 44.* 🕐 *9am–1pm, 3–7pm (Jun–
Sept: 4–8pm) daily.* 🚫 📷 ♿

⛩ Acropolis of Monte Sirai
3 km (2 miles) S of Carbonia.
🕐 *Jun–Sept: 9am–1pm, 4–8pm daily.
Oct–May: 9am–5pm daily.* 📷 📷

**Underground burial chambers in
the necropolis of Monte Sirai**

Calasetta 🔟

Road map B6. 🏠 *2,800.* 🚌 ⛴
ℹ️ *Piazza Municipio 10 (0781 885 34).*

The SECOND LARGEST village on
the island of Sant'Antioco
(*see p72*) and a trading port
for Carloforte, Calasetta was
founded in 1769 to house the
Ligurian fishermen arriving
from the Tunisian island of
Tabarca. The straight streets
with their two-storey houses
lead to the main square. Here,
the parish church has a bell
tower of Arab derivation. The
road heading south along the
western coast offers a
panoramic view of alternating
cliffs, coves and beaches.

Urns that held the ashes of babies in the Tophet outside Sant'Antioco

Sant'Antioco **⑱**

Road map B6. 🏘 *13,000.* 🚌
ℹ️ *Via Nazionale 175 (0781 84 05 92).*
📅 *29 Jun: San Pietro.*

S ANT'ANTIOCO is the main town on the island of the same name. The island is connected to Sardinia by a causeway and remains of a Roman bridge are still visible from the road. The *faraglioni,* two large menhirs, stand on one side. According to legend these are the petrified figures of a nun and a monk, turned to stone as they tried to elope.

The town was founded by the Phoenicians in the 8th century BC and named Sulki. It soon became a major port in the Mediterranean, due to the trade in minerals, including gold, extracted from the area. Ptolemy, the Greek astronomer, gave it the name of *insula plumbaria* (island of lead). The Carthaginians used the port during the second Punic War *(see p34),* but this alliance was harshly punished by the victorious Romans. Under the Roman Empire the town flourished, until continuous pirate raids during the Middle Ages led to its gradual decline.

The picturesque town centre climbs away from the sea and its characteristic houses have small wrought-iron balconies. The main street, **Corso Vittorio Emanuele**, is shaded by an avenue of trees. Above the town is the church of **Sant'Antioco**, built in the 6th century with a Greek cross plan and central dome, but modified in the 11th century.

According to tradition the remains of the island's patron saint, Sant'Antioco, are buried in the catacombs, reached via the transept. The body of the martyr is said to have floated here after he was killed by the Romans in Africa. Some catacombs are open to the public. The chambers are less than 2 m (6 ft) high and some are deco-rated with frescoes.

In nearby Via Regina Margherita, the Monte Granatico building is now occupied by the **Antiquarium**. This museum contains Phoenician and Roman earthenware, jewels and other objects found in the area, including urns from the nearby Tophet necropolis.

The **Museo Etnografico** is housed in a former wine-making plant. The large central hall contains kitchen equipment used to make cheese and cultivate grape-

vines. The weaving section has spindles and looms on display, once used for the processing of wool and *byssus,* a fine filament taken from the *Pinna nobilis,* the largest bivalve mollusc in the Mediterranean. Under the arcade outside, original wine-making equipment and implements used for raising livestock are on display.

Dominating the town is the red stone **Castello Sabaudo**, rebuilt by the Aragonese in the 16th century. Just outside town, on a cliff overlooking the sea, the bleak **Tophet** is a Phoenician sanctuary and necropolis. This burial ground was used for the ashes of still-born babies, or those who died shortly after birth. Nearby is the Carthaginian **Necropolis** with about 40

Fresco in the catacombs of Sant'Antioco

underground family tombs. This area was later used by the Romans for the ashes of their dead. The tombs occupy the upper part of town and were used as catacombs during the Early Christian period.

🏛 **Sant'Antioco**
Via Necropoli. 📞 *0781 830 44.*
Catacombs 🕐 *9am–noon, 3–6pm daily.* 🚫 ✅

Cala Domestica, north of Sant'Antioco *(see p68)*

⏷ Antiquarium

Via Regina Margherita 113. 📞 *0781 835 90*. ◐ *9:30am–1pm, 3:30–7pm daily*. 🎫 *combined ticket with Museo Etnografico, Tophet*.
🚫 ♿

⏷ Museo Etnografico

Via Necropoli. 📞 *0781 84 10 89*. ◐ *9:30am–1pm, 3:30–7pm daily*. 🎫 *combined ticket*. ♿

⏷ Tophet

Via Castello. 🛈 *Archeotur (0781 835 90)*. ◐ *9:30am–1pm, 3:30–7pm daily*. 🎫 *combined ticket*.

Tratalias ⑲

Road map B6. 🏙 *1,182*. 🚍

THIS VILLAGE in the Sulcis region was the seat of the diocese until 1413. The façade of the Pisan Romanesque cathedral of **Santa Maria**, consecrated in 1213, is divided horizontally by a row of little arches surmounted by a rose window. The tympanum is curious, in that the last section of a stairway juts out from it.

The sides and apse are decorated with pilasters and blind arches. Inside, the three naves are separated by large, octagonal pillars. An altarpiece from 1596 depicts St John the Baptist and St John the Evangelist with the Madonna and Child.

Cathedral of Santa Maria, Tratalias

Santadi ⑳

Road map C6. 🏙 *4,100*. 🚍 🛈 *Via Vittorio Veneto 1 (0781 94 10 00)*. 📅 *first Sun in Aug: Matrimonio Mauritano*.

BUILT ON THE BANKS of the River Mannu, Santadi's old town sits on the higher, north side. Some traditional architecture made from rough volcanic rock is still visible in the medieval centre. Evidence that the area has been inhabited since the nuraghic age can be seen in the copper, bronze, gold and earthenware objects found here, which are now on display in the Museo Archeologico in Cagliari (*see p58*). Local tools and furniture can be seen at the **Museo Etnografico Sa Domu Antigua**. The shop here sells typical Sulcis handicrafts.

ENVIRONS: On a plateau southwest of the town is the 7th-century BC Phoenician fortress, **Pani Loriga**. Continuing south for 5 km (3 miles) are two caves, the **Grotta Is Zuddas**, with splendid formations of stalagmites and stalactites, and the **Grotta Pirosu**, where archaeological finds such as a votive lamp and a Cypriot-style tripod were found.

The necropolis at Montessu

North of Villaperuccio, the **Montessu Necropolis** has typical *domus de janas (see p33)* tombs, some of which still have traces of the original yellow and red wall facing. Other tombs were probably used for worship.

The August festival, Matrimonio Mauritano (Mauretanian Wedding), is a ceremony that may have started with the North Africans who settled here during the Roman era.

⏷ Museo Etnografico Sa Domu Antigua

Via Mazzini 37. 📞 *0781 95 59 83*. ◐ *9am–12:30pm, 3–7pm daily*.

🏛 Grotta Is Zuddas and Pirosu

Benatzu. 🛈 *Cooperativa Monte Meana (0781 95 57 41)*. ◐ *Jun–Sept: 9:30am–noon, 2:30–7pm daily; Oct–May: tours only, noon & 4pm daily*. 🎫

⏷ Montessu Necropolis

Località Peruccio. 🛈 *0781 84 10 89*. ◐ *9am–1pm, 3–7pm daily*. 🎫 🎟

MONTE ARCOSU

The mountains in the Sulcis region are covered with forests of cork oak, holm oak, strawberry trees and heather, from which the granite peaks seem to emerge. This area extends for about 7,000 hectares (17,300 acres), interrupted only by a rough road that connects Santadi and Capoterra along the Mannu and Gutturu Mannu river valleys. There are plans to make the area into a National Park: the World Wide Fund for Nature (WWF) has purchased 300 hectares (741 acres) of land on the slopes of Monte Arcosu to protect the Sardinian deer, which roamed the entire island until 1900, but is now restricted to a few isolated areas. Other forest mammals include fallow deer, wild cats, boar and martens. Among the birds found here are the golden eagle, peregrine falcon and goshawk. This nature reserve is open all year

Stag in the Monte Arcosu reserve

and visitors can stay overnight in refuges. There are well-marked nature trails as well as unmarked wild walks, although an official WWF guide is obligatory in some areas. The Cagliari-based Cooperativa Quadrifoglio (*070 96 87 14*) has information regarding accommodation and trekking. To reach the reserve, take the road east from Santadi along the Gutturu river.

The sheltered beach at Baia Chia

Baia Chia ㉑

Road map C6. ℹ *Via Provinciale 41, Domus de Maria (070 923 62 93).*

THE SOUTHERN COAST (Costa del Sud) is an area of high sand dunes and white beaches that extend as far as the Capo Spartivento headland. Junipers grow in the sand and there is marshland frequented by egrets, purple herons, grebes and other migratory aquatic birds. The area is due to become the centre of a regional nature reserve.

Along the coastal road, the hamlet of Chia is a popular tourist destination set among orchards and fig trees. A rough road leads to the sheltered bay of Chia, flanked on one side by the 17th-century **Torre di Chia**, and on the other by red cliffs covered with maquis vegetation.

At the foot of the tower you can visit the remains of Phoenician **Bithia**. This ancient city, mentioned in the writings of Ptolemy and Pliny the Elder, had been covered by the sea for centuries and has not yet been completely excavated.

Remains of a Punic and Roman necropolis are visible, as are the ruins of a temple probably dedicated to the god Bes. Earthenware pots and amphorae from the 7th century BC have been discovered in the sand, and traces of Roman wall paintings and mosaics decorate porticoed houses. Ancient Punic fortifications can be seen near the base of the watchtower and an elliptical cistern has also been found.

⋔ Bithia
Domus de Maria, Località Chia.
◷ *at all times.*

ENVIRONS: Along the coast as far as the promontory of Capo Spartivento, where there are spectacular views, is a series of bays, dunes and pine forests that can be reached on foot.

The Roman theatre at Nora

Nora ㉒

Road map C6. ℹ *070 920 91 38.*
◷ *9am–sunset daily.* 🖼 🎫 ♿

FOUNDED UNDER Carthaginian rule in the 9th–8th centuries BC, the ancient city of Nora was built on a spit of land jutting out to sea. The town became the island's most important city, a role it continued to enjoy under the Romans. In AD 238, Nora became the capital of the Roman province of Sardinia.

Repeated Saracen raids and the lack of fertile land finally forced the inhabitants to abandon the city in the Middle Ages and the three ports were gradually covered up by the incoming sea.

The ruins of the ancient city extend as far as the headland of Capo di Pula, covered with

The promontory of Capo Spartivento overlooking the southern coastline

maquis and dominated by the Spanish **Torre del Coltelazzo**.

An impressive vestige of the Carthaginian city is the raised Temple of Tanit, the goddess of fertility. Little else remains of the Punic period, although rich findings in the tombs testify to active trading.

The Roman city is well represented. Left of the entrance are the 4th-century Terme di Levante, Roman baths decorated with mosaics. Nearby is a 2nd-century AD theatre and the large rectangular Forum behind it. South of the theatre, the mosaics in the *frigidarium* and *caldarium* of the baths are decorated with white, black and ochre tesserae. Paved roads and the city's extensive sewage system are also still visible.

Many finds, including Punic inscriptions in which the name of the island of Sardinia is first mentioned, are kept in Cagliari's Museo Archeologico Nazionale *(see p58)*.

Some earthenware objects found at the site are on display in the small **Museo Civico Archeologico**.

The nearby Romanesque church of **Sant'Efisio**, built by French Victorine monks in the 11th century, is the site of an annual procession from Cagliari *(see p26)*.

🏛 **Museo Civico Archeologico**
Corso Vittorio Emanuele 67.
📞 *070 920 96 10.*
🕐 *9am–8pm daily.* ✍

The popular resort of Poetto, between Quartu Sant'Elena and Cagliari

Quartu Sant'Elena ㉓

Road map C6. 🏠 *66,000.*
🚌 🚊 *Cagliari.* ✈ *Elmas.* ℹ *070 860 11.* 🎭 *14 Sep: Sant'Elena.*

SITUATED ON THE OUTSKIRTS of Cagliari, Quartu Sant'Elena has grown to become one of the island's largest cities. It lies at the edge of the salt flats and marsh of the same name which are a favourite breeding and nesting ground for flamingoes.

The medieval church of **Sant'Agata** stands in the town's main square, Piazza Azuni. From here Via Porcu leads to the **Casa Museo Sa Dom 'e Farra**, literally "the house of flour". This large country house, converted into a museum, features over 14,000 traditional farm and domestic tools and equipment collected over the years by Gianni Musiu, a

Golden pen found at Nora

former shepherd. Each of the museum's rooms is dedicated to different farm activities: displaying saddles and leather harnesses to wagons and blacksmiths' bellows. One of the more curious objects is the snow-cooled icebox. Gathered in the Barbagia region, the snow was taken to Cagliari on muleback and kept cold in large straw-lined containers stored underground.

The farmstead consisted of the owner's home and living quarters for farm labourers. Other rooms around a large courtyard were used for various domestic and farm activities such as milling, bread-making and tool repair.

A bus ride southwest of Quartu Sant'Elena brings you to the beach resort of Poetto, a favourite with local people.

🏛 **Casa Museo Sa Dom 'e Farra**
Via Eligiu Porcu 143. 📞 *0781 85 40 09.*

FORESTA DEI SETTE FRATELLI

The Forest of the "Seven Brothers" was named after the seven peaks that can be seen from Cagliari and which tower over the holm oak forests and maquis. Run by the *Azienda Foreste Demaniali (070 279 91)*, the forest covers an area of 4,000 hectares (9,800 acres), replanted with pine, eucalyptus and cypress trees, and reaching an altitude of 1,023 m (3,355 ft). It is also one of the few areas inhabited by the rare Sardinian deer, now almost extinct. The mountain has many mule trails, once used by coal merchants; one of these footpaths begins at the forest headquarters at Campu Omo on the N125. To drive into the mountains take a right turn past the Arcu 'e Tidu pass on the N125.

Densely wooded Foresta dei Sette Fratelli, which extends over seven hills

THE EASTERN COAST

MILE AFTER MILE OF PASTURES AND ROCKS *characterize the interior of eastern Sardinia, falling away to inaccessible cliffs on the coast, refuge for the rare monk seal. The coastline of the Golfo di Orosei is now part of the Parco Nazionale del Gennargentu, a vast nature reserve founded to protect golden eagles and moufflon.*

There are no towns of any great size along the Eastern coast but there are some good seaside resorts around Arbatax and Villasimius. Except for a few stretches, the road runs inland, so that most of the beaches can be reached only after walking a long way or by driving on dirt roads. The largest towns are Orosei, Muravera and Dorgali, also situated in the interior at a certain distance from the coast. The historical reasons for this go back to the endemic malaria that afflicted the island until after World War II and, before that, the constant pirate raids which plagued the coasts for centuries. This is still unknown Sardinia, the interior the domain of shepherds and their flocks, and the southeast yet to be discovered by tourism. Until recently the region of Sarrabus was isolated because of the absence of negotiable roads. The only way of reaching it was via a narrow-gauge railway from Cagliari, which followed the contours of the valleys. It is still in operation, and offers a delightful opportunity to take a trip back into the past. Sarrabus today attracts visitors who prefer to stray from the beaten track. Further north, the Ogliastra region, with its sandy beaches which vary from pearly grey to a startling reddish colour, has rugged mountains and hills where time seems to have stood still, pastoral life has not been invaded by the 21st century and strong traditions survive. The Baronie region, in contrast, has the towns of Siniscola and Orosei, with good public transport systems and a fast modern motorway, making the area more accessible.

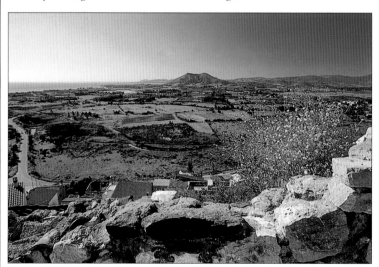

The alluvial plain around Posada, seen from the Castello della Fava

◁ Steep limestone cliffs on the Golfo di Orosei

Exploring the Eastern Coast

S PLENDID NATURAL scenery and prehistoric
archaeological sites around Dorgali and
Orroli are the main attractions of the Eastern
Coast. The cliffs along the coast are steep,
and the most secluded coves in the Golfo di
Orosei (Cala Sisine, Cala Luna, Cala Golo-
ritze) are most easily reached by boat. The
alternative is a lengthy walk, best tackled in
hiking boots. The countryside is marvellous
however, and the trek rewarding. The main road
winding through the region is the Orientale Sarda.
There is a proposal – supported by the local people
but vehemently opposed by environmentalists – to
widen this road into a fast access motorway.

A glimpse of the Golfo di Orosei, near Baunei

Sights at a Glance

0 kilometres   10

0 miles   10

Key

▬▬	Motorway
▬▬	Major road
▬▬	Minor road
▬▬	Scenic route
▬▬	River

Panoramic view of the foothills of Mount Gennargentu

(Map labels: POSADA ⑪, SINISCOLA ⑩, MONTE ALBO TOUR ⑨, ORO... ⑦, GALTELLÌ ⑧, Nuoro, DORG... ⑤, THE ORIENTALE SARDA ROAD ①, CODULA DI LUNA, Lago Fluminendosa, G..., ORROLI ⑱, Mu...)

Rocky outcrops of reddish granite at Arbatax

3 **SANTA MARIA
NAVARRESE**

2 **ARBATAX**

**VNARGENTU
TIONAL PARK**

ANUSEI N198

15 **BARÌ SARDO**

13 **JERZU**

19 **PERDASDEFOGU**

A TRIP ON THE
TRENINO VERDE

lumendosa

16 **MURAVERA**

Cagliari

**COSTA
REI**

SEE ALSO

• **Where to Stay** pp174–5

• **Where to Eat** pp184–5

17 **VILLASIMIUS**

LFO DI
ROSEI

Pisan tower at Orosei

GETTING AROUND
The Orientale Sarda road
(N125) is winding and
slow. The road leading to
the interior from Tortolì to
Nuoro is faster, thanks to
the tunnel that avoids the
Arcu Correboi pass and
goes directly from the
Barbagia to Ogliastra.
There is also a north-south
coach service. The
Ogliastra plain (Tortolì and
Arbatax) is connected to
Cagliari by the Ferrovie
Complementari della
Sardegna narrow-gauge
train; the trip takes about
eight hours. It is slow, but
the line goes through
wonderful scenery.

One of the rocky coves on the Eastern
Coast near Cala Luna

The Orientale Sarda Road ●

ALONG THE EASTERN PEAKS of the Gennargentu National Park *(see pp82–3)*, the N125, or the "Orientale Sarda" route, connects Olbia to Cagliari. The most spectacular stretch is between Dorgali and Baunei, 63 km (39 miles) of winding road hewn out of the rock by Piedmontese coal merchants during the mid-1800s. These "foreigners" carved a road through the remote mountain valleys and felled trees that were sent to the mainland. The deforestation that resulted has proved irreversible.

Flumineddu River Valley ②
This stretch of the N125 road goes through rugged terrain with cliffs and a fine view of the Flumineddu river valley under the peaks of Monte Tiscali. There are many places where you can stop to enjoy the wonderful scenery.

Dorgali ●

GROTTA DEL BUE MARINO

GOLFO DI OROSEI

Genna Silana Pass ③
This is the highest point of the tour at 1,017 m (3,336 ft). Stop here to get a dramatic view of the Gorroppu ravine. A footpath from Pischina Urtaddalà descends to the Flumineddu river bed.

Flumineddu

N125 (Orientale Sarda)

Codula di Luna

Codula di Sisine

GENNARGENTU NATIONAL PARK

Urzulei ④
Built on different levels on the slopes of Punta Is Gruttas, Urzulei was once an isolated town difficult to reach. The stone church of San Giorgio di Suelli dates from the 15th century.

Baunei ⑤
The white houses of this mountain village stand out under the limestone crags.

KEY

▬ Major road

▭ Minor road

— River

0 kilometres   5

0 miles   5

Cala Gonone ①

A 400-m (1,300-ft) tunnel
cut out of the limestone
rock leads to the popular
seaside resort of Cala
Gonone. A winding road,
with fabulous views of the
sea, white rocks and the
maquis, continues to the
Grotta del Bue Marino where
there have been sightings of
the rare monk seal *(see p17).*

San Pietro ⑥

A rough track with
precipitous hairpin
bends climbs to a
wooded plateau where
wild pigs graze. At the
end is the Golgo ravine,
295 m (967 ft) deep. A
little further along is the
18th-century church of
San Pietro. Shepherds
still make offerings here
and a rural festival takes
place from 28–29 June.

The holiday resort of Cala
Moresca, at Arbatax

Arbatax ②

Road map D4. 👥 *1,100.* 🚂 🚌 🚢
🛈 *Tortolì (0782 600 700).* 📅 *2nd
Sun in Jul: Madonna di Stella Maris.*

THE SMALL TOWN of Arbatax
lies on the northern tip of
the Bellavista promontory, a
red porphyry cliff that
plunges into the
sea. The port,
guarded by a
Spanish tower, is
the terminus for
the narrow-gauge
trains arriving
from Cagliari.
Ferries from
Cagliari, Olbia
and the Italian
mainland also
dock here.

This stretch
of coast has
clear, clean
water and
enticing coves

The Aragonese tower at Santa
Maria Navarrese

such as **Cala Moresca**, south
of Arbatax. Several tourist
resorts now cover this small
promontory, such as the
popular *Vacanze Club* village,
built to resemble a typical
Mediterranean village. The
solid wood doors and
wrought-iron grilles on the

windows were taken from the
abandoned village of Gairo
(see p89). Further south is
Porto Frailis, also protected
by a Spanish tower, and the
long, sandy Orrì beach. From
Arbatax footpaths lead up to
the lighthouse high on the
Bellavista promontory.

Santa Maria Navarrese ③

Road map D4. 👥 *1,500.* 🚌 🚌
🛈 *Piazza di Navarra (0782 61 08 23).*
📅 *15 Aug: Festa dell'Assunta.*

THIS SEASIDE resort was
named after the lovely
country church around which
it developed. It is said that
this three-aisle construction,
with a semicircular apse, was
built in the 11th century by
the daughter of the king of
Navarra after she had been
saved from a shipwreck.

In the church courtyard
is a gigantic wild olive
tree that is
reputed to be
over a thousand
years old.

The beautiful
beach at Santa
Maria Navarrese
is bordered by
a pine forest
and protected
by a Spanish
watchtower.
Opposite this
is the huge
Agugliastra (or
Sa Pedra Longa) rock, a slim
limestone pinnacle that rises
up 128 m (420 ft) from the
sea. Boat services from the
little port of Santa Maria
Navarrese will take visitors to
the stack, as well as to Cala
Luna, Cala Sisine and Cala
Goloritzè, further up the coast.

The rocky Ogliastra island viewed from Capo Bellavista

Gennargentu National Park ❹

Peonies in flower

THE PARK EXTENDS OVER 59,102 hectares (146,000 acres) of some of the wildest, most mountainous landscape in Sardinia, and includes the island's highest peak, Punta La Marmora. Established in 1989, most of the park lies in the province of Nuoro. There are 14 towns in this protected area, but few tarmac roads, and the steep-sided valleys and bare peaks give the area an isolated air. The unspoilt nature of the park makes it fascinating for walkers, geologists and naturalists alike. The climb up Punta La Marmora (1,834 m, 6,015 ft) is rewarding, and the limestone desert of Supramonte is one of Italy's spectacular sights. Monte Tiscali hides the prehistoric rock village of Tiscali *(see pp104–5)*, and the ravines of Su Gorroppu and the Su Gologone spring are unmissable. The coast to the east, home to the endangered monk seal, is one of Europe's loveliest. When walking, it is advisable to take an up-to-date map and plenty of water.

The Wild Cat
Larger than the domestic cat, the wild cat lives on Gennargentu and Supramonte.

Bearded vulture

Moufflon

Refuge

JONNI

N128

DÈSULO

Marten

ARITZO

Punta La Marmora

Griffon vulture

0 kilometres   15

0 miles   15

The Mount Gennargentu Massif
In winter the barren peaks and the lower slopes, carpeted in oak and chestnut trees, are sometimes covered by snow.

THE HIGHEST PEAK IN SARDINIA: PUNTA LA MARMORA

The massif of Gennargentu, whose name means "door of silver", reaches its peak in Punta La Marmora which, at 1,834 m (6,015 ft) above sea level, is the highest point on the island. The landscape here is quite barren and wild. The sky is populated by raptors circling around in search of prey and with a bit of luck you might be able to see, in the distance, small groups of moufflons, or mountain sheep.

Hikers on the top of Punta La Marmora

The Crests of Supramonte
The peaks rise to the east of Gennargentu and their slopes descend towards the sea.

VISITORS' CHECKLIST

Road map D4. ℹ️ *EPT Nuoro, Piazza Italia 19 (0784 323 07 or 0784 300 83); WWF Nuoro, Piazza Santa Maria della Neve 8 (0784 328 88)* 🅦 *www.wwf.it Pro Loco Dorgali, Via La Marmora 181 (0784 93 305); Desulo Town Hall (0784 61 92 11).*

The Monk Seal
The monk seal (Monáchus albiventer), thought to be extinct, has been sighted in recent years in the Golfo di Orosei. Tourism has been blamed for the fall in population.

KEY

▬▬	Major road
▭▭	Minor road
—	River

TIPS FOR TRAVELLERS

Ascending Punta La Marmora
From Desulo, follow the road to Fonni for about 5 km (3 miles) until you come to the S'Arcu de Tascusì pass, then take the asphalt road on the right until you reach a fork. Follow the dirt road on the right for 100 m (328 ft) and then take the right-hand road leading to the Girgini holiday farm. Skirt around it by keeping to the left. In a little less than 4 km (2 miles), take the right-hand fork and continue for 5 km (3 miles) until you reach the control cabin for an aqueduct. Leave your car here and follow the road on the right on foot until you reach the end, then proceed up the valley floor on the left until you reach the crest. From here you can continue up to the summit (an hour and a half on foot).

Su Gorroppu
This wild gorge, with its steep sides, can only be scaled by expert climbers.

Displays of exhibits at the Museo Archeologico in Dorgali

Dorgali ❺

Road map D3. 🏘 *8,500.*
ℹ *Pro Loco (0784 933 05).*
🎉 *16–17 Jan: Sant'Antonio Abate.*

THE CHARMING TOWN OF Dorgali lies on a ridge that descends from Monte Bardia and is 30 km (19 miles) from Nuoro and a little less than 10 km (6 miles) from the sea at Cala Gonone. Dorgali is predominantly an agricultural centre, but it is

Santa Caterina parish church in the centre of Dorgali

also important for locally produced crafts such as leather, ceramics and filigree jewellery, as well as rug- and carpet-weaving.

In the old part of town the buildings are made of dark volcanic stone. These include several churches: Madonna d'Itria, San Lussorio and the Maddalena. The central square, Piazza Vittorio Emanuele, is dominated by the façade of the parish church, Santa Caterina, home to a large carved altar.

Dorgali's **Museo Archeologico** contains an important collection of objects from nuraghic sites, as well as finds from sites dating back to Punic and Roman times. Some of the finest nuraghic pieces come from the nearby site of **Serra Òrrios**. The museum also provides information on visits to the rock village of Tiscali, another major nuraghic site *(see*

pp104–5). The town is known for its wine, and the local wine-making cooperative and the local dairy can be visited.

Nuraghic dwelling at Serra Òrrios

🏛 **Museo Archeologico di Dorgali**
Scuola Elementare, Via La Marmora.
📞 *0784 961 07.* ⭘ *9:30am–1pm, 4:30–7:30pm (Oct–Apr:3–5pm).* 🎫 ♿
⋔ **Serra Òrrios**
ℹ *0784 933 05.* ⭘ *9am–noon, 4–7pm (Oct–Apr: 3–5pm).* 🎫 🎫

THE NURAGHIC VILLAGE OF SERRA ÒRRIOS

At Serra Òrrios – about 10 km (6 miles) to the north-west of Dorgali and 23 km (14 miles) east of Nuoro – lies one of Sardinia's best preserved nuraghic villages, which dates from the 12th–10th centuries BC. The 70 round dwellings, each with a central hearth, are arranged in at least six groups around large central spaces with a well. Small places of worship have also been found in the village.

Main Temple

Group of Dwellings

Codula di Luna ❻

A THREE-HOUR WALK down the "Codula
Illune", or Valley of the Moon, will
take you from the Supramonte to the
sea. The path is straightforward to
follow, although there is little shade
from the sun in summer. The track
runs through aromatic maquis scrub,
and passes shepherds' huts on the
way, as well as the entrances to
enormous caves, many of which
have not yet been fully explored.

The beautiful, secluded beach of Cala Luna,
backed by a small lake

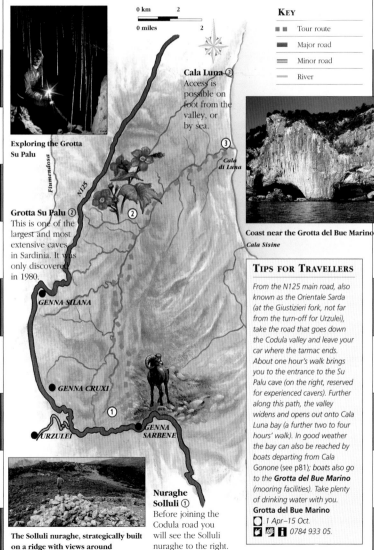

KEY

🔲 🔲 Tour route

▬▬ Major road

▭▭ Minor road

▬ River

Cala Luna ③
Access is
possible on
foot from the
valley, or
by sea.

*Cala
di Luna*

**Exploring the Grotta
Su Palu**

Grotta Su Palu ②
This is one of the
largest and most
extensive caves
in Sardinia. It was
only discovered
in 1980.

Coast near the Grotta del Bue Marino
Cala Sisine

GENNA SILANA

GENNA CRUXI

URZULEI   **GENNA
SARBENE**

**Nuraghe
Solluli** ①
Before joining the
Codula road you
will see the Solluli
nuraghe to the right.

The Solluli nuraghe, strategically built
on a ridge with views around

TIPS FOR TRAVELLERS

*From the N125 main road, also
known as the Orientale Sarda
(at the Giustizieri fork, not far
from the turn-off for Urzulei),
take the road that goes down
the Codula valley and leave your
car where the tarmac ends.
About one hour's walk brings
you to the entrance to the Su
Palu cave (on the right, reserved
for experienced cavers). Further
along this path, the valley
widens and opens out onto Cala
Luna bay (a further two to four
hours' walk). In good weather
the bay can also be reached by
boats departing from Cala
Gonone (see p81); boats also go
to the* **Grotta del Bue Marino**
*(mooring facilities). Take plenty
of drinking water with you.*

Grotta del Bue Marino

⬛ *1 Apr–15 Oct.*

☑ 🈲 🅸 *0784 933 05.*

The Chiesa delle Anime at Orosei

Orosei ❼

Road map D3. 🏠 *6,000.* 🚌
ℹ️ *Pro Loco (0784 99 83 67).* 🎉 *Easter Week, 26 Jul, San Giacomo.*

THE HISTORIC CAPITAL of the Baronia region is situated about 5 km (3 miles) inland, and has a bustling, well-kept historic centre with churches, archways and small, white-washed stone buildings over-looking flowered courtyards.

The town of Orosei was probably founded in the early Middle Ages and its golden age occurred under Pisan domination, when it was ruled by the barons of the Guiso family. Orosei developed into an important harbour with moorings alongside the Cedrino river. After yielding to Aragonese rule, the town began to decline as a result of malarial disease, repeated pirate raids and the gradual silting up of the river.

The portal of Santa Maria 'e Mare

A labyrinth of alleys leads to the central Piazza del Popolo, where three churches stand. At the top of a flight of steps is **San Giacomo Maggiore** with an 18th-century façade and terracotta-tiled domes. Opposite is the **Chiesa del Rosario**, with a Baroque façade, and the **Chiesa delle Anime**, founded by the brotherhood of monks that participates in the Easter Week ceremonies.

Sant'Antonio Abate, once an isolated rural sanctuary, is now surrounded by the expanding town. Local handicrafts are on display in the Pisan tower inside the precincts of Sant'Antonio. The 17th-century Sanctuary of the Madonna del Rimedio, also once isolated, is now part of the outskirts and is surrounded by *cumbessias*, the houses used by pilgrims each September.

Monte Albo Tour ❾

THE MASSIVE WHITE limestone ridge that gave this mountain its name (*albo* means white) extends like a bastion between the Barbagia and Baronia regions. There are magnificent panoramic views from the maquis-covered slopes of the mountain. The area is destined to become a reserve to protect 650 plant species as well as moufflons, wild boar and raptors. Part of this tour follows a narrow road along the base of the limestone cliffs.

Lodè ②
This small town amid olive trees and maquis is the home of the Annunziata sanctuary, with its whitewashed, red-roofed *cumbessias*. On 22–23 May the sanctuary becomes a pilgrimage site.

Bitti ③
This lively town *(see p100)* lies in pretty countryside surrounded by clusters of oak and wild olive trees.

The Annunziata Sanctuary, Lodè

KEY

▬▬ Tour route

═══ Other roads

━━━ River

0 kilometres   4

0 miles   4

ENVIRONS: Near the mouth of the Cedrino river is **Santa Maria 'e Mare**, founded in the 13th century by Pisan merchants. The church is full of ex votos, and on the last Sunday in May it is the focus of a pilgrimage, when a statue of the Madonna is taken down the river on a boat, followed by a flotilla of boats.

At the mouth of the estuary the river divides into two. The northern part flows into an artificial canal, the southern half feeds the Su Petrosu marsh. This is where to find coots, moorhens, mallards and purple gallinules. The shallows are home to avocets, stilts, grey heron and egrets.

Galtellì ⓪

Road map D3. 🏛 *2,400.* 🚉
ℹ *Pro Loco, Orosei (0784 998 367).*
🎎 *16–17 Jan, Sant'Antonio Abate.*

L YING ON THE SLOPES of Monte Tuttavista, Galtellì was the most important town in the region during the Middle Ages. Until 1496 it was the regional bishopric, as can be seen in Roman-esque San Pietro, the former cathedral built in the 12th century. After this era the town began to decline thanks to the ravages of malaria and frequent pirate raids, but traces of its glorious past have been pre-served in the parish church of Santissimo Croci-fisso, which contains fine 16th- and 17th-century wooden statues.

The historic centre of Galtellì is still pretty, with its whitewashed buildings and small, well-kept houses.

ENVIRONS: One of the most interesting sights in this area is Monte Tuttavista. A dirt road and then a footpath take you to Sa Pedra Istampada ("the perforated rock"), a wind-sculpted arch 30 m (98 ft) high. There are splendid views from the summit.

Near the village of La Traversa, 12 km (8 miles) from Galtellì, is the Tomba di Giganti (giants' tomb) of **Sa Ena 'e Thomes**, a very impressive prehistoric monument with a 3-m (10 ft) stele hewn out of a single block of granite.

The Sa Ena 'e Thomes "giants' tomb" near La Traversa

Sant'Anna ①
This pass is 624 m (2,050 ft) above sea level, and offers splendid scenic views. The road winds up among cliffs, euphorbia bushes and cluster pines.

TIPS FOR TRAVELLERS

Length: 76 km (47 miles). This tour takes about two hours by car, but allow half a day to include the stops.
***Stopping-off points:** the Sant'Anna roadman's house and the town of Bitti (see p100).*

View of Monte Albo

Lula ④
This town in Barbagia has a famous sanctuary, which is dedicated to St Francis. Thousands of worshippers participate in the saint's feast day celebrations from 1–10 May, events described by Grazia Deledda in *Elias Portolu*.

The road leading up Monte Albo ⑤
The 20 km (12 miles) of this hillside road run along the northern slope of the mountain through pastures and maquis. On the right are steep limestone walls streaked with pink.

Siniscola ❿

Road map D2. 🏔 *11,000.* 🚌
ℹ️ *Via Monfalcone 17 (0784 87 70 13).* 🎭 *18 Aug: Sant'Elena.*
🌐 *www.siniscola.net*

SET AT THE FOOT of Monte Albo, the once agricultural town of Siniscola was an important trading centre in the 14th century under the principality of Gallura *(see p36).* Since then, the town has grown in a haphazard manner around the medieval centre. On the lively main street, Via Sassari, the 18th-century parish church of **San Giovanni Battista** is decorated with a fresco cycle representing the life of St John the Baptist. The town is also well known for its local pottery studios.

ENVIRONS: A straight road northeast from Siniscola leads to **La Caletta**, a small tourist port with a wide sandy beach, 4 km (2 miles) long. Heading southwards, the N125 passes the fishing village of **Santa Lucia**. Probably founded by emigrants from the island of Ponza, the village is guarded by a Spanish watchtower. Today Santa Lucia is a popular summer resort, with a pine forest that extends behind the beach. Continuing southwards, a long walk along the shore

The church at Santa Lucia

will take you to the white sand dunes and juniper bushes of **Capo Comino** (also accessible from the N125).

The headland of Capo Comino consists of rounded rocks and pebble beaches and is overlooked by a lighthouse. A two-hour walk along the seashore and pine forest will take you to **Berchida beach**, where there is a huge rock called *S'incollu de sa Marchesa* (The Marquise's Throat). Eels and grey mullet populate an area of marshland here.

An alternative excursion is to take the rough track that turns right from the N125 after the Berchida river.

Spanish tower at Santa Lucia

Winding through the maquis it leads to a splendid white sand beach and clear blue sea. On the way, the road passes the remains of the nuraghic settlement of Conca Umosa.

Posada ⓫

Road map D2. 🏔 *1,200.* 🚌

PERCHED ON TOP of a limestone bank covered with euphorbia and lentiscus, this village is dominated by the ruins of **Castello della Fava**. The castle was built in the 12th century by the rulers of Gallura, who were later conquered by the principality of Arborea before passing under Aragonese dominion *(see p36).* In the Carthaginian era this place was known as the colony of Feronia.

The town still retains its medieval character, with winding alleyways connected by steep stairways, arches and tiny squares. The grey stone houses have been preserved and the castle has also had a face-lift. Wooden steps lead to the top of the castle's square tower where there is a panoramic view of the sea, the mouth of the Posada river and the surrounding plain covered with fruit orchards.

ENVIRONS: Inland, 9 km (5 miles) west of Posada, is the artificial lake of Posada. The pine forests and fine views make this a popular spot.

Lanusei ⓬

Road map D4. 🏔 *6,500.* 🚶 🚌 🚌
🎭 *22 Jul: Santa Maria Maddalena.*

THIS LARGE, austere-looking town, situated on a hillside at 600 m (1,926 ft), overlooks the plain that descends to the

The white sand dunes at Capo Comino

The village of Posada and the Castello della Fava

sea. It was once a health retreat due to its excellent climate, high altitude and the many walking trails in the surrounding forest. The town was built on various levels and still has some aristocratic buildings of interest.

Jerzu ⑬

Road map D4. 🏠 3,600. 🚌
🎉 13 Jun: Sant'Antonio; 25 Jul: San Giacomo; 4 Aug: Sagra del Vino.

Tall, sharp pinnacles of rock, known locally as *tacchi* (high heels), are an impressive sight as they emerge from the maquis on the mountainous approach to Jerzu. This modern town is built on several levels up the hillside with houses of two storeys or more overlooking the main street. Steep

Wine labels from Jerzu

side streets in the lower quarter lead to older houses with many original features.

Jerzu's economy is based mainly on viticulture and small vineyards cling to the steep slopes around the town. The area produces about 10,000 tonnes of grapes from which the local wine cooperative makes the good red wine Cannonau DOC, one of the most famous in Sardinia.

The most important holiday is the feast day of Sant'Antonio da Padova, on 13 June. One of the town's churches is dedicated to the saint.

Environs: At Ulassai, 7 km (4 miles) northwest of Jerzu, is the limestone **Grotta Su Màrmuri**, (*Il Marmo*, "the marble", in Italian). Steps descend to reveal spectacular pools and stalagmites.

🛖 **Grotta Su Màrmuri**
ℹ️ Via Dante 69 (0782 798 59).

Gairo ⑭

Road map D4. 🏠 2,000. 🚌 🚏
🎉 third Sun in Sep: Nostra Signora del Buoncammino.

Gairo Sant'Elena lies in the Pardu river valley, a deep ravine with impressive limestone walls. The present-day village was built after 1951, when Gairo Vecchio had to be evacuated after excessive rain that autumn caused a series of landslides. All that remains of the abandoned village are gutted houses without doors and windows. The entire area has spectacular scenery.

Barì Sardo ⑮

Road map D4. 🏠 4,500. 🚌
🎉 29 Aug: San Giovanni Battista; 8 Sep: Nostra Signora di Monserrato.

This agricultural centre is set in fertile countryside filled with vineyards and orchards. The name of the town is derived from the Sardinian word for marshes, *abbari*. In the oldest part of town, around the district of San Leonardo to the south-west, original stone houses are still visible. Here, the parish church, **Beata Vergine del Monserrato**, has a Rococo bell tower dated 1813. The town is also known for its textiles: tapestries, rugs and linen cushions and bedcovers.

Environs: On the coast, east of Barì Sardo, **Torre di Barì** is a pleasant seaside resort that developed around the 17th-century Spanish tower built to defend the town from pirates. It has a sandy beach and small pine forest. The festivities for San Giovanni Battista, known here as *Su Nenneri*, are unusual. In a ritual to encourage a good harvest, grain and vegetable seedlings are cast into the sea.

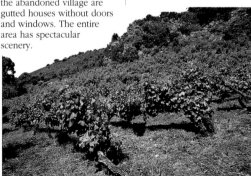

The vineyards at Jerzu produce Cannonau, Sardinia's best-known wine

The basalt rock promontory at Capo Ferrato, south of Muravera

Muravera 16

Road map D5. 🏘 *4,500.* 🚌 *Via Macchiavelli 3 (070 993 07 60).* 📅 *14–15 Aug: l'Assunta.*

MURAVERA LIES at the mouth of the Flumendosa river, in the middle of an area of fruit orchards. It is a modern tourist town, catering to the resort complexes that have grown up along the coast. In ancient times this was the Phoenician city of Sarcapos. Today, the only building of any historical interest is the church of **San Nicola**, off the main street, which retains its original 15th-century chapels.

ENVIRONS: Muravera is an ideal starting point for trips along the coast and into the valleys of the interior. To the east, the beach around **Porto Corallo** is long and sandy, interrupted by small rocky headlands. Near this tourist port is another **Spanish tower** which, in 1812, was used as a stronghold in one of the rare victories of the Sardinians over the Muslim pirates.

Northwards, 11 km (7 miles) along the SS125, also known as the Orientale Sarda road *(see p80)*, are the remains of the **Castello di Quirra** and the small Romanesque church of **San Nicola**, the only church in Sardinia built of brick.

To the south, the coast around **Capo Ferrato** is also beautiful, with basalt rocks, small white sandy coves and pine trees. Past the headland of Capo Ferrato is the **Costa Rei**, a stretch of straight coastline with beaches and tourist villages. The sea bed at the bay of **Cala Sinzias** further to the south consists of long slabs of rock, giving the water a strikingly clean and transparent look.

Inland, the route towards Cagliari along the SS125 offers spectacular scenery, with red rock among myrtle, juniper and strawberry trees. A trip down the Flumendosa river valley, beyond San Vito, also offers spectacular scenery.

Castiadas is a hamlet behind the Costa Rei, set around a 19th-century prison amid vineyards and citrus trees. From the late 19th century to the 1950s the area was occupied by a prison farm, where prisoners worked on the land.

Villasimius 17

Road map D6. 🏘 *2,800.* 🚌 🚌 *Via Marconi 12 (070 79 15 46 14).* 📅 *Jul: Madonna del Naufrago.*

WITH ITS HOTELS, residences and second homes, this modern town is the leading seaside resort on the south-eastern coast. Villasimius lies on the northern edge of a promontory that extends to **Capo Carbonara**. At the centre of the headland is the **Notteri marsh**, separated from the sea by Simius beach, a long stretch of sand. In the winter the marsh is a popular stopping-off point for migratory flamingoes. On the very tip of the promontory the lighthouse offers a sweeping view of the coast and the tiny islands of **Serpentara** and **Cavoli** in the distance. The stretch of water between the two islands is shallow and has

THE TOWN OF THE LAUNEDDAS

Northeast of Muravera is San Vito, an agricultural town that thrived in past centuries thanks to the silver mines on Monte Narba. In the centre of town, the parish church with its twin bell towers over the façade is worth a visit. San Vito is known for its tradition of craftmanship, in particular the flute-like instrument, the *launeddas*, which was originally played by shepherds *(see p25)*. Luigi Lai, Sardinia's most famous player of this ancient instrument, lives here and makes the instrument himself. Other crafts at San Vito include fine embroidery and basket-weaving with juniper twigs.

Luigi Lai, one of Sardinia's most famous *launeddas* players

The long beach separating the sea from Notteri marsh, south of Villasimius

witnessed many shipwrecks over the years. Off the island of Cavoli, at a depth of 10 m (33 ft), is the statue of the *Madonna dei Fondali* (Our Lady of the Sea Floor) by local sculptor Pinuccio Sciola. Excursions by glass-bottomed boat leave from the quay at Porto Giunco to view the submerged statue. This port is protected by the **Fortezza Vecchia**, a star-shaped fortress built in the 17th century. The sea around the headland is rich in fauna and flora and is popular with scuba divers.

Orroli ⓲

Road map C4. 🏃 3,300. 🚌
ℹ️ *Largo Aldo Moro (0782 84 70 06).* 📷 *30 Jun: Santa Caterina.*

THE TOWN of Orroli lies in a hollow in the rather barren Pranemuru plateau, at the edge of the Flumendosa valley. The area is dotted with numerous archaeological sites, such as the necropolis of **Su Motti** where *domus de janas* tombs are cut out of the rock.

Other archaeological sites in the area include the ruins of the **Arrubiu Nuraghe**, 5 km (3 miles) southeast of Orroli. This complicated, pentagonal site is larger than the one at Su Nuraxi *(see pp64–5).* The complex, made of red stone, was built around an 11th–10th-century BC central tower which, according to experts, was 27 m (88 ft) high. Five towers, probably dating from the 7th century BC, connected by tall bastions, were built around the complex, and an outer defensive wall was added in the 6th century BC. The ruins of the nuraghic village, consisting of round and rectangular dwellings, lie around the nuraghe.

Another interesting site is the nearby **Su Putzu** nuraghe, which has numerous dwellings in excellent condition.

🏛 Su Motti
4 km (2 miles) SE of Orroli. 📞 *0782 84 72 69.* ⭕ *by appt only.* 🏃 🎫
🏛 Arrubiu Nuraghe
📞 *0782 84 72 69.* ⭕ *9:30am–1pm, 3–8:30pm (Oct–Apr: 9:30am–5pm).* 🏃

The Arrubiu Nuraghe near Orroli

Perdasdefogu ⓳

Road map D4 & D5. 🏃 2,500. 🚌
📷 *12 Sep: San Salvatore.*

AN ISOLATED mountain village in the lower Ogliastra area, Perdasdefogu lies at the foot of the striking *tacchi*, vertical limestone walls that tower over the maquis *(see p89).* The road that meanders northeast towards Jerzu is one of the most scenic in Sardinia. It runs along a plateau at the base of these dolomitic walls, offering a spectacular view of the sea and Perda Liana peaks in the distance. Along the way is the rural church of **Sant'-Antonio**, set in a meadow at the foot of Punta Coróngiu, one of the most impressive of the limestone *tacchi*.

View from the headland of Capo Carbonara, south of Villasimius

A Trip on the Trenino Verde ⓴

Lake Alto Flumendosa, on the southern side of Gennargentu

IT TAKES ALMOST FIVE hours to travel 160 km (99 miles) on the narrow-gauge *trenino verde* (little green train), but the reward is a trip backwards in time through some of the wildest landscapes in Sardinia. The line passes through the softly rolling hills of Trexenta, carpeted with almond and olive trees, to the rugged mountains of Barbagia di Seui, where the train runs along the foot of a magnificent *tònnero*, with a broad view of its vertical limestone walls. The route follows the craggy contours of the mountain and there are so many bends that it is easy to lose your sense of direction. The train makes two hairpin turns through the town of Lanusei in order to get over a steep slope. The only drawback is the timetable: travellers cannot make the return trip on the same day.

Flumendosa

Villanovatulo ⑥
This isolated shepherds' village has a view of the Flumendosa river basin. The walls of the houses have murals by Pinuccio Sciola.

The Trenino Verde
This picturesque train skirts the hillsides, well away from the road amid unspoilt scenery. As well as the timeless landscape, you can appreciate the atmosphere of a forgotten age.

Lago di Flumendosa

N198

VISITORS' CHECKLIST

🛈 *Cagliari (070 57 93 03 46).*
Trenino Verde 📞 *070 58 02 46.* @ *treninov@tin.it*
🖥 *www.treninoverde.com*
Train timetable *May–Sep: from Arbatax, 7:50am and 2:30pm daily; from Mandas, 8:27am and 3:10pm daily; mid-Jul–Aug: from Arbatax, 9:10am daily; from Mandas, 4:44pm daily. Oct–Apr: private hire only.*

Mandas ⑧
69 km (43 miles) from Cagliari, Mandas is the leading agricultural town in the area. The church of San Giacomo, with statues of San Gioacchino and Sant'- Anna, is worth a visit.

Orroli ⑦
Surrounded by oak forests, the town of Orroli lies on a basalt tableland crossed by the Flumendosa river. Look out for the Arrubiu nuraghe *(see p91).*

Montarbu Forest ③
This is one of the best preserved forests in Sardinia, where moufflons live among ash, holm oak and yew trees. A striking feature here are the *tònneri*, massive vertical limestone walls.

Lanusei ②
This village lies on the slope of a hill commanding a fine view of the sea *(see p88)*.

Tortolì ①
The capital of the Ogliastra region is 3 km (2 miles) from the sea, on the edge of a large marsh which attracts thousands of migratory birds in winter. Watch out for the ruins of Castello di Medusa.

Interior of the Trenino Verde

Sadali ⑤
Lying in the middle of a karstic plateau, Sadali boasts a 7-m (23-ft) waterfall fed by springs that flow into an underground chasm. There are numerous caves, such as Is Janas, 205 m (672 ft) long with an underground lake and impressive stalagmites and stalactites.

Seui ④
The village of Seui, on the side of a steep valley, retains some traditional stone houses. The 17th-century Spanish prison is now occupied by the Civic Museum of Rural Culture with displays of traditional farm utensils and reconstructions of an 18th-century kitchen and bedroom.

0 kilometres 4

0 miles 4

KEY

▬▬ Train route

▬▬ Major road

▬▬ Minor road

▬ River

The train passing near Orroli

TIPS FOR TRAVELLERS

Refreshments are not served on the train and the few stations en route are not equipped to offer restaurant facilities, so it is advisable to take along something to eat and drink. Going towards Mandas, the best views can be appreciated from the left-hand side of the train (and vice versa).

The "normal" train, called TL, is superior to the AT (single-unit rail diesel car), which is noisier and less comfortable.

CENTRAL SARDINIA AND BARBAGIA

THE CENTRAL REGION OF SARDINIA *is the area that most vividly reflects the ancient character of the island. Rugged mountains are marked by shepherds' trails and villages perch over steep valleys. The inhabitants of this isolated region are known as hardy and proud and have retained many aspects of their traditional way of life.*

The name Barbagia derives from the Latin word *barbària*, used by the Romans to designate the inaccessible regions of the interior inhabited by "barbarians" (any culture that did not share the values and beliefs of the Roman civilization). Inhabited since prehistoric times and rich in archaeological sites, such as the nuraghic village of Tiscali *(see pp104–5)*, the heart of Sardinia resisted Roman invasions for many centuries and preserved its nuraghic religious rites up to the advent of Christianity.

Getting to know this rugged land requires some effort, since the roads are slow and winding, road signs are sometimes missing and many sights can be reached only via rough dirt tracks. The people, however, are often hospitable and tradition is still an essential part of local life. The churches and villages come to life during the colourful folk festivals, the patron saints' feast days and at religious festivities. At Mamoiada the *Mamuthones* lead the Mardi Gras processions wearing forbidding masks, cow bells and sheepskins *(see p102)*.

The mountainous landscape dominates central Sardinia. Trekkers can enjoy walks from the rocks of Supramonte di Oliena to the dense forests of holm oak on the slopes of Monte Novo San Giovanni *(see p107)* and the chestnut woods along the old railway near Belvì *(see p109)*.

The local cuisine is flavoured with herbs from the maquis, such as rosemary and thyme, while the handicrafts draw inspiration from pastoral life. Woven carpets, baskets and pottery with traditional motifs can be seen in Nuoro's Museo Etnografico *(see p99)*.

A shepherd and his flock in the high summer pastures at Pietrino

◁ **Wind-battered cork oak, a common sight in the Barbagia**

Exploring Central Sardinia and Barbagia

NUORO IS THE CAPITAL of Sardinia's interior region: to the east lies the Supramonte mountain range, with Oliena, Orgòsolo and Dorgali at its feet, while to the west the valleys descend towards Lake Omodeo and Macomer.

In this landscape of hills and steep limestone walls (the *tònneri* formations) are some of the most important towns in the region: Mamoiada, Bitti and Sarule. To the south is the Gennargentu massif, carpeted with forests, on the slopes of which are typical mountain villages such as Gavoi and Fonni. Heading northeast and skirting the slopes of Monte Ortobene, which towers above the city of Nuoro, the road descends among almond trees and vineyards towards the Baronia region.

Barren slopes on the Gennargentu mountain range

SIGHTS AT A GLANCE

A mural painted on rocks near Orgòsolo

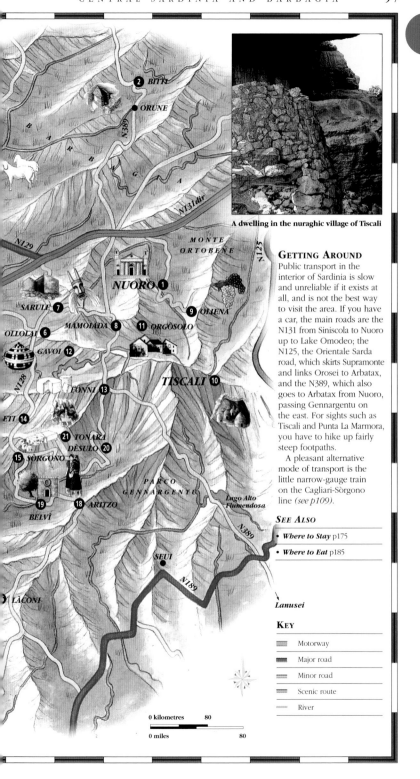

A dwelling in the nuraghic village of Tiscali

MONTE ORTOBENE

NUORO ❶

SARULE ❼   OLIENA ❾

OLLOLAI ❻   MAMOIADA ❽   ORGÒSOLO ❶❶

GAVOI ❶❷

TISCALI ❶❶

FONNI ❶❸

ETI ❶❹

TONARA ❷❶   DÈSULO ❷❶

SÒRGONO ❶❺

PARCO GENNARGENTU

Lago Alto Flumendosa

BELVÌ ❶❾   ARITZO ❶❽

SEUI

LÀCONI

Lanusei

GETTING AROUND

Public transport in the interior of Sardinia is slow and unreliable if it exists at all, and is not the best way to visit the area. If you have a car, the main roads are the N131 from Siniscola to Nuoro up to Lake Omodeo; the N125, the Orientale Sarda road, which skirts Supramonte and links Orosei to Arbatax, and the N389, which also goes to Arbatax from Nuoro, passing Gennargentu on the east. For sights such as Tiscali and Punta La Marmora, you have to hike up fairly steep footpaths.

A pleasant alternative mode of transport is the little narrow-gauge train on the Cagliari-Sòrgono line *(see p109)*.

SEE ALSO

• **Where to Stay** p175

• **Where to Eat** p185

KEY

▦	Motorway
▦	Major road
▦	Minor road
▦	Scenic route
▦	River

0 kilometres   80

0 miles   80

Nuoro ●

NÙGORO, AS THE LOCALS still call their city, is one of Sardinia's most important centres. The city began to expand in the 14th century, but by the 18th century there was social unrest and riots erupted. In 1746 the Piedmontese prefect, De Viry, described the city as "a hotbed of bandits and murderers". A decree in 1868 that put an end to the common use of farmland culminated in a popular rebellion known as *Su Connottu.*

Traditional costume   At the beginning of the 20th century Nuoro became the heart of the island's cultural life, producing political and social writers such as Grazia Deledda. The city became the provincial capital in 1926, and today it is the commercial heart of Barbagia.

Santa Maria della Neve

The huge granite blocks in Piazza Sebastiano Satta

Exploring Nuoro
The city is set in spectacular surroundings on a granite plateau beneath Monte Ortobene. Its isolated position and relatively recent exposure to tourism have helped to preserve local culture, traditions and costumes.

The modern city retains many picturesque streets and buildings in the old centre. Corso Garibaldi, once known as Bia Maiore, leads up to the quarter of San Pietro and the city's Neo-Classical cathedral, **Santa Maria della Neve** (1836). Near Corso Garibaldi is the whitewashed Piazza Sebastiano Satta, paved in 1976 with large granite blocks.

Nuoro is the birthplace of some of Sardinia's most notable men and women of letters, who at the end of the 19th century injected new life into the island's culture. Apart from Grazia Deledda, other native literary figures are politician and essayist Attilio Deffenu (1893–1918) and poet Sebastiano Satta (1867–1914).

🏛 Civico Museo Speleo-Archeologico
Via Leonardo da Vinci. ☏ 0784 300 83. ⬤ *for restoration.*
This museum combines the collections of fossils and fossil plants of the *Gruppo Speleologico Nuorese,* with archaeological finds excavated over many years in the area. Exhibits range from Neolithic to medieval objects, including the skeletons of an ancient hare, *Prolagus sardus,* a giant otter, *Lontra gigante,* and a collection of cave finds. Also of interest are Bronze Age menhir statues from Làconi, and nuraghic bronze statuettes. Finds from the Roman era include belt buckles and other everyday household objects.

🏛 Museo Deleddiano
Via Grazia Deledda 28. ☏ 0784 25 80 88. ⬤ *to the public.*
Grazia Deledda's birthplace retains the atmosphere of a mid-19th-century Sardinian home. The house has been arranged according to her own description, set out in her novel *Cosima,* with objects marking the stages of her career. The courtyard leads to what was the kitchen garden (now the venue for cultural events), while the upper floors are given over to displays of the covers of her books, programmes for her plays, and a copy of the diploma for the Nobel Prize for Literature.

GRAZIA DELEDDA (1871–1936)

Grazia Deledda won the Nobel Prize for Literature in 1926 in recognition of her perceptive portrayal of the power and passions in the primitive communities around her. Born in Nuoro in 1871, she has become a symbol of Sardinian culture and an example of the island's prolific artistic production. The eventful and difficult years of her early career are described in the auto-biographical novel *Cosima* (1937). Her world of fiction revolves around Barbagia, with its mysteries and strong sense of identity. Among her best-known novels are *Elias Portolu* (1900), *Cenere* (1903), and *Canne al Vento* (1913). She died in Rome in 1936.

The author Grazia Deledda

The whitewashed Museo Etnografico in Nuoro

VISITORS' CHECKLIST

Road map D3. 38,000.
Ente Provinciale per il Turismo,
Piazza Italia 19 (0784 300 83).
19 Mar: San Giuseppe; 6 Aug:
San Salvatore; last Sun in Aug:
Processione del Redentore.

solemn procession known as
the *Processione del Redentore*
in which representatives from
almost every town in Sardinia
take part *(see p28)*.

Traditional costume from Dèsulo,
Museo delle Tradizioni Sarde

⚜ Museo Etnografico

Via Antonio Mereu 56 & Via Salis 54.
0784 24 29 00. Jun–Sep:
9am–8pm daily; Oct–May: 9am–1pm,
3–7pm daily.

The Museum of Sardinian life
and popular traditions was
designed in the
1960s by
architect
Antonio
Simon
Mossa. The
aim of the
project was to
recreate a typical
Sardinian village,
with courtyards,
alleys and stairways, as a
setting for artifacts, objects
and costumes representing
Sardinian daily life.

On display in this popular
ethnographic museum are
traditional pieces of furniture,
such as a 19th-century chest
and cover and silver jewellery
used to adorn aprons or hand-
kerchiefs. Characteristic costumes worn daily or on special
occasions by women are also
on show, as are different types
of traditional bread moulds,
looms and hand-woven car-
pets. One room is dedicated to
carnival masks and costumes.

The museum also has a
library specializing in
anthropological literature, an
auditorium and an exhibition
centre. Every other October,
the museum features a festival
of ethnographic and anthropological films.

Chest and cover in the
Museo Etnografico

ENVIRONS:

🏔 Monte Ortobene

East of Nuoro.
Nuoro was founded on the
granite slopes of this mountain
and the inhabitants have
always held it in high regard.
To reach its
wooded areas,
take the N129
Orosei road
east out of the
city. The road
passes the
church of **Nostra
Signora della
Solitudine**, where
Grazia Deledda is
buried. At the summit is a
statue of the Redentore (Christ
the Redeemer) that overlooks
the city below and next to it
is the church of **Nostra
Signora di Montenero**. On
the last Sunday in August this
church is the focus of the

⋂ Necropoli di Sas Concas

N128. 0784 24 29 00.
daily.
To visit this necropolis, take
the N131 15 km (9 miles)
west out of Nuoro and then
the N128 southwards for 3 km
(2 miles) towards Oniferi. The
complex consists of a series of
domus de janas, some decorated with bas reliefs, such as
the *Tomba dell'Emiciclos*
(Tomb of the Hemicycle). The
area is unattended, so a torch
for the tombs may be useful.

The Sagra del Redentore procession on Monte Ortobene

Su Tempiesu well-temple near Bitti

Bitti ❷

Road map D3. 🏛 *3,800.* 🛈 *Town Hall (0784 41 51 24).* 📅 *23 Apr: San Giorgio.*

THIS PASTORAL village has recently become known thanks to the *Tenores de Bitti* musical group, whose interpretations of traditional Sardinian close harmony songs have won them acclaim throughout Europe *(see pp24–5).* Experts say the local dialect is the one that most resembles Latin.

The 19th-century church of **San Giorgio Martire** stands in the central Piazza Giorgio Asproni. In the nearby parish home is a fine small collection of local archaeological finds.

ENVIRONS: Not far from Bitti on the road to Orune (watch out for the signs, which can be difficult to follow) is the **Su Tempiesu** well-temple. This consists of several chambers made of large square basalt stones, and houses the sacred well. The well water was used

in nuraghic rituals. A little way east of Bitti are five churches, Santo Stefano, Santa Maria, Santa Lucia, San Giorgio and *Babbu Mannu* (Holy Ghost). These become lively during religious festivities.

Bono ❸

Road map C3. 🏛 *4,100.* 🛈 *Town Hall (079 79 02 19).* 📅 *31 Aug: San Raimondo Nonnato.*

SET AT THE FOOT of the Gocèano mountain range, Bono is an ideal starting point for trips to the wooded Monte Rasu and the Foresta di Burgos. In the centre of town is the parish church of **San Michele Arcangelo**, which has been rebuilt several times over the years. Inside is a curious clock driven by the weight of four cannonballs, shot at the town during the 1796 siege, when the government troops were driven out by the city's inhabitants. This episode is re-enacted every year during the traditional festival held on 31 August. On this day the largest pumpkin from the local kitchen gardens is awarded to the person who comes in last in the festival horse race as a facetious sign of recognition of the "valour" of the routed army. Until recently, this pumpkin was

rolled down the mountain to the valley to symbolize the government troops escaping from the local inhabitants.

In early September Bono plays host to the colourful *Fiera dei Prodotti Tipici Artigiani del Gocèano,* a fair featuring typical handicrafts from the Gocèano region.

ENVIRONS: From the Uccaidu pass, northwest of Bono, you can hike up the ridge to the summit of Monte Rasu at an altitude of 1,258 m (4,125 ft). From here there are magnificent sweeping views of the Foresta di Burgos and surrounding mountain range as well as most of Sardinia.

The countryside between Bono and Burgos

Burgos ❹

Road map C3. 🏛 *1,100.*

THE HAMLET of Burgos lies below a cone-shaped peak in the Gocèano mountains. The town was founded in 1353 by Mariano d'Arborea and is dominated by the ruins of

The village of Burgos, dominated by the 12th-century castle

Small Giara horses in the Foresta di Burgos

Burgos Castle, built much earlier, in 1127. The castle was the scene of many battles between the Sardinian principalities and mainland colonists during the Middle Ages. It was from here that in 1478 Artaldo di Alagon's troops marched from the castle to the battle of Macomer, marking the end of Sardinian independence and the start of Aragonese dominion. Inside the outer defensive walls, further fortifications surround a restored tower. The entrance to the tower was once through a wooden stairway that could be raised in case of a siege.

San Nicola, near Ottana

ENVIRONS: The **Foresta di Burgos**, 5 km (3 miles) northwest of Burgos, is a well-kept forested area with holm oak and cork oak trees, cedars, conifers and some chestnut trees. The area is also known for the small Sardinian Giara horses that graze in fenced-off pastures.

Ottana **5**

Road map C3. 🏠 2,700. 🚹 Town Hall (0784 758 30). 🎭 Carnevale.

OTTANA LIES IN the valley of the river Tirso, not far from the slopes of the Barbagia di Ollolai region.

In the Middle Ages the town was an important religious centre. On the southern outskirts of town is the church of **San Nicola**, once the cathedral of the regional diocese. It was built in 1150 in austere Romanesque style, with black and purple trachyte ashlars showing strong Pisan influence. Inside is a 14th-century polyptych showing the Madonna flanked by the bishop of Ottana and Mariano d'Arborea, count of Gocèano. In the apse is a 16th-century wooden crucifix.

Almost abandoned in the 16th century due to an outbreak of malaria, Ottana was chosen in the 1970s as an industrial development site,

Typical masked figures dressed for the Carnival at Ottana

promoted by ENI, the National Hydrocarbon Corporation. The industries have not produced the expected profits, however, and the ecological problems are so serious that the entire project is to be abandoned.

Carnival is a popular festival in Ottana, when locals dress in sheepskin and bells and wear bull-like masks (*see p29*).

Ollolai **6**

Road map C3. 🏠 1,800. 🚹 Town Hall (0784 514 99). 🎭 24 Aug: San Bartolomeo.

Asphodel, used in traditional basket-weaving at Ollolai

THE VILLAGE of Ollolai was once the medieval administrative centre of the Barbagia di Ollolai region, an area that included the northern part of Barbagia and still retains the name today. The town's decline began in 1490 after a terrible fire destroyed most of it and today it is a small hamlet.

Some original houses decorated with dark stone doorways are visible in the old centre and there are still a few craftsmen who weave the traditional asphodel baskets in their courtyards.

ENVIRONS: A short distance west of Ollolai is the church of **San Basilio**. A traditional rural religious festival is held here on 1 September. A rough road climbs up to S'Asisorgiu peak to an altitude of 1,127 m (3,700 ft). From here there are fabulous views of the surrounding mountain range and the summit is popularly known as "Sardinia's window".

Sarule seen from the nearby hills

Sarule ❼

Road map C3. 🏛 *2,100.* 🛈 *Town Hall (0784 760 17).* 🎭 *8 Sep: Madonna di Gonare.*

SARULE IS A VILLAGE of medieval origin which has preserved its tradition of carpet-weaving. Along the main street you can still see the workshops where these vividly coloured carpets with stylized figures are woven on antique vertical looms and then sold on the premises.

Perched on a spur overlooking the village is the sanctuary of **Nostra Signora di Gonare**, one of the most sacred shrines in Sardinia. The church was built in the 13th century for the ruler of the principality, Gonario II di Torres, and by the 16th century it had already become a famous pilgrimage site. The sanctuary was enlarged in the 17th century with a dark stone exterior and austere buttresses.

To reach the sanctuary, a rough road heads east from Sarule and climbs up Monte Gonare for 4 km (2.5 miles). This granite rock mountain is interspersed with layers of limestone and outcrops of schist covered in vegetation. The mountain slopes are populated by many species of birds, including partridges, turtle doves, woodpeckers, shrikes and various birds of prey. The forest has holm oaks and maples, while in the spring the undergrowth is enlivened by brightly coloured cyclamen, peonies and morning glory. The road ends at an open space with pilgrims' houses *(cumbessias)*, and a winding footpath up the bluff through the holm oak forest leads to the sanctuary. From here there are marvellous views of Monte Ortobene towering over Nuoro, Monte Corrasi near Oliena, and the Gennargentu mountains in the distance.

From 5–8 September a lively festival takes place at the sanctuary for the Madonna di Gonare, to which pilgrims travel on foot from all of the neighbouring villages. As well as religious festivities, a horse race is held, and the square resounds with poetry readings and sacred songs sung in traditional dialect.

The sanctuary of Nostra Signora di Gonare at Sarule

Mamoiada ❽

Road map D3. 🏛 *2,700.* 🛈 *Town Hall (0784 567 00).* 🎭 *17 Jan, Carnival Sun & Shrove Tue: Mamuthones procession.*

SOME OLD BUILDINGS, possibly of Aragonese origin, are still visible among the modern houses that line the main street of Mamoiada. In 1770 the town was mentioned by the Savoyard viceroy, Des Hayes, as a place of some interest with numerous vineyards and an exceptional number of sheep. Flocks are still taken every summer to the slopes of Barbagia di Ollolai to graze.

TRADITIONAL FESTIVALS IN THE BARBAGIA

S'Incontru, the procession held in the streets of Oliena on Easter day, commemorates the resurrection of Christ and his subsequent encounter with the Virgin Mary. On this occasion, and during the festivities in honour of San Lussorio on 21 August, you can admire the colourful traditional costumes and watch the impressive procession of horsemen through the streets of the town.

The *S'Incontru* procession

At Mamoiada the lively celebrations on the night of Sant'Antonio Abate (17 January), Shrove Tuesday and the last night of Carnival, all revolve around the figures of the *Mamuthones* and *Issohadores*. The former wear tragic masks and shepherds' garb, with a set of cow bells tied on their backs. The bells jangle in time with their rhythmical steps as they go through the village to the main square, where there is music and dancing all evening. The *Issohadores*, with their red waistcoats, are more colourful: they "capture" spectators and drag them inside the circles of the traditional round dance *(see p25)*.

The carnival *Mamuthones* at Mamoiada

A typical street in the town of Oliena

Mamoiada is best known for the dark, forbidding masks of the *Mamuthones*, who appear in the village streets on the feast days of Sant'Antonio Abate (17 January), the Sunday of Carnival and in particular on Shrove Tuesday, during the Barbagia's most famous Carnival celebrations *(see p29)*.

ENVIRONS: About 5 km (3 miles) southwest of Mamoiada, along a secondary road towards Gavoi, is the **Santuario di San Cosimo**. This typical rural church has a central structure surrounded by *cumbessias,* lodgings for pilgrims to the sanctuary. The present-day church dates from the 17th century and its main feature is the single nave. At the end of the nave, recent restoration has brought to light an Aragonese niche with columns and an architrave made of volcanic rock.

A further 6 km (4 miles) to the south is the **Santuario della Madonna d'Itria**, an imposing church with *cumbessias.* Here, on the last Sunday of July, there is a horse race around the church, known as *Sa Carrela*.

Oliena ❾

Road map D3. 🏘 *8,000.* 🛈 *Town Hall (0784 28 02 00).* 🎭 *Easter am: S'Incontru; 21 Aug: San Lussorio.*

THE APPROACH to Oliena towards evening, along the northern road from Nuoro, is an unforgettable sight. The lights of the town shine at the foot of the steep white mass of Supramonte, which rises

eastwards towards the Golfo di Orosei. The countryside is covered in vineyards, which yield the famous Sardinian wine Cannonau.

Some original houses, built around courtyards with external stairways and pergolas and brightly coloured rooms, are still visible along the narrow streets and alleyways. There are also several religious buildings, such as the church of **Santa Croce**, said to be the oldest in the town. Rebuilt in the 17th century, it has a bell tower decorated with an unusual trident motif.

The **Jesuit College** on Corso Vittorio Emanuele II is a reminder of the arrival of this religious order in Oliena. From the beginning of the 17th century onwards, the Jesuits encouraged the town's economy by promoting wine-making and the breeding of silkworms. Next door to the Jesuit college, the church of **Sant'Ignazio di Loyola** has wooden statues of Sant'Ignazio and San Francesco Saverio,

as well as an altarpiece depicting San Cristoforo.

Oliena, known for its good wine, is also famous for its jewellery, cakes and the traditional costumes worn by the women: a black shawl, interwoven with silk and gold, and a light blue blouse.

There are two important festivals at Oliena that end with impressive processions: *San Lussorio* in August and *S'Incontru* on Easter morning.

ENVIRONS: South of Oliena, it is possible to take various hiking tours on the rugged and spectacular rocks of the **Supramonte di Oliena**. Starting from the Monte Maccione refuge, you can cross the chain and descend into the Lanaittu valley floor.

The **Su Gologone** natural springs are 8 km (5 miles) east of Oliena. The waters, which have cut channels through the mountain rock, are refreshingly cool in summer and turn into an extremely cold, rushing torrent in winter. Su Gologone is the largest spring in Sardinia, with an average production of 300 litres (66 gallons) per second. It lies in a pleasant wooded area ideal for picnics in the shade.

For many years speleologists have been exploring the depths of the underground cave of **Grotta Sa Oche**, in the Supramonte mountains. Every year divers penetrate further underground into the Supramonte mountains to study the various aspects of this natural phenomenon.

The Su Gologone natural spring at the foot of Supramonte

Tiscali ⑩

ALITTLE OVER A CENTURY AGO some woodcutters, travelling over the mountain range that dominates the Lanaittu valley, discovered a nuraghic settlement hidden in the depths of an enormous chasm in Monte Tiscali. The village of Tiscali, which had been inhabited up to the time of the Roman invasion, consists of a number of round dwellings with juniper wood architraves around the doors and roofs. Years of neglect have led to the partial deterioration of the site, but it is still one of the most exciting nuraghic finds in Sardinia, in particular because of its unique position. The climb to Tiscali can be tiring and is over rocky ground.

The Path to the Village
Red arrows on the rocks in-dicate the way to the village.

The chasm had no natural springs, so the inhabitants collected water that dripped down the walls of the rock.

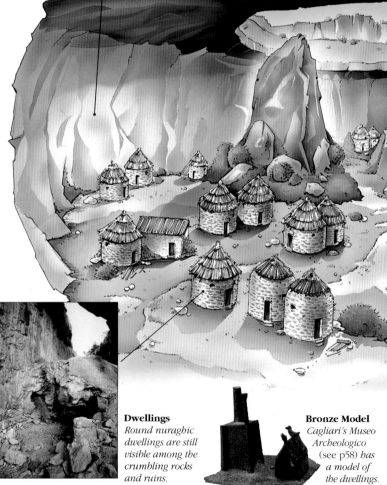

Dwellings
Round nuraghic dwellings are still visible among the crumbling rocks and ruins.

Bronze Model
Cagliari's Museo Archeologico (see p58) has a model of the dwellings.

VISITORS' CHECKLIST

Road map D3. ☐ 9am–7pm
(Oct–May: 5pm). 🎫 🚻
ℹ️ Town Hall, Dorgali (0764 961
13) or Pro Loco, Dorgali (0784
933 05). Monte Maccione refuge,
Oliena organizes tours and hikes.
📞 0784 28 83 63.

View of Monte di Tiscali
*Hidden inside this 518-m (1,700-ft) high mountain,
the nuraghic village of Tiscali was discovered in
the 19th century. Archaeological
excavations did not begin until
many years later.*

Entrance to the Chasm
*The difficult terrain and steep
walls were the best defence for
the inhabitants of Tiscali.*

TIPS FOR TRAVELLERS

*From Oliena take the road east
towards Dorgali. After about 5 km
(3 miles), take the right-hand turn
for Su Gologone. Just before the
hotel of the same name (see
p175), take the dirt road to the
left that goes to the Lanaittu
plain. Proceed along the floor of
the valley (keeping to the left)
until the road becomes too
difficult for vehicles. Clear red
arrows on the rocks and trees
indicate the footpath to the
chasm of Tiscali. The walk will
take you about an hour.*

*It is possible to make other
trips in this area, although it is
advisable to go with a guide.
Places to head for include the
gigantic Gole di Su Gorroppu
ravines, parts of the caves of Su
Bentu, Sa Oche or S'Elicas Artas,
or the climb down to the Codula
di Luna valley (see p85).*

The roofs were
made of juniper
wood.

The walls of the
dwellings were made
of limestone blocks.

THE NURAGHIC VILLAGE OF TISCALI

*This reconstruction of the nuraghic village shows how the
settlement would have looked. A crater opening allows natural
light in and steps from the entrance made the descent easy.*

MURALS IN SARDINIA

Sardinian murals began to appear on walls at Orgòsolo in the 1960s and soon became a feature of many of the island's villages and towns. The most famous of these is San Sperate *(see p62)*, the home town of the artist Pinuccio Sciola. The themes of this particular artistic genre are satirical, political or social. The styles vary greatly but are always characterized by bright colours. Even in the open country you may come across faces, shapes, hands and penetrating stares painted onto the boulders, rocks or cliffs. The *Associazione Italiana Paesi Dipinti* (Italian Association of Painted Towns) was founded to preserve and publicize the towns with these murals and also to encourage creativity and cultural exchange between different regions.

Mural at Orgòsolo

Mural on a wall at San Sperate

A mural painted on rock near Orgòsolo

Orgòsolo ⓫

Road map D3. 🏠 *4,800.* ℹ *Town Hall (0784 40 09 01).* 🎪 *first Sun of Jun: Sant'Anania; 15 Aug: Festa dell'Assunta.*

THIS CHARACTERISTIC village in the interior of the island has been compared to an eagle's nest and a fortress, perched precariously on the mountainside. The villagers are known as rugged and hardy shepherds, proud of their lifestyle and traditions. Rampant banditry in the 1960s was documented in Vittorio De Seta's film *Bandits at Orgòsolo*, in which the hard life of the shepherds and their mistrust of the government is narrated with cool detachment. The passion of the locals for social and political issues is also visible in the hundreds of murals painted on the walls of houses and on the rocks around Orgòsolo. The images describe the harsh life of the shepherds, their struggles to keep their land and Sardinian traditions, as well as injustices committed in other parts of the world.

Simple low stone houses can be seen along the steep and narrow streets of the town and some original features are still visible on a few isolated houses. On Corso Repubblica, the church of **San Pietro** retains its 15th-century bell tower. Traditional dress, a brightly coloured apron embroidered with geometric patterns and a saffron-yellow headscarf, is still worn by some local women.

In summer two popular local festivals draw large crowds: the Assumption Day Festival on 15 August and Sant'Anania's feast day on the first Sunday of June.

ENVIRONS: Just outside Orgòsolo is the 17th-century church of **Sant'Anania**. The church was built where the saint's relics are said to have been found. Orgòsolo is an ideal starting point for excursions up to the surrounding Supramonte mountains, where open pastures are interspersed with dense forests of oak.

A road leads to the **Funtana Bona**, 18 km (11 miles) south of Orgòsolo. These natural springs emerge at an altitude of 1,082 m (3,550 ft), at the foot of the limestone peak of **Monte Novo San Giovanni**, 1,316 m (4,316 ft) high. From here it is also possible to reach the shady **Foresta di Montes**, a forest of holm oak that stretches out to the south.

Sculpted detail on San Gavino, Gavoi

Gavoi ⓬

Road map C3. 🏠 *3,100.* ℹ *Town Hall (0784 531 20).* 🎪 *last Sun of Jul: rural festival at Sanctuary of the Madonna d'Itria; second Sun after Easter: Sant'Antioco's feast day.*

FOR MANY CENTURIES this village was famous in Sardinia for the production of harnesses and bridles. Today its most characteristic product is cheese, including *fiore sardo* pecorino, made from sheep's milk *(see p181)*. The centre of town is dominated by the pink façade of the 14th-century church of **San Gavino**, which overlooks the square of the same name. Some of Gavoi's oldest and most characteristic streets begin here. A stroll down these narrow alleys will reveal historic buildings with dark stone façades and balconies overflowing with flowers, such as the two-storey building on Via San Gavino.

In the little church of **Sant' Antioco**, in the upper part of town, dozens of ex votos in gold and silver filigree are pinned to the wall. There is also a fine statue of the saint, whose feast day is celebrated the second Sunday after Easter.

View of the Lago di Gusana seen from Gavoi

Fonni ⑬

Road map D3. 👥 *4,600.* ℹ️ *Town Hall (0784 570 22).* @ *comunedifonni@ tiscalinet.it* 📅 *first Sun & Mon in Jun: Madonna dei Martiri feast day.*

FONNI IS ONE of the highest towns in Sardinia, lying at an altitude of 1,000 m (3,280 ft). Its economy relies on tradition and tourism, offering locally made produce, such as traditional sweets, as well as fabrics and rugs known for their fine workmanship. Although recent new building has slightly diminished its charm, at first sight the town gives the impression of sprouting from the mountainside.

On the edge of town is the Franciscan **Madonna dei Martiri** complex, which dates from the 17th century. Inside is a curious statue of the Virgin Mary made from pieces of ancient Roman sculptures.

The town's major festival is held in mid-June to celebrate the return of the shepherds and their flocks from the winter pastures.

On the road towards Gavoi, 4 km (2 miles) west of Fonni, is the **Lago di Gusana**, a large artificial lake. Its tranquil shores, surrounded by holm oaks, make it a popular spot.

Teti ⑭

Road map C4. 👥 *900.* ℹ️ *Town Hall (0784 680 23).* 📅 *third Sun in Sep: San Sebastiano.*

PERCHED ON the rocky mountains that dominate Lago di Cucchinadorza, the village of Teti distinguishes itself by its small museum, the **Museo Archeologico Comprensoriale**. Run by a team of enterprising young local people, the museum illustrates with clarity and detail the history of the area's ancient nuraghic settlements (in particular the village of S'Urbale and the sacred precinct of Abini). The display cases contain pieces found during excavations, including everyday objects used by the nuraghic people. One hall has a reconstruction of a round dwelling dating from about 1000 BC.

Bronze statuettes found at Teti, Cagliari Museo Archeologico

Inside are spinning tools, pots, small axes and granite mills. In the middle of the house is the area used as a fireplace.

The halls of the lower floor are used for temporary exhibitions on local culture and traditions, such as traditional costumes and handicrafts.

ENVIRONS: About one kilometre (half a mile) southwest of Teti is the entrance to the nuraghic archaeological site of **S'Urbale**. The village was inhabited from 1200 to 900 BC, and the ruins of many prehistoric dwellings are still visible. The ancient nuraghic village of **Abini** is found 10 km (6 miles) to the north of Teti.

🏛 **Museo Archeologico Comprensoriale**
📞 *0784 681 20.* 🕐 *9am–12:30pm, 3–8pm (Oct–May: 3–5:30pm).*
📷 ✏️ ♿

FORESTA DI MONTES

At the foot of the rocky bluffs of Monte Novo San Giovanni and Monte Fumai is the largest holm oak forest in Europe. Although many trees were destroyed in the past by fires – often started by shepherds in order to acquire more grazing land – the vast forest is once again increasing in size thanks to replanting, and today it attracts visitors from all over the island. Even in the heat of the summer, a walk through this area and the plateau around the River Olai is very enjoyable, as the dense forest offers shade from the sun and there is a chance to see sheep and pigs, as well as asphodels in bloom. The many footpaths around the Funtana Bona forest headquarters offer opportunities for hiking and mountain-biking.

Monte Novo San Giovanni

The rural Sanctuary of San Mauro, near Sòrgono

Sòrgono **⓯**

Road map C4. 🏠 *2,100.* 🛈 *Town Hall (0784 62 25 20).* 📅 *26 May: San Mauro feast day.*

The Pisan fountain at Sòrgono

S ET IN A DENSELY cultivated area of orchards and vineyards, famous for producing Cannonau wine *(see p182)*, Sòrgono has been an important town since Roman times. Today it is the administrative centre of the Mandrolisai area.

Two rather dilapidated sites in the town are worth a visit; the 17th-century **Casa Carta**, featuring a typical Aragonese window, and a medieval fountain of Pisan origin.

Just west of town is one of the most interesting and oldest rural sanctuaries in Sardinia, the **Santuario di San Mauro**. This imposing church is surrounded by the traditional *cumbessias*, the houses used by the pilgrims during their stay at the sanctuary. The building is a mixture of local architectural features and the characteristic Gothic-Aragonese style.

A fine stairway flanked by two stone lions leads to the grey trachyte façade, which boasts a beautiful carved Gothic rose window. Numerous inscriptions are recorded on the stones of the church, some many centuries old and others more recent, carved by pilgrims to commemorate their visits to the sanctuary.

The interior of San Mauro has a single vault and is interrupted only by an arch that leads into the presbytery. Here there are a Baroque altar and some statues.

Various buildings were added to the original church to accommodate pilgrims and offer them adequate dining facilities, in particular during the San Mauro feast day. One of Sardinia's most important livestock and horse fairs used to be held on this day in the grounds of the sanctuary.

Not far from the church are two further sites worth visiting: the **Tomba di Giganti di Funtana Morta** (Tomb of the Giants) and, on a hilltop overlooking the church, the **Talei Nuraghe**, built with large granite stones and partly into the surrounding rock.

Làconi **⓰**

Road map C4. 🏠 *2,500.* 🛈 *Town Hall (0782 86 62 00).*

T HE TOWN of Làconi is built around a rocky spur of the Sarcidano mountain range, with panoramic views of the surrounding countryside. Another striking feature of the town is the ruins of **Castello Aymerich** in the park above the town. Only a single tower from the original fortress, built in 1053, remains. The rest of the castle includes later additions such as the 15th-century hall and the 17th-century portico. The magnificent park around the castle includes a botanical garden and waterfall, and today it is a popular destination for walks and picnics.

Once the seat of the local noble overlords, Làconi has preserved the Neo-Classical **Palazzo Aymerich**, built in the first half of the 19th century by architect Gaetano Cima from Cagliari. Near the 16th-century parish church is the birthplace and small museum of **Sant'Ignazio da Làconi**, a miracle worker who lived here in the second half of the 18th century. There is also a monument in his honour in the square.

ENVIRONS: The area around Làconi has many prehistoric remains. Among these are the anthropomorphic menhirs, single stones on which ancient sculptors carved human features. These can be seen at Perda Iddocca and Genna 'e Aidu, but it is advisable to be accompanied by a local guide.

The ruins of Castello Aymerich at Làconi

The Cagliari – Sòrgono Railway ⑰

THE TRAIN RIDE BETWEEN CAGLIARI and Sòrgono is a slow approach to the foothills of the Gennargentu mountain range (the journey takes four-and-a-half hours, while you can cover the same distance by car in two hours). The narrow-gauge railway nevertheless offers a scenic route through spectacular mountains and an insight into travel from another age. DH Lawrence described the trip in his book *Sea and Sardinia* (1921). In the first stretch, up to Mandas, the train goes over the rolling hills of Trexenta. It then climbs up to the road house at Ortuabis, an area of thick vegetation with a backdrop of mountain peaks, and on beyond Belvì through a wood of dense tree heathers.

Lush scenery *and waterfalls characterize the stretch between Làconi and Meana.*

Around the village *of Meana Sardo, dense vegetation fills the valleys. Meana has stone houses, and the parish church of San Bartolomeo has a Renaissance façade. There are also several nuraghi in the vicinity.*

Chestnut and hazelnut *woods cover the foothills of the Gennargentu. Near the station at Belvì you can visit the* Museo di Scienze Naturali *(Natural Science Museum) (See p110).*

Làconi *is a popular tourist destination in the Sarcidano region.*

San Pantaleo Cathedral, *at Dolianova, is a Romanesque building built by the Pisans. Inside is a 5th–6th-century christening font, vestige of the original early Christian basilica that stood on this site.*

| 0 km | 10 |
| 0 miles | 10 |

TIPS FOR TRAVELLERS

ℹ️ *Ufficio Orari e Concessioni (070 49 13 04).*

📷 *Guided tours require a minimum of 25 people and are available from May to August by appointment only. There is also a restricted Summer-only train timetable.* 🚆

KEY

▭▭ Train route

▬ Motorway

▬ Major road

▬ Minor road

— River

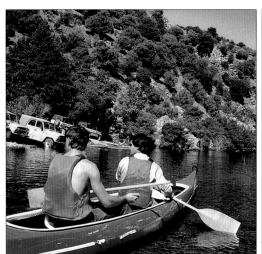

Canoeing on the Flumendosa river near Aritzo

Aritzo ⑱

Road map C4. 🏠 *1,700.* 🛈 *City hall (0784 62 92 23).* 🎭 *second Sun in Aug: Sant'Isidoro.*

THE SMALL TOWN of Aritzo was once famous for selling snow, at a very high price, packed in straw-lined boxes and transported throughout the island during the hot summer months. Under Aragonese rule, the town had the privilege of being governed by its own inhabitants, locally elected.

There are still many traces of the old town. Some houses retain typical stone façades and long, wooden balconies. Among the most important buildings are the **Casa degli Arangino** (in Neo-Gothic style) and the impressive 17th-century stone **Aritzo prison** on Via Maggiore.

The market for snow no longer exists, but the town has continued its tradition of making wooden furniture, such as hand-carved wedding chests. These are sold from the craftsmen's workshops.

The good climate, the high altitude and panoramic views of the surrounding mountains make Aritzo a pleasant tourist destination in the summer. Rodeos are a popular attraction outside town and interesting walking tours and horseback rides take place

towards the Gennargentu massif and the upper Flumendosa river valley. Here canoeing on the river is a popular activity.

ENVIRONS:
Just north of Aritzo is the **Tacco di Texile**, a vertical limestone pinnacle, 975 m (3,200 ft) high, in the

Wedding chest made by Aritzo craftsmen

shape of a mushroom. From here there are spectacular views of the mountains of the Barbagia region.

During the Middle Ages, the humble saint Efisio lived in this area. For many years he preached to the local inhabitants and eventually converted them to Christianity.

Belvì ⑲

Road map C4. 🏠 *810.* 🛈 *City Hall (0784 62 92 16).* 🎭 *28 Aug: Sant'Agostino feast day.*

THE VILLAGE of Belvì lies in a dominating position overlooking the Iscra river valley, which is full of fields of hazelnut trees and orchards.

In the past it must have been an important economic and trading centre, as the surrounding mountain region, Barbagia di Belvì, has also adopted the name.

The narrow-gauge railway which connects Cagliari and Sòrgono runs along the stretch of road near the village. The route goes through magnificent scenery as well as tackling a thousand tortuous bends and high viaducts (*see p109*).

In the village, several old houses are still visible. One of these, on the main street, Via Roma, houses the private **Museo di Scienze Naturali** (Natural Science Museum). Founded in the 1980s by a group of enthusiasts (including a German naturalist who lived in Belvì for almost ten years) it has interesting palaeontology and mineralogy departments, as well as occasional exhibitions of its collection of typical Sardinian fauna and insects.

🏛 **Museo di Scienze Naturali**
Via San Sebastiano 54. 📞 *0784 62 94 67.* ⏰ *by appt only.* 🖼 🔧

The rodeo held near Aritzo

Overlooking Dèsulo

Dèsulo ⑳

Road map C4. 🏠 *3,200.* ℹ️ *Pro Loco (0784 61 98 87).* 🎉 *Second Sun of Pentecost, Corpus Domini.*

PERCHED AT AN altitude of 895 m (2,900 ft) on the slopes of Gennargentu, the village of Dèsulo was not converted to Christianity or ruled by outsiders until the 7th century. Unfortunately, unregulated building development has had a devastating impact on the village and has almost eliminated the traditional schist houses. It is still quite common, however, to see villagers in traditional dress.

Chestnuts

The local economy is based on sheep-raising and the ancient tradition of cultivating the chestnut groves and mountain pastures. Until quite recently, the inhabitants, skilled in wood-carving, used to travel to the various markets and fairs throughout Sardinia to sell their hand-made spoons, cutting boards and other wooden objects, as well as locally grown chestnuts.

The parish church of **Sant'Antonio Abate**, and other churches such as the **Madonna del Carmelo** and **San Sebastiano**, are worth a visit for a series of colourful wooden statues sculpted in the mid-1600s. But the main reason to visit this village is its natural scenery and the splendid views of the highest peak on the island. There are plans to give the area National Park status, incorporating it into the Gennargentu National Park. Dèsulo is a favourite destination for hikers keen to attempt the arduous climb up Gennargentu and Punta La Marmora *(see p82)*. As groups of walkers and mountaineers become more common, a number of hotels and hostels catering for this new form of tourism have been built.

Tonara ㉑

Road map C4. 🏠 *2,600.* ℹ️ *Town Hall (0784 638 23).* 🎉 *second Sun in Aug: Sagra del Torrone.*

IN THE PAST the economy of Tonara was based largely on the chestnut and hazelnut groves that surround the town, and on other products typical of a mountain environment. Since tourism discovered this side of the mountain, the local production of cow bells, *torrone* (nougat) and hand-woven rugs has become famous. During the local festivals in the town square, blacksmiths forge the celebrated Tonara bells by hammering the metal on specially shaped stone moulds. The inhabitants will be more than willing to tell you how to arrange to see craftsmen at work and purchase traditional rugs. The atmosphere of a typical mountain village can still be seen in the shepherds' houses, which have not changed in over a century.

Tonara is another popular starting point for excursions to the Gennargentu massif. One of the most interesting is the tour to **Punta Mungianeddu** (1,467 m, 4,800 ft). A road climbs through holm oak and chestnut woods to reach the summit, from which there are magnificent views.

Stone used as a mould for making cow bells at Tonara

SARDINIAN NOUGAT

Nougat (*torrone* in Italian) is one of the most common sweets in the culture and tradition of central Sardinia. Every local fair or festival will have stalls selling the delicious, hard nougat made in Tonara, Dèsulo or one of the other mountain villages. The main ingredients are almonds, walnuts, hazelnuts, various qualities of honey and egg whites (in some cases the yolk is also used). Cooking – during which the mixture has to be stirred continuously – takes more than five hours. The different styles of nougat are created by variations in the type of honey, the flavour of the nuts or number of eggs used. There are many nougat confectioners and, no matter how big or small the premises, visitors are always welcome to watch the preparation and choose a favourite flavour. Blocks of nougat are cut for you while you wait. One excellent outlet is Signora Anna Peddes in Tonara, at No. 6 Via Roma; she makes particularly delicious and fragrant nougat.

The Nougat Festival at Tonara

THE WESTERN COAST

EACH YEAR THOUSANDS OF FLAMINGOES *choose the marshes and wetlands of western Sardinia as their favoured place for overwintering, creating clouds of pink against the vegetation of the maquis. The coastline is vulnerable to the cool mistral, and years of strong winds have sculpted massive dunes along the shore.*

The natural harbours and fertile land in this part of Sardinia have attracted foreign ships for centuries. The Phoenicians discovered the safe harbours of Sulki and Tharros as well as the great commercial potential of the obsidian from the slopes of Monte Arci. The Romans and Spaniards also left their mark at Bosa, the latter transforming Alghero into a Catalonian town.

The area around Oristano is one of the largest wetland areas in Europe. As well as freshwater pools and marshy lakes, there are saltwater lagoons, sandbanks and sand dunes. A combination of the waters of the Tirso river and the mistral is responsible for this particular ecosystem. Over the course of centuries massive dunes have formed at the river mouth, whipped up by the violent winds from the west, effectively blocking the flow of water out to sea. At the beginning of the 20th century, this marshland was infested with malaria-transmitting mosquitoes but, thanks to land reclamation in the 1930s and the Rockefeller-funded anti-malaria campaign, the soil can now be cultivated without risk. Today this is one of the most fertile areas in Sardinia, producing spring vegetables for sale to mainland Italy, as well as olives and citrus fruits. Vineyards cover the land around Oristano and near the beaches in the Sinis region, yielding quantities of white Vernaccia wine. The coastline is lovely – small beaches and seaside resorts nestle against sand dunes shaded by thick pine forests. Some beaches are made of grains of translucent quartz, which suits wild lilies. Some stretches of cliff, wild and rocky, can only be reached by boat or after a lengthy trek.

The historic town of Bosa seen from the Temo river

◁ **A lateen-sail dinghy off the coast near Stintino**

Exploring the Western Coast

T HE WESTERN COAST OF SARDINIA offers a wide variety of activities – whether you prefer to explore the towns and countryside, or relax on a beach at places like Is Arenas, Is Arutas or Bosa Marina. There are extensive nature reserves teeming with wildlife, and fortified cities with Romanesque cathedrals. One of Sardinia's best-known wines, Vernaccia, is made in this region, from the vineyards north of Oristano. At Tharros you can explore the ruins of a Phoenician coastal town, founded in the 8th century BC. The relatively short distances between sights and the flattish terrain, especially in the Sinis and Campidano di Oristano regions, make this area ideal for cycling tours. Walkers may prefer the hiking trails and riders can choose from the bridle paths that converge at the riding school in Ala Birdi. At the headland of Capo Caccia you can explore caves and grottoes, some of which extend for kilometres under the cliff.

CAPO CACCIA

MAR DI SARDEGNA

BOSA

Limestone rocks at Capo Caccia and the island of Foradada

SEE ALSO

- *Where to Stay* pp175–6
- *Where to Eat* pp185–6

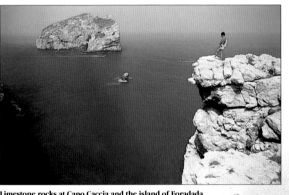

Archaeological excavations at Tharros

CUGLIERI ⑭

SAN SALVATORE

⑯

Stagno di Cabras

⑰ **SAN GIOVANNI DI SINIS**

⑱ **THARROS**

⑮ **CABRAS**

PAULILÀT

GOLFO DI ORISTANO

⑲ **ORISTANO**

⑳ **SANTA GIUSTA**

SA LUSSUR

N292

N388

⑳ **ARBOREA**

N131

FORDONGIA

ALES ㉔

N442

Sanluri ↓

View towards the fishing village of Stintino

SIGHTS AT A GLANCE

Traditional fisherman's house, San Giovanni di Sinis

GETTING AROUND

The coastal road is quite good but not especially fast; the same is true of the roads connecting the villages and those used for mountain tours. The SS131, known as the Carlo Felice road, goes from Oristano to Sassari. There are good railway connections from Oristano to Cagliari, Olbia and Porto Torres, the main ports for ferry connections.

KEY

- Motorway
- Major road
- Minor road
- Scenic route
- River

0 km   10

0 miles   10

Street-by-Street: Alghero ●

42

Old street number

IN THE EARLY 12TH CENTURY, the aristocratic Doria family from Genoa decided to establish two strongholds in Sardinia, which became Castelgenovese (now Castelsardo) and Alghero. Because of the abundant quantities of algae off the coast, the latter city was named Alquerium – *s'Alighera* in Sardinian dialect and *l'Alquer* in Catalan. After a very short period of Pisan rule, Alghero was conquered by the Aragonese in 1353, and has always been the most Spanish city on the island. The old centre lies within the ancient fortified quarter and the local economy is based on tourism and handicrafts – particularly jewellery and other items made of coral.

★ San Francesco
Parts of this jewel of Catalan architecture date back to the first half of the 14th century. The lovely cloister becomes an open-air concert venue in summer.

Porta Terra tower

PIAZZA CIVICA

The Maddalena tower and ramparts

MAGELLANO

VIA ROMA

LUNGOMARE

LUNGOMARE

Torre di Sant'Erasmo

Torre della Polveriera

LES QUATRO CANTONADES

Sign in Catalan
The street signs in Alghero are still written in Catalan.

Lungomare
Each seafront road (lungomare) *is named after a great explorer from the past. The buildings are painted in sunny Mediterranean colours.*

★ Duomo Doors
Built in the mid-1500s, the carved doorway, together with the bell tower, is the oldest part of Alghero's cathedral.

KEY

– – – – – – Suggested route

San Michele
This Baroque church contains two stucco altars dating from the second half of the 17th century.

Torre di San Giovanni

VISITORS' CHECKLIST

Road map B2. 🕍 *41,148.*
✈ *Alghero Fertilia, 24 km (15 miles) N.* ℹ️ *079 97 90 54.*

Torre dell'Esperò Real
This is one of the towers in the walls surrounding Alghero. It overlooks Piazza Sulis, the heart of city life.

Chiesa della Misericordia

Via Carlo Alberto is the most elegant street in the city. In the summer months craftsmen set out their coral jewellery to tempt visitors to buy.

Torre San Giacomo

Chiesa del Carmelo

The Al Tuguri Restaurant
This small restaurant in the historic centre of Alghero offers some of the best food in Sardinia. Al Tuguri specializes in fresh fish cooked according to old Catalan recipes.

0 metres   50
0 yards   50

★ Ramparts
Positioned between the old city and the sea, the ramparts are now popular places for strolling, especially on warm evenings.

STAR SIGHTS

★ **San Francesco**

★ **Duomo Doors**

★ **Ramparts**

Exploring Alghero

DESPITE THE CONSIDERABLE DAMAGE wrought by Allied bombardments in World War II, the heart of the old city is, for the most part, intact and can easily be explored on foot. The main roads from Bosa (to the south) and Sassari (to the northwest) lead to the city walls, and the best way to explore is to leave your car outside and walk around the narrow, high-sided streets of the old city. Strongly influenced by Spanish culture, Alghero remains the most Spanish city in Sardinia. The Alghero dialect is closely related to that of Catalonia, so much so that since 1970, street signs have been printed in Italian and Catalan, and you are likely to hear as much Catalan spoken on the streets as Italian.

⊞ Porta a Terra
Piazza Porta a Terra.
This 14th-century city gate now has a rather stranded air, as most of the associated fortifications were demolished to make room for present-day Via Sassari. The gate was once known as Torre degli Ebrei (dels Hebreus in Catalan), or Tower of the Jews, because of the contribution made by the Jewish community to Catalan king Pietro III's conquest of the city. The tower was originally one of two gates. A drawbridge linked Porta a Terra and the large Gothic arch which is now a war memorial. The ground floor, covered by a stone vault, is now used as a small exhibition centre.

A window at Palazzo d'Albis

⊞ Torre dell'Esperò Real
Piazza Sulis.
Facing Piazza Sulis, the heart of city life, is the impressive Torre dell'Esperò Real

The massive Torre dell'Esperò Real

(Tower of the Royal Spur), which was built in its present form in the first half of the 16th century, to replace an older military structure. This 23-m (75-ft) high tower has an interesting interior with a number of superimposed chambers connected by means of a spiral staircase.

⊞ Lungomare and Forte de la Magdalena
Around sunset locals and tourists alike enjoy the pleasant stroll along the seafront. Starting from the south, Lungomare Dante is followed by Lungomare Cristoforo Colombo and Lungomare Marco Polo, which has a series of ramparts with towers (the Torre di San Giacomo, the Mirador rampart, the Torre de la Polvorera, the Torre de Castilla), leading to the port. Not far from the steps which run from the seafront to the old Porta a Mare city gate, is Forte de la Magdalena,

the city's most important Spanish fortification. On its walls a plaque commemorates Giuseppe Garibaldi's landing here on 14 August 1855.

⊞ Palazzo d'Albis
Piazza Civica (Plaça de la Dressana).
This 16th-century palace with twin lancet windows is also known as Palazzo de Ferrera. It is a rare example of Catalan civic architecture, and is famous for having hosted Charles V in October 1541.

The old town, Alghero

The emperor stopped at Alghero with his fleet on the way to Algiers, and was very flattering in his reactions to the city. According to tradition, the emperor spoke to the populace from the balcony of Palazzo d'Albis, and had the following to say about the city: "Bonita, por mi fé, y bien assentada". ("Beautiful, by my faith, and quite solid") and told the inhabitants "Estade todos caballeros" ("You are all gentlemen"). The monarch's sojourn ended with a massive requisition of cattle, which he needed for the Spanish troops. The animals were then slaughtered after an impromptu bullfight, held by the palazzo in Piazza Civica.

⚑ Cattedrale di Santa Maria
Piazza Duomo. 📞 *079 97 92 22.*
🕐 *6:30am–noon, 5–8pm.*
The doorway of Alghero's Cathedral opens out onto the small Piazzetta Duomo. The cathedral, dedicated to Santa Maria, was first built in the 14th century. In the mid-1500s the building was restructured in the Catalan-

View of the harbour and broad seafront in Alghero

inspired late Gothic style. The unusual octagonal bell tower dates from the same period.

In the interior there is a striking difference between the layout of the central part, which is late Renaissance, and that of the 16th-century Gothic presbytery. Items of Catalan jewellery are on display in the sacristy.

Displays of coral jewellery

Via Principe Umberto

This narrow street, which begins at the Cathedral, was one of the main arteries in the old walled city. Of interest are the Casa Doria (16th century), Palazzo della Curia and, in Piazza Vittorio Emanuele II, the 19th-century Savoyard Teatro Civico.

San Francesco and Cloister

Via Carlo Alberto. ☎ 079 97 92 58.
◻ 8am–noon, 5–8pm.
San Francesco may very well be the most important Catalan monument in the whole of Sardinia. Built at the end of the 1300s and then partially rebuilt when some of the structure collapsed,

the church clearly displays different stylistic influences. The bell tower is Gothic, with a hexagonal body set on a square base. The cupola, dressed with multi-coloured tiles, has become the symbol of Alghero.

The two-aisle, white sandstone interior still has Baroque altars made of carved wood and, under the star-spangled Gothic vault of the presbytery, there is an 18th-century altar. The sculptures include a *Dead Christ* and *Christ at the Column*.

The cloister, accessible from the sacristy, is well worth a visit. It is an eclectic sandstone construction, built in different periods. The lower part dates from the 14th century, while the upper part was added in the 1700s. The 22 columns are in two sections, with round or polygonal bases and sculpted capitals. During the summer music season, the Estate Musicale Internazionale di Alghero, concerts and other cultural events are held in these lovely surroundings. In other seasons of the year events and art exhibitions are held in the old refectory.

The Beaches

The port of Alghero has never been an important trading place, partly because of its position and the low-lying coast. There is no heavy industry here, and consequently the sea is not polluted. A series of resorts can be found just outside the old town. The best-known beach is the Bombarde, a

strip of pure white sand bordered by crystal-clear sea, 8 km (5 miles) northwest of the city. Another good beach nearby is the Lazzaretto, which owes its name to the hospital for the poor which was there during the period of the black plague. When the weather is clear, the impressive vertical profile of Capo Caccia stands out on the horizon.

ENVIRONS: To the north is the coastal town of **Fertilia**, a small yacht harbour built during the Fascist era as the centre of the land reclamation programme. Just north is the mouth of the Calich lagoon, where eels, gilthead bream and mullet are raised. Nearby you can still see the 13 arches of the Roman bridge at the ancient city of Carbia. At one time the bridge connected Carbia to Portus Nympharum, now Porto Conte bay. A few minutes away stands the site of **Palmavera Nuraghe**. This prehistoric complex contains two towers and a courtyard surrounded by a barbican.

Entranceway to the prehistoric site of Palmavera Nuraghe

Porto Torres ❷

Road map B2. 🏛 *22,000.*
🛈 *079 51 50 00.*

T HE CHIEF PORT in northern
Sardinia lies in the Golfo
dell'Asinara. Porto Torres was
known to the Romans as
Turris Libisonis, and was once
a prosperous colony. Trade
with the city of Kàralis
(today's Cagliari) was carried
out along the main road on
the island. Relations with
Rome were very close, as can
be seen from the ancient
mosaics at the Foro delle
Corporazioni in Ostia Antica.

After a lengthy period of
decline that began in the
Middle Ages, Porto Torres
began to recover in the 19th
century, when it became the
port for Sassari, and again in
the 20th century with the development of local industries.

The basilica of **San Gavino**
is one of the most important
Romanesque churches
in Sardinia, built in
the Pisan style
in 1111.
Noteworthy
elements are
the portal in
the northern
façade, with
its 15th-century
bas relief, and
the other Gothic
doorway, which
shows Catalan
influences.

**Gold bracelet from the
Porto Torres excavations**

Inside there is a crypt, with
access to an area of late
Roman-Early Christian ruins,
as well as the 18th-century
statues of the martyrs Gavino,
Proto and Gianuario, and a
medieval inscription celebrating emperor Constantine.

The **Terme Centrali**
archaeological area presents a
reasonably faithful picture of
an ancient Roman quarter,
and the **Antiquarium
Turritano** contains finds
from the excavations here.
Not far away, the 135-m
(440-ft), seven-arched **Ponte
Romano** (Roman bridge)
crosses the Mannu river.

ENVIRONS: A short distance
from here lies one of the
most interesting sites in
ancient Sardinia, the pre-

San Gavino, in Porto Torres

nuraghic **Santuario di Monte
d'Accoddi**. From Porto
Torres, head towards Sassari
along main road SS131; a
short distance after the Sorso
junction (at kilometre marker
222.3) a signposted road
leads to the archaeological
site. The sanctuary dates from
the Copper Age (2450–1850
BC) and provides the only
example of a megalithic altar
in the entire western
Mediterranean.

The shape is that
of a truncated
pyramid with a
trapezoid base,
supported by
walls of stone
blocks. On the
southern side, a
ramp leads to the
top, about 10 m
(33 ft) high, while
the base is about
30 m by 38 m
(98 ft by 124 ft).

Around the altar you can
see foundations for houses,
some sacrificial stone slabs
and fallen menhirs. A group
of *domus de janas* (rock-cut
tombs) was once part of this

complex. The material found
at this site, including
ceramics, is on display at
the Museo Nazionale in
Sassari *(see p163).*

🏛 **Antiquarium Turritano**
📞 *079 51 44 33.* ◯ *9am–7:30pm
Tue–Sun.* 📷 ✔ ♿
∩ **Santuario di
Monte d'Accoddi**
◯ *at all times.* 📞 *32 84 83 99 95.*

Stintino ❸

Road map B2. 🏛 *1,200.*
🛈 *City Hall (079 52 30 53).*

T HE ROAD to Capo Falcone,
the northwestern tip of
Sardinia, passes by the large
wind turbines at the Alta
Nurra ecological energy plant.
Beyond this is the pleasant
fishing village of Stintino
(named from the Sardinian
word *s'isthintinu,* or narrow
passageway, the traditional
name for the inlet where the
village lies). Now a holiday
town, Stintino was once
important for its tuna fishing
grounds, off the island of
Asinara. In the summer, at
the old harbour, there is an
exhibition devoted to the
subject of Sardinian tuna
fishing traditions. The two
ports, Portu Mannu and Portu
Minori, have facilities for
aquatic sports of all kinds.

North of Stintino, the road
skirts the coastline as far as
Capo Falcone. The place is
still "defended" by a tower on
its highest point and by the
two Spanish fortifications at
Pelosa and Isola Piana, in the
inlet of Fornelli, opposite the
island of Asinara.

Portu Mannu, one of the two harbours in Stintino

The barren cliffs on the island of Asinara

Asinara ❹

Road map B1. ⓘ *079 50 08 86.*

Tᴴɪꜱ ʀᴜɢɢᴇᴅ ɪꜱʟᴀɴᴅ is closed to visitors because of the Fornelli maximum security prison here, and it is still administered by the Italian Ministry of Justice. Asinara is less than 18 km (11 miles) long and 6 km (4 miles) wide and ends at the headland of Scomunica. The island's ecosystem is unique in the entire western Mediterranean and, because of its rare or endangered animal species, the island has been incorporated into the recently established Gennargentu National Park *(see pp82–3)*.

In fact, the pristine coastline and lack of traffic on its 50 sq km (19 sq miles) make Asinara an ideal refuge for raptors, various species of sea birds, moufflons and wild boar. There is also a rare species of small endemic albino donkey, after which the island must have been named (*asino* meaning donkey). The rocky, volcanic terrain still supports a small holm oak forest, and the typical low-level maquis brush shields numbers of rare plants.

Albino donkey from Asinara

Asinara can only be visited by naturalists and zoologists who have been authorized to carry out research by the island's prison administration.

Argentiera ❺

Road map B2.

Mᴀɴʏ ᴘʟᴀᴄᴇꜱ ɪɴ Sardinia still carry reminders of the island's former mining industries. At Argentiera, not far from the modern town of Palmadula, the ancient Romans, and the Pisans in the Middle Ages, dedicated themselves to mining the precious metal that gave its name to the area (*argento* means silver).

In the 19th century, mining complexes, with wooden and masonry buildings, were constructed along the coast, and the mined silver could then be transported by sea to other destinations, where it could be processed and eventually sold.

In recent years restoration and restructuring projects, many of which are yet to be completed, have changed the face of the town, but it still remains one of the most fascinating examples of industrial archaeology in Sardinia.

In the summer, the tranquil bay at Argentiera, with its crystal-clear water, is a great favourite with visitors.

The old mine buildings at Argentiera

Capo Caccia ❻

Towering above the sea, the Capo Caccia promontory, with a lighthouse perched on the outermost point, offers wonderful views of Alghero. Wild pigeons, swifts, peregrine falcons and herring gulls nest in the crevices and gullies of the precipitous cliffs. On the western side of the headland – opposite the barren profile of the island of Foradada – 656 steep steps (known as the Escala del Cabirol, or Roe-deer's Staircase) take you down the cliff to the fascinating caves of the Grotta di Nettuno (Neptune's Grotto). The cave can also be reached in about three hours by boat from Alghero.

Griffon vulture
Only a few of these rare creatures survive in Sardinia.

Herring gulls
These birds nest in cliff crevices and ravines.

Gabbiano reale

Torre del Tra

Torre Pegna

Cala d'infer

Peregrine falcons
These raptors prefer calm, open spaces with rocky cliffs – Capo Caccia is a favoured ground.

Capo Caccia
In the past this promontory was frequented by travellers and prominent naturalists such as Alberto La Marmora. The name Capo Caccia derives from the caccia, or wild pigeon hunting, that was once popular here.

Grotta Verde
The name of this large cave, Green Grotto, derives from the colour of the moss and other plants that cover the stalagmites and stalactites. On the shores of a small lake at the far end of the gallery, ancient graffiti have been discovered.

Escala del Cabirol
From the ridge of land separating the headland from the lighthouse point, the Escala del Cabirol steps wind down to the entrance of the Grotta di Nettuno.

Punta del Quadro

Punta del bollo

Lago La Marmora

Isola Foradada

Grotta di Nettuno
Neptune's Grotto, one of the most picturesque caves in Sardinia, was first explored in the 1700s. The grotto extends for 2,500 m (8,200 ft), while the guided tour covers 200 m (650 ft).

Romanesque Santo Stefano, at Monteleone Rocca Doria

Monteleone Rocca Doria **7**

Road map B3. ⚇ 140.

Situated on the top of the Su Monte cliff (420 m, 1,380 ft), the little village of Monteleone Rocca Doria has a sweeping view of Lake Temo and the Nurra plain. It is tranquil today, although inhabitants look back proudly on a noble, warlike past. In the 13th century the Doria family from Genoa built a fortress here which was totally destroyed in 1436 after a ferocious three-year siege by troops from Aragon, Sassari, Bosa and Alghero.

Many inhabitants departed to found the town of Villanova Monteleone, but a few people remained behind. Monteleone was not included in development programmes and, at one point, locals tried to improve their lot by putting the village up for sale. In the centre of Monteleone is the 13th-century Romanesque parish church, **Santo Stefano**.

Bosa **8**

See pp126–7.

Macomer **9**

Road map C3. ⚇ 12,000.
🛈 *Town Hall (0785 79 08 00).*
🎨 *17 Jan: Sant'Antonio Abate.*

Built on a platform of volcanic rock, Macomer is one of the most important commercial centres in the interior of Sardinia. Macomer developed around key communication routes – the Carlo Felice road (the N131 that runs through most of the island) and the railway – and owes its prosperity to agriculture, livestock raising, dairy products and light industry, while retaining traces of its past. The parish church of **San Pantaleo** is an example of 17th-century Spanish Gothic. On the evening of 17 January the traditional *Sa Tuva* celebration is held in honour of Sant'Antonio Abate. The event takes place in the large square in front of Santa Croce, and a huge bonfire lights up the entire quarter.

San Pantaleo, in Macomer

Environs: Not far from the town centre, near the Carlo Felice road, a short walk will take you to the impressive **Santa Barbara Nuraghe**. Its sheer size means that it dominates a series of smaller towers and ramparts.

Sedilo **10**

Road map C3. ⚇ 2,700.
🛈 *0785 56 00.* 🎨 *5–8 Jul: S'Ardia at Santu Antine sanctuary.*

The rocky terrain in the Abbasanta plateau gave the people of Sedilo the raw material to build their houses. There are still a few originals remaining, representing a style that has virtually disappeared. The main sight of interest is the church of **San Giovanni Battista** in the centre of town. However, Sedilo's most notable claim to fame is the **Sanctuary of Santu Antine**, otherwise known as San Costantino, or Constantine, after the early champion of Christianity who is much revered in Sardinia. The church, with the typical *cumbessias* houses for pilgrims, stands on a cliff overlooking Lake Omodeo. Within the precinct there are numerous nuraghic sculptures on display, including the so-called *Perda Fitta*, a monolith which, according to legend, is actually the body of a woman who was turned into stone because she was disrespectful towards the patron saint.

The open space opposite the sanctuary is the setting for the annual *S'Ardia*. This horse race ends the July festivities commemorating the Great's victory over Maxentius in the battle of the Milvian Bridge in AD 312. The inside walls of Santu Antine are covered with quantities of ex votos.

The S'Ardia horse race run around the Santu Antine sanctuary, Sedilo

The Losa nuraghe near Abbasanta

Ghilarza ⓫

Road map C3. 🏛 *4,700.*
ℹ *Town Hall (0785 540 38).*

A**N UNFINISHED** Aragonese tower stands in the centre of Ghilarza, but the place is known principally as the town in which the famous Italian political thinker and writer Antonio Gramsci spent his childhood years. A small door on Corso Umberto leads to the **Casa di Gramsci**, now occupied by a research and study centre. There is also an exhibition of historical material relating to the Communist leader, who died in prison during the Fascist era. On the second floor is the small bedroom that was Gramsci's from 1898 to 1908.

ENVIRONS: A short distance from Ghilarza, on the road to Nuoro, you will find the beautiful church of **San Pietro di Zuri**, which was relocated, along with the village of the same name, after the artificial lake Omodeo was created in 1923. The original church dates from 1291. The building was commissioned by Mariano d'Arborea, and carried out by architect Anselmo da Como. The architecture is prevalently Romanesque, with some interesting details which anticipate the transition towards the Gothic style.

🏛 **Casa di Gramsci**
Corso Umberto 57. 📞 *0785 541 64.*
🕐 *10am–noon, 4–7pm.*

Abbasanta ⓬

Road map C3. 🏛 *2,700.*
ℹ *Town Hall (0785 542 29).*

T**HIS VILLAGE,** the centre of which still has some old traditional houses made of dark local basalt stone, revolves around the parish church of Santa Cristina, with its impressive Renaissance-inspired architecture. Situated in the middle of a highly developed agricultural region, Abbasanta owes its importance to its strategic position near main artery routes, both ancient and modern.

In the vicinity are two of the most important archaeological sites in the whole of Sardinia: the **Losa Nuraghe** and the **Santa Cristina** nuraghic complex near Paulilàtino *(see p137).* In order to reach the Losa

Nuraghe, take the Carlo Felice road towards Cagliari until you reach kilometre marker 123 (indicated on a road sign). Here, a turning to the right leads to the entrance to the archaeological site, which is fenced off. Together with the monuments at Barùmini *(see pp64–5)* and Torralba *(see pp22–3)*, this nuraghic complex is one of the most important remaining from the immediate pre-Punic period.

In the middle of this vast structure is a keep thousands of years old, dating from the second millennium BC, while the ramparts were built some centuries later. The outer defensive walls were the last to be built, and date from the 7th century BC.

Inside the nuraghe you can visit three roofed chambers with a great many niches, which were probably used for storage. A spiral staircase leads to the upper floor, which has a terrace above.

All around the main structure are the foundations of a series of later buildings, dating from the Bronze Age to the Middle Ages.

A small **Antiquarium** stands about 100 m (328 ft) from the nuraghi themselves. It houses an interesting exhibition of plans and illustrations of a number of nuraghic monuments in this part of Sardinia.

Losa Nuraghe
SS Carlo Felice 123.5 km. 📞 *0785 548 23.* 🕐 *8:30am–sunset daily.* 🏛 ✔

ANTONIO GRAMSCI

Antonio Gramsci was born at Àles in 1891 of humble family. After completing his studies at Turin, he entered politics full-time. He was one of the co-founders of the radical weekly *L'Ordine Nuovo* and in 1921 helped to found the Italian Communist Party, later becoming its Secretary-General. He was elected to parliament but was arrested by the Fascists in 1926 and given a 20-year prison sentence. He did not see freedom again, dying in prison in 1937. The complete edition of his writings, *Quaderni del Carcere* (Prison Notebooks) was not published until 1976. *Lettere dal Carcere* (Letters from Prison) are a moving statement of his sufferings as a prisoner.

The young Gramsci

Bosa

DOMINATED BY the Castello dei Malaspina, the pastel-coloured houses of Bosa lie on the right bank of the Temo river, the only navigable river in Sardinia. The town was originally founded by the Phoenicians on the opposite bank of the river. In the Middle Ages, under threat from constant pirate raids, the townspeople sought the protection of the Malaspina family on the slopes of the hill of Serravalle. Bosa was granted the status of

Locally made jewellery

royal city under Spanish rule and always maintained a close relationship with the Iberian peninsula. The town today is still fascinating, with the buildings of the Sas Conzas quarter mirrored in the calm waters of the river. In the Sa Costa medieval quarter, a labyrinth of cobble-stone alleys and steps, you can still see women sitting outside their homes making lace. Environmentalists say the nearby seaside is the cleanest in Italy.

Interior of the Cathedral in Bosa, with Baroque ornamentation

🔒 Cathedral
Piazza Duomo. **(** 0785 37 32 86.
⏲ 7am–7pm daily.
Dedicated to the Virgin Mary, the Cathedral was rebuilt in the 19th century in the majestic late Baroque Piedmontese style. In the interior is a statue of the *Madonna and Child*, of the Catalan school, sculpted in the 16th century. On either side of the main altar are two marble lions killing dragons. The side altars are made of multi-coloured marble.

🏛 Corso Vittorio Emanuele II
The main street in Bosa, paved with stone, runs parallel to the river. It is lined with aristocratic buildings and goldsmiths' workshops where filigree and coral jewellery are made.

🏛 Pinacoteca Civica
Casa Deriu, Corso Vittorio Emanuele II 59.
(0785 37 70 43.
⏲ May–Oct: 10am–1pm, 6–10:30pm daily.
Casa Deriu is a typical 19th-century Bosa building which has been transformed into an exhibition centre. The first floor features traditional locally made products such as cakes,

Detail of the architrave of San Pietro

wine and bread, as well as a display of old black-and-white photographs. On the second floor is a fine re-construction of the elegant Deriu apartment, with its olive wood parquet, frescoed vaulted ceiling, majolica tiles from Ravenna and locally made lace curtains.

The top floor houses the Pinacoteca Civica (municipal art gallery), featuring the collection of Melkiorre Melis, a local artist and one of the leading promoters of 20th-century applied arts in Sardinia.

The works on display span a 70-year period of graphic art, oil painting, ceramics and posters. Also shown here are the Arab-influenced works of Melis, executed while he headed the Muslim School of Arts and Crafts in Tripoli.

🏛 Castello Malaspina
Via Ultima Costa 14. **(** 0785 37 32 86. ● for restoration.
Built in 1112 by the Malaspina dello Spino Secco family, this castle is still impressive, even though only its towers and outer walls have survived. It was enlarged in the 1300s and covers a large area. Very little remains of the castle itself: only parts of the wall on the northeast corner, at the foot of the main tower. The tower was built of light ochre trachyte in the early 1300s and is being restored. Inside the walls the only

View of Bosa from the Temo river, with fishing boats

Aerial view of Bosa Marina with its Aragonese tower

building left standing is the church of **Nostra Signora di Regnos Altos**, built in the 14th century. Restoration carried out in 1974–5 brought to light a cycle of Catalan school frescoes, one of the few left in Sardinia. From the ramparts there are splendid views of the church of San Pietro, the lower Temo river valley and the red roofs of the Sa Costa quarter. You can walk down to the centre of town by following the steps skirting the walls that once defended Bosa to the east.

Sas Conzas
The buildings on the left bank of the Temo river were once used as tanneries. Abandoned years ago after a crisis in the leather goods market, the buildings are still waiting to be restored. In the meanwhile a small restaurant is housed here. The Sas Conzas quarter

can best be admired from the palm-lined street on the other side of the river, Lungotemo De Gasperi, where the fishermen of Bosa moor their boats.

San Pietro
☐ ask custodian at cathedral for key.
About 1 km (half a mile) east of the left bank of the Temo stands the church of San Pietro, built in red trachyte stone, one of the most interesting of Sardinia's Romanesque churches. It was built in different periods, beginning in the second half of the 11th century, while the bell tower, apse and side walls were added the following century. The façade combines some elements of Romanesque with touches of

Bosa coat of arms

French Gothic, imported by the Cistercian monks. On the architrave of the doorway is a singular *Madonna and Child with Saints Peter, Paul and Constantine*. It is unfortunately difficult to arrange a visit to the interior.

ENVIRONS: Bosa Marina, just over 2 km (1 mile) from the centre of town, has a lovely secluded beach with dark sand. Isola Rossa is linked to the mainland by a long jetty. The Aragonese tower is open in July and August and hosts temporary exhibitions.
The coastline between Bosa and Alghero is spectacular. Part of the Trenino Verde route *(see pp92–3)* goes from Bosa Marina to Macomer, skirting the Pedras Nieddas (black stones) beach before going up the Rio Abba Mala valley to Modolo, Tres-nuraghes and Sindia.

The Castello Malaspina in Bosa

VISITORS' CHECKLIST

Road map B3. 🚐 *7,786.*
🚌 🚉 🛈 *Pro Loco (0785 37 61 07).* 🎭 *Easter Week: Settimana Santa Bosana; 29 Jun: boat pro-cession on river; first Sun of Aug: Santa Stella Maris; second Sun of Sep: Sagra di Nostra Signora di Regnos Altos.* 🅦 *www.bosa.net*

The paired horse race held during Carnevale at Santu Lussurgiu

Santu Lussurgiu ⑬

Road map B3. 👥 *2,900.* 🚉
ℹ️ *Via Santa Maria 40.* 📞 *0783 55 10 34* 🎭 *Carnevale: horse race in town centre; 2–3 Jun: Horse Fair; 21 Aug: San Lussorio.*

Santu Lussurgiu lies at 500 m (1,640 ft) above sea level on the eastern slope of Mount Montiferru, laid out like an amphitheatre on the edge of a volcanic crater, and surrounded by olive groves.

The historic centre is fascinating, with its steep, narrow streets and tiny squares surrounded by beautiful tall stone houses painted in bright colours. Some have decorated architraves and wrought-iron balconies. In Via Roma, an elegant 11-room 18th-century building houses the **Museo della Tecnologia Contadina**, (Museum of Rural Culture), founded by the local Centro di Cultura Popolare. The "Su Mastru Salis" collection is the work of Maestro Salis, the museum curator, who in over 20 years has collected more than 2,000 objects related to the culture and traditions of Santu Lussurgiu.

A guided visit to this interesting museum is like making a trip backwards in time. Room after room contains fascinating displays of everyday objects used by the farmers, shepherds and coal merchants who worked at the foot of Mount Montiferru. Some of the most interesting exhibits are in the sections given over to spinning and weaving, cooking and crafts. The room devoted to wine-making is also interesting. Equipment includes a fulling-mill, the implement used to soften and felt fabric. Over 40 of them were once in use in the Santu Lussurgiu area.

In the upper part of town is the 15th-century church of **Santa Maria degli Angeli**, which has a fine 18th-century carved wooden altar.

There are still craftsmen in Santu Lussurgiu who specialize in making knives and fittings for horse-riding (bridles, bits, saddles and leather riding boots).

At Carnevale the street in front of the museum is turned into a track for a breakneck horse race between pairs of riders dressed as knights.

The Museum of Rural Culture

FLAMINGOES IN THE SALE PORCUS RESERVE

The Sale Porcus marsh is one of the largest reserves on the Sinis peninsula, its many white sand dunes covered with maquis vegetation. In winter and spring over 10,000 flamingoes and thousands of cranes, wild geese, cormorants and mallards make their home here, making the area look like an East African lake. In summer, drought reduces the water level, transforming the lake into a white area with a thick, hard salty crust that you can walk across. The Flamingo Centre is run by the Lega Italiana per la Protezione di Uccelli (LIPU), the Italian Society for the Protection of Birds. The exhibition here illustrates the life cycle of the birds and the centre is also the starting point for all paths through the Sale Porcus marsh.

🦩 **Oasi LIPU Sale Porcus**
🕐 *daily.* 📞 *0783 52 81 00.* ✉️
🌐 *www.sitogea.net*

Flamingoes in the Sale Porcus reserve

One of the seven springs at San Leonardo de Siete Fuentes

ENVIRONS: A few kilometres from Santu Lussurgiu there is a forest of pine, holm oak and oak near the village of **San Leonardo de Siete Fuentes**, which is famous for its seven springs of radioactive, diuretic water that flow out of seven fountains at a constant temperature of 11°C (52°F). The streams pass through a wood popular for family outings. In the centre of town is the small church of San Leonardo, which once belonged to the Knights of Malta. It was constructed with dark trachyte stone in the 12th century, and acquired its present Romanesque-Gothic appearance the following century. The single-nave interior bears the insignias of the Knights of Malta. Opposite the church stands a small public library.

In early June, San Leonardo plays host to an important saddle-horse fair.

🏛 **Museo della Tecnologia Contadina**
Via T Meloni 1. 📞 *0783 55 06 17.*
🕐 *by appt only.* ♿ ✦

Cuglieri ⑭

Road map B3. 🏘 *3,400.*
ℹ️ *Viale Regina Margherita (0785 398 39).* 🎉 *Good Friday: procession and 'Iscravamentu; 5 Aug: Madonna della Neve.*

THE AGRICULTURAL town of Cuglieri lies 500 m (1,640 ft) above sea level on the western slopes of Mount Montiferru, with a panoramic view of the sea. It is dominated by the striking church of **Santa Maria della Neve**, which has an 18th-century façade and twin bell towers. The walk up to the church is lovely, winding through alleyways and stepped streets lined with tall stone houses.

The square in front of Santa Maria offers a fine view of the town and the coast between Santa Caterina di Pittinuri and Porto Alabe.

Santa Maria della Neve, in Cuglieri

ENVIRONS: The coast is 15 km (9 miles) away on main road 292. **Santa Caterina di Pittinuri** is a seaside town set around a white-stone inlet enclosed by a limestone cliff, where the Spanish Torre del Pozzo tower stands. This stretch of coast is scenic, with rocky headlands and white sand and pebble beaches. The most famous sight is **S'Archittu**, a large natural bridge created by coastal erosion. A dirt road off main road 292, between Santa Caterina di Pittinuri and S'Archittu, goes to the ruins of the Punic-Roman city of **Cornus**, the setting for the last battle between the Romans and Sardinian-Carthaginians headed by Amsicora (215 BC).

In the 9th century the city was abandoned because of repeated Saracen raids and the inhabitants founded a new city, Curulis Nova, present-day Cuglieri, on the nearby mountainside. The dirt road peters out just before the Early Christian town of Columbaris, while the acropolis of Cornus is visible on the hill to the southwest. Although the archaeological site may seem abandoned, it still has some sarcophagi and the remains of a three-nave basilica. It seems likely that all of these date back to the 6th century.

The cliff with the famous S'Archittu di Santa Caterina natural bridge at Pittinuri, near Cuglieri

Aerial view of the Cabras marsh area

Cabras ⑮

Road map B4. 🏛 *10,000.* 🅿
ℹ *Via Palestro 2 (0783 29 39 71).*

THE TOWN of Cabras lies
a short distance from
Oristano, and is characterized
by its old, one-storey houses.
It stands on the edge of the
largest freshwater lake and
marsh in Sardinia (2,000
hectares, 5,000 acres), and is
connected to the sea via a
series of canals.

The presence of both fresh
and salt water attracts coots,
marsh harriers, peregrine
falcons and purple gallinules.
The water itself is rich in
mullet and eels.

In the past, local fishermen
used long, pointed boats,
called *is fassonis*, which were
made of dried rushes and
other marsh plants, using a
technique similar to that
known to the Phoenicians.
Another Phoenician survival
is the marinading technique
called *sa merca*, in which
fresh fish is wrapped in plant
leaves from the lake and left
to soak in salt water.

ENVIRONS: At the northern
end of the Golfo di Oristano
is the **Laguna di Mistras**.
Separated from the sea by
two sandbars, in wetlands
of international scientific
importance, this lagoon

makes an ideal habitat for
flamingoes, cormorants, grey
heron and ospreys. The
nearby Mar 'e Pontis marshland is also rich in ornitho-
logical interest. At the
Peschiera Pontis, once a fish
farm, you can still see the old
sluices and gratings.

San Salvatore ⑯

Road map B4. ℹ *Cabras.*
🎉 *end of Aug–first Sun in Sep: Corsa
degli Scalzi di San Salvatore.*

TYPICAL WHITE houses for
pilgrims, or *cumbessias*,
surround the country church
of San Salvatore. They are
occupied for nine days each
year in late August and early
September, for the novena of
the saint's feast day.

In the 1960s the church's
central square was used as a
location for "spaghetti
westerns". San Salvatore was
built in the 17th century on
the site of a nuraghic
sanctuary for the worship of
sacred waters. In the 6th
century the site was transformed into an underground
church. In the left-hand nave
stairs lead to the hypogeum,
which has six chambers: two
rectangular ones flanking a
corridor leading to a circular
atrium with a well, around
which three further chambers
lie. The hypogeum was partly
hewn out of the rock; the
vaulted ceilings are made of
sandstone and brick. On the
walls are graffiti of animals
(elephants, panthers and
peacocks) and heroes and
gods (Hercules fighting the

The annual Corsa degli Scalzi (barefoot race) at San Salvatore

Marsh samphire, a typical plant growing in the Cabras marshes

Nemean lion, Mars and Venus with a small winged cupid). There are even Arabic writings about Allah and Mohammed, and numerous depictions of ships, which experts believe are ex votos.

The Latin letters RVF, interlaced as in a monogram and repeated several times, seem to derive from the Phoenician language and are said to stand for "cure, save, give health".

On the first Saturday in September, the feast day of San Salvatore is celebrated. The event is marked with a barefoot (*scalzi*) race in memory of local youths, who, in the Middle Ages, left the village to escape from the Saracens but returned to save the statue of the saint.

Just east of the sanctuary are the ruins of the Domu 'e Cubas Roman baths.

San Giovanni di Sinis ⑰

Road map B4. **⋔** *40.* **🛈** *Cabras.*

AT THE EDGE OF THE Sinis peninsula there is a bathing resort that was once famous for its fishermen's huts made of wood and reeds (*see p115*). Today only a few have survived; the largest group lies east of the motor-way, not far from the famous archaeological site of Tharros (*see pp132–3*).

As you enter the small village of San Giovanni di Sinis you will see the early Christian church of **San Giovanni** which, together with San Saturnino in Cagliari, is the oldest in Sardinia. It was built in the 5th century, though much of the present-day church was the result of 9th- and 10th-century rebuilding. The three-nave interior is barrel-vaulted.

ENVIRONS: Near San Giovanni di Sinis is the WWF **Torre 'e Seu** reserve, where some of the last dwarf palms in the area survive. A dirt road at the northern end of San Giovanni di Sinis leads to the reserve. At the gate there is a path to the sea and the Torre 'e Seu Spanish tower.

THE VERNACCIA WINE OF SARDINIA

The countryside north of Oristano is one of the most fertile areas in Sardinia, carpeted with grapevines, orange groves and olive trees. The cultivation of tangerines dates from the 14th century, thanks to the Camaldolite monks from the large monastery at Bonarcado. However

Vernaccia grapes

viticulture is a great deal older: wine jugs, glasses and amphoras have been found at Tharros (*see pp132–3*). The Vernaccia made in Oristano is perhaps Sardinia's most famous white wine and is produced in the towns of San Vero Milis, Cabras, Zeddiani, Narbolia, Riola and Baratili. The wine is full-bodied and strong, with 15 degrees of alcohol, and is aged for at least three years in large oak barrels. You can tour the wine-producing area, and pause for a wine-tasting at the Cantina Sociale della Vernaccia, where the entrance is framed by an impressive 18th-century gate.

The 18th-century gate, Cantina Sociale

Wine barrels in the Cantina Sociale della Vernaccia

Rows of Vernaccia vines

Tharros ⑱

1st-century AD oil lamp

The city of tharros was founded by the Phoenicians in around 730 BC, on a spit of land called Capo San Marco, which offered safe anchorage for cargo-laden ships from all around the Mediterranean. By the 6th and 5th centuries BC, Tharros had become a flourishing port and this prosperity continued under the Romans, from 238 BC on. With sea on two sides, this is one of the most intriguing ancient sites in the Mediterranean. Only a third of the area has been unearthed so far. The southern section contains the Punic and Roman city, with baths, houses and sanctuaries, while to the north lies the Tophet, the nuraghic village of Murru Mannu and the Roman walls.

7th–6th century BC necklace
Made of gold and cornelian, this necklace was found in the southern necropolis.

The necropolis, of Roman origin, was used until the 3rd century AD.

San Giovanni Spanish tower

Capo San Marco
The tip of the Sinis peninsula, Capo San Marco was settled in the Middle Neolithic era. In the Bronze Age the area was fortified with nuraghi.

Section of the Punic Walls
Squared blocks of basalt and sandstone were used alternately in the 4th-century BC walls, which were 4 m (13 ft) thick.

STAR SIGHTS

★ **Cistern**

★ **Corinthian Columns**

Ancient Baking Oven
The bakery dates from Roman times. It is still possible to recognize the millstone, which was turned by mules and slaves, and the basins made of basalt, used to mix flour and knead dough.

Drainage System

A drain ran along the middle of the paved road. The system was linked to the rows of houses on either side of the street.

VISITORS' CHECKLIST

Road map B4. *San Giovanni di Sinis.* ℹ *Cooperativa Penisola Sinis (0783 37 00 19).* ◯ *9am–9pm summer, 9am–5pm winter.*

Arena   Tophet   Sanctuary of Demeter

The Castellum Acquae was a square construction used as a cistern. The vault was supported by eight brick pillars. It dominates the Compitum, the small piazza in the centre of Tharros.

Head of Goddess

Found in the Punic necropolis, this 5th-century BC head is now in Cagliari museum (see p58).

Baths

★ **Corinthian Columns**
These columns have become the symbol of Tharros, but are not in fact the originals. They were reconstructed by one of the many groups of archaeologists who have worked on this site.

Baths

★ **Cistern**
Made of large blocks of sand-stone, this well supplied water for the sacred rites celebrated in the temple adorned with Doric half columns.

Oristano ⑲

Interior of Cathedral dome

PLACED AT THE NORTHERN BORDER of the Campidano region, between the mouth of the Tirso river and the Santa Giusta marshlands, Oristano is the largest town in western Sardinia. It was founded in 1070, after the powerful and prosperous city of Tharros was abandoned, the inhabitants defeated by constant pirate raids. The period between 1100 and 1400 saw the rise of the city under enlightened rulers such as Mariano IV and his daughter Eleonora, who controlled most of Sardinia. Oristano became the provincial capital only in 1974. The town stands in the middle of a fertile plain with a network of pools, well-stocked with fish. The historic centre, once protected by the city walls, is small and mostly a pedestrian-only zone.

The Cathedral of Oristano with its octagonal campanile

🔒 Cattedrale
Piazza Mannu. 📞 0783 786 84. ⏰ 7am–noon, 3:30–8:15pm daily. 📷 ♿

Dedicated to the Blessed Virgin Mary, the Cathedral was built in 1228 by Lombard architects and masons for Mariano di Torres. It was totally rebuilt in the 17th century in the Baroque style and now displays a mixture of influences. The remaining original elements are the octagonal bell tower with its onion dome and brightly coloured majolica tiles, the bronze doors and the Cappella del Rimedio, which has a fine marble balustrade decorated with Pisan bas relief sculpture depicting Daniel in the lions' den. The Renaissance choir behind the main altar is another important work. The rich and varied Tesoro del Duomo, the cathedral treasury, is housed in the chapterhouse, and silverwork, vestments and illuminated manuscripts can be seen upon request. On Piazza del Duomo are the Palazzo Arcivescovile (archbishop's palace) and the Seminario Tridentino.

♖ Torre di Mariano II
Piazza Roma.

Also called Torre di San Cristoforo or Porta Manna, this sandstone tower at the northern end of the former city walls was built in 1291 by the ruler of the Arborea principality, Mariano II. This and the Portixedda tower, just opposite, are the sole surviving remains of the old city walls. At the top of the tower is a large bell made in 1430. The Torre di Mariano is open on its inner façades and looks over Piazza Roma, the heart of city life, with its fashionable shops and outdoor cafés.

♖ Corso Umberto
This pedestrian street, also known as Via Dritta, is the most elegant in Oristano with impressive buildings such as Palazzo Siviera, once the residence of the Marquise

---

THE KNIGHTS OF THE STAR

The Sa Sartiglia procession and tournament is centuries-old and is held on the last Sunday of Carnival and on Shrove Tuesday. It was probably introduced in 1350 by Mariano II to celebrate his wedding. On 2 February the procession leader, *su Componidori*, is chosen. On the day of the event he is dressed by a group of girls. A white shirt is sewn on him, his face is wrapped in fasciae and covered with a woman's mask, and a bride's veil and black hat are placed on his head. He then leads a procession of knights, trumpeters and drummers through the city to the tournament grounds by the Arcivescovado and the Cathedral. At a given signal the tournament begins. The leader has to run his sword into the hole in the middle of a star hanging from a string, and pick it up. If he succeeds, this signals a prosperous year.

The Sa Sartiglia tournament at Oristano

d'Acrisia, which has a dome on top, and Palazzo Falchi, built in the 1920s. Oristano's smartest shops are found here and it is the most popular street for the traditional evening stroll.

🏛 Piazza Eleonora D'Arborea

This long, irregular, tree-lined square is named after the ruler who established the famous Carta de Logu body of laws in 1392. A 19th-century statue of Eleonora stands in the middle of the square. This piazza also boasts noble buildings such as Palazzo Corrias and the Palazzo Comunale, the town hall, once the Scolopi monastery. The octagonal church of San Vincenzo was part of the monastery.

🏛 San Francesco

Piazza Mannu. **℡** 0783 782 75. **○** 7–11:30am, 5–7pm daily. 📷
This Neo-Classical church was built over the remains of a Gothic church which was completely destroyed in the early 19th century. The façade has six columns with Ionic capitals. In the interior is one

of the most interesting statues in Sardinia: a crucifix executed by an unknown late 14th-century Catalan artist. Another important work, by Pietro Cavaro, depicts *The Stigmata of San Francesco.*

Eleonora d'Arborea

🏛 Santa Chiara

Via Garibaldi. **℡** 0783 780 93. **○** 5–6pm daily.
The Gothic church of Santa Chiara was built in the 14th century. The façade displays sandstone ashlars, a severe rose window and small bell gable. The interior has wooden Gothic corbels with carved animal figures.

🏛 Antiquarium Arborense

Palazzo Parpaglia, Via Parpaglia 37. **℡** 0783 79 12 62. **○** 9am–2pm, 3–8pm daily. 🧥 📷 ♿
Housed in the Neo-Classical Palazzo Parpaglia, this museum features archaeological finds from Tharros, an art gallery and a section given over to medieval Oristano. The gallery has interesting altarpieces in Catalan style: the San Martino *retablo* (15th century)

VISITORS' CHECKLIST

Road map B4. 🏘 32,000.
🚌 🚏 ℹ EPT, Piazza Eleonora 19, (0783 368 31).
Antiquarium Arborense 🎫 ticket is also valid for a guided tour of the historic centre.

attributed to the workshop of the Catalan artist Ramon de Mur; the *Retablo di Cristo* (1533), by followers of Pietro Cavaro, of which only nine panels remain; and the *Retablo della Madonna dei Consiglieri (*1565) by the Cagliari artist Antioco Mainas, representing the councillors of Oristano kneeling before the Virgin Mary.

The archaeological collection contains over 2,000 Neolithic obsidian scrapers, bone hair slides, small amphoras from Greece and Etruria, and Roman glass objects and oil lamps. These all belong to the Collezione Archeologica Efisio Pischedda.

Among the most notable objects in the collection are a terracotta mask used to ward off evil spirits, scarabs made out of green jasper, and carved gemstones from the Roman period.

ORISTANO

Antiquarium Arborense ②
Cattedrale ①
Corso Umberto ④
Piazza Eleonora ③
Santa Chiara ⑦
San Francesco ⑥
Torre di Mariano II ⑤

0 metres 200
0 yards 200

KEY

🚌 Coach station

🅿 Parking

ℹ Tourist information

✝ Church

Fishermen using *fassonis*, traditional sedge boats, on the Santa Giusta lake

Santa Giusta 🄴

Road map B4. 🏘 *4,200.*
ℹ *Via Amsicora 17 (0783 35 96 14).*
🎉 *14 May: Sagra di Santa Giusta.*

Tᴴɪꜱ ᴀɢʀɪᴄᴜʟᴛᴜʀᴀʟ ᴛᴏᴡɴ, built on the banks of the Santa Giusta lake and marsh, was built over the ruins of the Roman city of Ottona. The cathedral of **Santa Giusta**, a jewel of Pisan Romanesque architecture blended with Arab and Lombard elements, stands on the rise as you enter the town. The cathedral was built in the first half of the 12th century and has a narrow façade, with a triple-lancet window. The

columns in the interior are in various styles, and originally came from the nearby Roman cities of Neapolis, Tharros and Othoca. From the sacristy there is a lovely view of the lake, one of the best fishing areas in Sardinia, where you can still see the long *is fassonis* sedge boats of Phoenician derivation. On the feast day of Santa Giusta in May, a lively regatta is held here. The local gastronomic speciality is *bottarga* (salted mullet roe).

Soapstone scarab found in Santa Giusta digs

🏛 **Santa Giusta**
Via Manzoni. 📞 *0783 35 92 05.*
🕐 *9am–noon, 3–7pm (2–6pm winter).*

Arborea 🄵

Road map B4. 🏘 *3,900.* ℹ *Via Roma (0783 80 13 07).* 🎉 *Good Friday: living representation of the Passion of Christ.*

Aʀʙᴏʀᴇᴀ ᴡᴀꜱ founded in 1930 during the Fascist period and was initially

named Mussolinia. The town was built on a regular grid plan typical of modern cities. All the civic buildings (school, parish church, hotel and town hall) are found in Piazza Maria Ausiliatrice, from which the main streets radiate.

The avenues are lined with trees and the two-storey Neo-Gothic houses are surrounded by gardens. In the **Palazzo del Comune** (town hall) there is a small collection of archaeological finds from excavations in the area, including the Roman necropolis of S'Ungroni, north of Arborea, discovered during work on land reclamation.

About 9 km (6 miles) to the southwest is the pretty fishing village of Marceddi, on the edge of the marsh of the same name, dominated by the 16th-century Torrevecchia.

🏛 **Palazzo del Comune**
Piazza Maria Ausiliatrice. 📞 *0783 803 31.* 🕐 *10am–1pm Mon–Fri, 3–6pm Mon–Thu.* 📷 ♿

Fordongianus 🄶

Road map C4. 🏘 *1,200.* ℹ *Via Traiano 7 (0783 601 23).* 🎉 *21 Apr & 21 Aug: Festa di San Lussorio.*

Aɴᴄɪᴇɴᴛ ꜰᴏʀᴜᴍ ᴛʀᴀɪᴀɴɪ was once the largest Roman city in the interior. Located in the Tirso river valley, it was fortified against the local Barbagia people. Today the centre consists of houses in

Cathedral of Santa Giusta, a masterpiece of Romanesque architecture

red and grey stone. One of the best preserved is Casa Madeddu, a typical old "Aragonese house" of the early 1600s with Catalan-style doorways and windows. On the same street is the 16th-century parish church of San Pietro Apostolo, in red trachyte, which has been almost entirely rebuilt. The **Roman Baths**, currently being restored, lie on the banks of the river. The rectangular pool still contains warm water from the hot springs and the local women use it to do their washing. The portico and the rooms with mosaic pavements are closed to the public at present.

A short distance south of Fordongianus stands the little rural church of San Lussorio, built by Victorine monks around AD 1100, over an early Christian crypt.

Earrings found at the Forum Traiani

Paulilàtino ㉓

Road map C4. 🏠 3,000. 🚹 *Via Pia 4 (0785 556 23).* 🎭 *second Sun in May: Sagra di Santa Cristina.*

T HIS RURAL VILLAGE at the edge of the Abbasanta basalt plateau is surrounded by olive groves and cork oak woods. The houses are built of dark stone and have Aragonese doorways and small wrought-iron balconies. The same stone was used to build the church of San Teodoro in the 17th century. This Aragonese Gothic church has a stained-glass rose window and a bell tower with an onion dome. **Palazzo Atzori** houses a museum of folk culture with domestic tools and objects on display.

🏛 Palazzo Atzori

Via Nazionale 127. 📞 0785 554 38.
🕐 9am–1pm all year; 3–5:30pm (Oct–Mar); 3:30–6:30pm (Apr–June) 4:30–7:30pm (Jul–Sept). ⬤ Mon. 🖼 📷 ♿

ENVIRONS: About 4 km (3 miles) from town, a turning off state road 131 takes you to the nuraghic village of **Santa Cristina**. A stone wall encloses the archaeological area, where there is a well temple dedicated to the local mother-goddess dating from the 1st millennium BC. The well is in a good state of preservation, and a broad stone stairway leads to its vaulted underground chamber. Nearby is an enclosure that was probably used for general assemblies. The sacred nature of this site has been maintained over the centuries with the construction of a church dedicated to Santa Cristina. Worshippers continue to flock to the church, which is surrounded by *muristenes*, houses intended for those who come here for novena on the saint's feast day.

To the right of the church, among the olive trees, another archaeological zone includes a well-preserved nuraghe and two rectangular nuraghic-age stone dwellings. The best preserved of these is 14 m (46 ft) long and 2 m (6 ft) high.

🏛 Santa Cristina

Km 114,300, SS131 Cagliari–Sassari.
🚹 *Cooperativa Archeotur (0785 554 38).* 🕐 9am–11pm (Winter: 9pm).

Steps leading to the temple of Santa Cristina at Paulilàtino

Panoramic view of Àles at the foot of Monte Arci

Àles ㉔

Road map C4. 🏠 1,700. 🎭 *first Sun in Aug: Santa Madonna della Neve.*

À LES, THE MAIN VILLAGE in the Marmilla area, lies on the eastern slope of Monte Arci. In the upper part stands the cathedral of San Pietro, built in 1686 by Genoan architect Domenico Spotorno, who used the ruins of the 12th-century church on this site as material for his construction.

Twin bell towers with ceramic domes rise above the elegant façade, while in the Baroque interior, the sacristy has lovely carved furniture and a rare 14th-century crucifix. The Archivio Capitolare contains elegant gold jewellery.

In the same square stand the Palazzo Vescovile and the seminary and oratory of the Madonna del Rosario.

Àles is also the birthplace of Antonio Gramsci (1891–1937) *(see p125)*. The house is marked with a plaque.

ENVIRONS: Àles is a good starting point for a hike to the top of Trebina Longa and Trebina Lada, the highest peaks on **Monte Arci**, the remnants of an ancient crater. Along the way you are likely to spot pieces of obsidian, the hard black volcanic glass which was cut into thin slices and used to make arrowheads, spears and scrapers. The obsidian of Monte Arci was in great demand, and not only supplied the whole of Sardinia, but was also sold throughout the Mediterranean in the 4th–3rd millennia BC.

THE NORTH AND THE COSTA SMERALDA

ORTHEASTERN SARDINIA'S *beauty is familiar from the classic images of a rugged coastline, beautiful inlets, sparkling turquoise sea and beaches of brilliant white sand. To the north, the islands crowded in the Straits of Bonifacio, a stone's throw from Corsica, have great appeal for those in search of unspoilt calm.*

The most well-known development in the northeast is the famous Costa Smeralda, founded by a consortium of financiers including the Aga Khan in 1962. In the space of 40 years, few areas in Sardinia have undergone such profound changes as the northeastern coastline. Villas and residential hotels have sprung up almost everywhere, and small harbours have been equipped as marinas. The surroundings are undeniably beautiful, with spectacular scenery at headlands such as Capo d'Orso and Capo Testa. The perfume of the Mediterranean maquis still manages to reach the beaches of pure white sand, and there are still unspoilt areas that have resisted the encroachment of holiday homes. Tourism brings its own problems however, and there is increasing recognition of the need for stricter controls on building, if the growing influx of visitors is not to damage the island's unique environment.

In the interior, the Gallura region displays quite a different character, with extensive forests of cork oak trees and rough, rocky terrain. Granite outcrops create enchanting landscapes like the Valle della Luna near Aggius *(see p152).* This part of Sardinia is characterized by its wholesome cooking, the continuing practice of traditional handicrafts and frequent reminders of its long history. As well as prehistoric nuraghe, an exceptional series of Romanesque churches survives in the Logudoro area *(see pp156–7),* culminating in the black and white striped stone church of Santissima Trinità di Saccargia *(see pp158–9).*

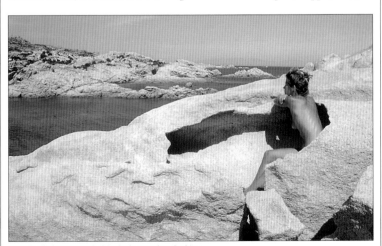

The island of Caprera, ideal for bathing and sunbathing

◁   Two coves on the island of Mortorio, separated by a thin strip of land

Exploring the North and the Costa Smeralda

THE PORT AND AIRPORT in Olbia handle most of the visitors headed not only for the Costa Smeralda holiday villages, but the rest of Sardinia as well. The appeal of the northern part of Sardinia is the beautiful long coastline, with magnificent beaches and wind-eroded cliffs. From Olbia the road winds northwards to Santa Teresa di Gallura, then turns westwards, beyond the Castelsardo headland, until it reaches Porto Torres. In the interior, Tempio Pausania, capital of the Gallura region, makes an excellent starting point for local tours.

The bear-like cliff at Capo d'Orso

SIGHTS AT A GLANCE

24 ISOLA RO

23
CASTELSARDO

*GOLFO
DELL'ASINARA*

Porto ←
Torres

*TOUR OF THE
LOGUDORO* **20**

22 *SASSARI*

21 *SANTISSIMA TRINITÀ
DI SACCARGIA*

PLOAGHE

MÓRES

OZIERI

A stretch of coast at Capo Testa

Macomer

0 kilometres 30

0 miles 30

THE MADDALENA ARCHIPELAGO 6

SANTA TERESA I GALLURA

PALAU 5

4 PORTO CERVO

COSTA SMERALDA

9 LUOGOSANTO 8 ARZACHENA

PORTO ROTONDO 3

2

GOLFO ARANCI

SANT'ANTONIO DI GALLURA 10

Lago di Liscia

11 CALANGIANUS

1 OLBIA

12 TEMPIO PAUSANIA

N199

MONTI

SAN TEODORO 16

14 BERCHIDDA

N125

Siniscola

N389

Posada

ALÀ DEI SARDI 17

PATTADA

18

17 BUDDUSO

GETTING AROUND

The Costa Smeralda area probably has the best public transport facilities in Sardinia, certainly in the summer. There are plenty of links with Olbia (and its airport) and the most important tourist resorts in the northeast. The main roads through the Gallura region are state road SS125, the famous Orientale Sarda, which connects Olbia and Palau; SS133 from Palau to Tempio Pausania and then Ploaghe; and SS199 from Olbia to Macomer.

Sailing along the Costa Smeralda

The Romanesque abbey church of Tergu

KEY

	Motorway
	Major road
	Minor road
	Scenic route
	River

SEE ALSO

- **Where to Stay** pp176–7

- **Where to Eat** pp186–7

The ruins at Cabu Abbas

Olbia ❶

Road map D1 & 2. 🏛 43,000. ⚓ ℹ
Azienda Autonoma Soggiorno (0789 214 53). @ aastolbia@tiscalinet.it

THE TOWN OF OLBIA is only 200 km (125 miles) from the port of Civitavecchia on the mainland of Italy, and has always been the main arrival point on the island, rather than the capital Cagliari. The building of the airport just outside Olbia, to serve the Costa Smeralda, has confirmed this role.

Olbia is a modern city and usually considered as a stop-off on the way to the coast. Of interest in the town are a Roman cistern in Piazza Margherita, proof of ancient Roman occupation, and the Romanesque **San Simplicio**. This church was built from the 11th century onwards and enlarged in the 13th century.

ENVIRONS: There are two interesting prehistoric sites near Olbia: the **Cabu Abbas** nuraghic complex (4 km, 2 miles to the northeast) and the **Sa Testa** holy well.

To reach Cabu Abbas from the old port of Olbia, go along Corso Umberto and then Via d'Annunzio. Once past the railway you will see the country church of Santa Maria Cabu Abbas. From here a dirt path winds up towards the top of the mountain, another 15 minutes on foot. The site offers a magnificent view of the island of Tavolara. There is a central well with a tower where remains of sacrifices – burnt bones and pieces of pottery – were found in 1937. This large megalithic zone extends for about 200 m (656 ft).

To reach the Sa Testa holy well, take road SP82 to Golfo Aranci as far as the Pozzo Sacro hotel. This site consists of a wide paved courtyard, from which 17 covered steps lead down to a well chamber.

Golfo Aranci ❷

Road map D1. 🏛 2,100.
ℹ *Town Hall (0789 468 49).*

THE NAME "ARANCI" means oranges, but you will not see orange groves here. Golfo Aranci owes its name to a mistaken interpretation of the local place-name *di li ranci*, meaning "some crabs".

Formerly a part of Olbia, the village of Golfo Aranci became an independent town in 1979. Since 1882 increasing numbers of ferries from the mainland have used Golfo Aranci as a stopping place. It is also the official port of call for the Ferrovie dello Stato (Italian State Railway) ferries.

The Porto Rotondo Yacht Club

Porto Rotondo ❸

Road map D1.
ℹ *Azienda Autonoma di Soggiorno di Arzachena (0789 826 24).*

PORTO ROTONDO is not so much a town as a large, well-planned tourist village which grew from nothing during the Costa Smeralda boom. The buildings, placed around the inevitable yacht marina, were designed to fit in as much as possible with the natural surroundings. The result is certainly pleasant, and Porto Rotondo has been a great success as a tourist resort, despite its perhaps slightly artificial air.

Mussel beds at sunset in the Bay of Olbia

Aerial view of Porto Rotondo

The Porto Rotondo quay and Piazzetta San Marco are lined with famous designer shops, and throughout the summer the cafés and restaurants are crowded with visitors, lunching, dining, meeting friends, listening to music and just watching the world go by. Out of season Porto Rotondo is quiet and even deserted.

The church of San Lorenzo, designed by Andrea Cascella, holds wooden statues by Mario Ceroli depicting Biblical figures.

Just outside Porto Rotondo is the pretty headland called Punta della Volpe, separating the Golfo di Marinella from the Golfo di Cugnana.

Architecture on the Costa Smeralda

NEARLY 40 YEARS have passed since a stretch of coastline in north-eastern Sardinia was transformed into the most exclusive tourist resort in the Mediterranean, the Costa Smeralda or Emerald Coast. Back in 1962 the beaches were the preserve of grazing cattle, then taken to overwinter on the islands of Mortorio, Soffi and Li Milani. The Consorzio Costa Smeralda was formed to transform the area. The group initially consisted of the landowners, but expanded to include property owners. Building regulations were established and an architectural committee was founded to supervise any new building in the area. The prominent architects Luigi Vietti, Jacques Couelle, Giancarlo and Michele Busiri Vici, Antonio Simon, Raimond Martin and Leopoldo Mastrella were appointed to design the resorts. The area has since changed beyond recognition. Luxury hotels, sumptuous villas and huge holiday villages have gone up, together with sporting facilities: the famous Yacht Club and one of the most attractive golf courses in the Mediterranean, as well as small villages such as Porto Cervo.

The Neo-Mediterranean style *is a combination of the various elements frequently seen in Mediterranean architecture.*

***In planning Porto Rotondo**, the architects decided that only native plants should be used, so trees such as pine, poplar and eucalyptus are banned because they would not blend in with the local strawberry trees, myrtle, lentiscus, oleanders and mimosa.*

The materials *used must be traditional – local stone, pebbles, curved tiles and brick.*

An aerial view of Porto Cervo

Porto Cervo ❹

Road map D1. ℹ️ *Azienda Autonoma Soggiorno di Arzachena (0789 826 24).*

THE HEART OF the Costa Smeralda and a paradise for VIPs, Porto Cervo is centred around two yacht harbours with some of the most spectacular private craft in the world. In summer there is a series of top sporting events, including regattas and golf tournaments. The traditional evening stroll along the quay is almost obligatory, with fashionable designer shops on one side, and luxury yachts on the other. The church of Stella Maris has a canvas attributed to the painter El Greco.

ENVIRONS: There are plenty of good beaches around Porto Cervo, such as Liscia Ruja to the south, framed by the sheltered Cala di Volpe.

Palau ❺

Road map D1. 👥 *3,300.* ℹ️ *Azienda Autonoma Soggiorno (0789 70 85 56).* **FAX** *0789 70 95 70.*

THE LOGICAL departure point for a trip to the Maddalena archipelago, Palau also owes its success to the appeal of the narrow-gauge Sassari-Tempio-Palau railway. Life here is rather frenetic in the summer and revolves around the ferry boat wharf and the yacht harbour. From Palau you can travel to some of the most fascinating and famous places on the coast, such as

the jagged Capo d'Orso (Bear Cape) promontory, which ends in a large, bear-shaped rock, sculpted by the wind.

To get to Punta Sardegna, take the road that goes up to Monte Altura and then go on foot to the beach of Cala Trana, on the tip of the headland. There is an extraordinary view of the coast and the islands, which is particularly lovely in the early morning

and at sunset, despite the fact that 21st-century construction work is slowly but surely spoiling the unique beauty of this part of Sardinia.

The Maddalena Archipelago ❻

See pp146–9.

Santa Teresa di Gallura ❼

Road map C1. 👥 *4,200.* ℹ️ *Azienda Autonoma Soggiorno (0789 75 41 27).*

THE AREA around Santa Teresa was inhabited in Roman times and was also important to the Pisans, who used the local granite for building. The present-day town was built from scratch during the Savoyard period. It has a regular grid plan with streets intersecting at right

Sunset at Palau, departure point for the Maddalena Archipelago

THE AGA KHAN AND THE COSTA SMERALDA

The Consorzio Costa Smeralda group of foreign investors was founded in 1962 with Prince Karim Aga Khan IV at its head. The Harvard-educated prince, rich and charismatic, was then in his mid-twenties. He is reputed to have spent more than 1,000 million dollars in creating an opulent jet-set playground, complete with yachting marinas, luxury hotels, villas and elegant restaurants along the Gallura coastline, all designed to harmonize with the rugged Sardinian landscape. The project has proved very successful: Porto Cervo and the nearby villages quickly became popular holiday spots, especially for the wealthy and famous of the international jet set, who can be seen on the quays of Porto Cervo in the summer.

Aga Khan IV

Overlooking Santa Teresa di Gallura

angles, in the middle of which is a small square and the church of San Vittorio. The local economy is based on fishing (including coral fishing) and tourism.

On the rocky headland stands the Torre Longosardo, a tower built in the 16th century during the Aragonese period; it affords a magnificent view of Porto Longone bay and, in the distance, the white cliffs circling the city of Bonifacio in Corsica, which is only 12 km (7.5 miles) away.

To the left the coast falls away to the beach of Rena Bianca, which ends not far from the Isola Monica, a tiny island which has the remains of an abandoned quarry.

The Capo Testa lighthouse

ENVIRONS: About 5 km (3 miles) away is **Capo Testa**, a rocky promontory connected to the mainland by a thin sandbar. The headland can be reached via a very pretty route around the bays of Colba and Santa Reparata. A walk through the ancient and modern quarries – which supplied the Romans with the granite for the columns in the Pantheon – accompanied by the sweet fragrance of the maquis will take you to the Capo Testa lighthouse.

Arzachena ❽

Road map D1. 🏠 *10,000.*
🛈 *Azienda Autonoma Soggiorno (0789 826 24).*

AROUND FORTY YEARS AGO, Arzachena was a peaceful shepherds' village in the interior. Today it is the centre of one of the most famous tourist resorts in the world, the Costa Smeralda, and has undergone considerable change. Towering above the houses is a curious rock formed by wind erosion, called the Fungo (mushroom), and there are many traces of prehistoric settlements in the vicinity. Among the most interesting sites for a tour are the **Albucciu Nuraghe**, the **Tomba di Giganti Coddu Vecchiu** and the **Li Muri Necropolis**.

⋔ Albucciu Nuraghe

☎ *0789 815 37.* ⭕ *At all times.*
From Arzachena, take the road to Olbia and after about 600 m (650 yds), at the end of town, follow the turn-off and

then take the footpath on the right. Once at the nuraghe, go up the ladder to the upper level, to visit the side section.

The protruding stone brackets that once supported the original wooden structure are still intact.

⋔ Tomba di Giganti Coddu Vecchiu

☎ *0789 815 37.* ⭕ *At all times.*
To get to the Giants' Tomb, take state road SS427 towards Calangianus and, after about 3 km (2 miles), take the turning to the right signposted Luogosanto. After about 1,800 m (1 mile) you join the Capichera road, and another 500 m (550 yds) on there is a path leading to the tomb, which lies to the right. In the middle of the funerary monument there is a stele 4 m (13 ft) high, surrounded by a semicircular wall of stone slabs set into the earth.

⋔ Li Muri Necropolis

☎ *0789 815 37.* ⭕ *At all times.*
Once outside Arzachena, follow signs for Calangianus (SS427) and then the right-hand turning for Luogosanto. Continue for about 4.5 km (3 miles) and take another turning to the right (a dirt road), which goes to the necropolis of Li Muri.

This site includes a number of ancient tombs: burial chambers surrounded by as many as five concentric circles of stones. These funerary circles constitute the most important monumental complex left from the era archaeologists now refer to as the Arzachena Culture.

The mistral whipping up the surf off Capo Testa

The Maddalena Archipelago ❻

Subalpine warblers

Sᴇᴠᴇɴ ɪsʟᴀɴᴅs (Maddalena, Caprera and Santo Stefano to the southeast, Spargi, Budelli, Razzoli and Santa Maria to the northwest) make up the Arcipelago della Maddalena. Beyond lie the Straits of Bonifacio, which became a marine reserve of international status at the beginning of 1997. Rugged, jagged coasts, rocks hewn by wind and water erosion, and tenacious maquis vegetation characterize this group of islands, known during the Roman period as *Cuniculariae*, or "rabbit islands". In the 18th century Maddalena was used as a military base – it is a convenient landing place and lay in a strategically important position. A tour of the island would be incomplete without a visit to Caprera, to see the places where the Italian hero Giuseppe Garibaldi lived and is buried.

Lᴏᴄᴀᴛᴏʀ Mᴀᴘ

RAZZOLI · SANTA MARIA

BUDELLI

SPARGI

LA MADDALENA

Spargi
Uninhabited, like Budelli, Razzoli and Santa Maria, this island has marvellously clear water and secluded beaches, making it an ideal site for swimmers, snorkellers and scuba divers.

A scenic route of just over 20 km (12 miles) runs around the island, providing magnificent views of the archipelago, Corsica and the four Corsican islands of Lavezzi.

Bird Life
The many rock formations in this archipelago are frequently visited by sea birds such as cormorants, to the delight of bird-watchers.

★ La Maddalena
This is the most important town in the archipelago. Town life centres around Piazza Umberto I and Piazza Garibaldi. There is a wide choice of boat trips to the nearby islands from the harbour.

Regattas
The west wind, an almost constant presence in the Maddalena archipelago, makes this a popular place for yachting competitions.

Guardia Vecchia is the highest mountain on the island. The Savoy rulers chose it as the site for the fort of San Vittorio, which is now occupied by a lighthouse.

Monte Teialone is the highest point on Caprera.

The Bridge over Passo della Moneta
Constructed in 1891, this bridge links the islands of Maddalena and Caprera.

SANTO STEFANO

CAPRERA

Caprera
The island of Caprera extends over nearly 1,600 hectares (3,950 acres).

★ **Tomb of Garibaldi**
The "hero of two worlds" was buried here on 2 June 1882.

STAR SIGHTS

★ **La Maddalena**

★ **Tomb of Garibaldi**

Exploring the Maddalena Archipelago

THE SMALL Maddalena Archipelago is a favourite with sailing fanatics, fans of underwater fishing and with people who appreciate tranquillity and unspoilt surroundings. Except for the two largest islands, the archipelago is uninhabited and, together with the many other small islands, make perfect summer destinations for boat trips, sunbathing and swimming in solitude.

The Sardinia Regional Naval headquarters at La Maddalena

La Maddalena

Road map D1. 🏘 *12,000.*
🛈 *Azienda Autonoma Soggiorno, Via XX Settembre 24 (0789 73 63 21).*
🚢 *from Palau.* 🎭 *20–22 Jul: Santa Maria Maddalena.*

The town that is now the capital of the island was founded in 1770 and replaced a small village built on the shores of the Cala Gavetta bay. After the unsuccessful invasion on the part of the French in 1793, British admiral Horatio Nelson stopped at La Maddalena in 1804 and in 1887 the entire Maddalena Archipelago was turned into a naval base by the Savoy rulers. On Via Amendola, which runs along the seafront, a series of 19th-century buildings bears witness to the rapid development of the town in this period. In Piazza Garibaldi, the Municipio (town hall) has on display a French bomb dating from France's attempt to conquer Sardinia in 1793.

In the evening, particularly in summer, the traditional evening stroll centres around Via Garibaldi. Not far away is the church of Santa Maria Maddalena, which has two candelabra and a silver cross given by Admiral Nelson to the island's inhabitants. La Maddalena is still the head-quarters of the Sardinia Regional Navy.

🛶 The Scenic Route

The road around the island is about 20 km (12 miles) long and goes through the Cala Spalmatore, Stagno Torto and Baia Trinita bays.

On your way from La Maddalena, you will see the church of the Trinità, then the turn-off for Monte Guardia Vecchia, on the summit of which is the Savoyard fort of San Vittorio, and lastly the island of Giardinelli, which is connected to La Maddalena by a narrow strip of land. Further north are Porto Massimo, the inlets of Abbatoggia and Cala d'Inferno, and the other large fortification on the island, Forte dei Colmi. In the first stretch of this tour is the **Museo Archeologico Navale "Nino Lamboglia"**, the maritime museum with finds from the "ship of Spargi", an ancient Roman cargo vessel discovered in the 1950s.

🏛 Museo Archeologico Navale "Nino Lamboglia"

Località Mongiardino. ⏰ *8:30am–1:30pm.* ⬤ *Sun & winter.* 📞 *0789 790 660.* 📷

Caprera

Road map D1. 🛈 *Azienda Autonoma Soggiorno della Maddalena (0789 73 63 21).*
This small island has 34 km (21 miles) of coastline, and is connected to the island of Maddalena by the 600 m (1,968 ft) Passo della Moneta bridge. Walkers will enjoy the climb up the steps to the top of Monte Teialone (212 m, 695 ft).

The island of Caprera became the property of Giuseppe Garibaldi in 1856. His estate is now part of the **Compendio Garibaldino** museum area. A visit here includes a fascinating tour of the stables, moorings and the Casa Bianca (white house) where Garibaldi lived. The stable still has a period steam-engine used for threshing, while the Casa Bianca contains mementos of Garibaldi's adventurous life: weapons, flags, portraits, the hero's clothes (including his famous

---

GARIBALDI AND CAPRERA

The legendary Italian hero and revolutionary Giuseppe Garibaldi escaped to the island of Caprera in 1849, after the fall of the Roman Republic. He returned in 1855 after the death of his wife Anita and decided to buy most of the island. The rest of the land was then given to him by some English friends. Garibaldi, who went on to play a key role in the unification of Italy, settled on Caprera permanently in 1857, and died here in 1882.

Giuseppe Garibaldi wearing the famous red shirt

The famous pink sand beach at Budelli

red shirt) and a model of the Battle of Solferino.

Garibaldi's favourite room was the salon, and he asked to be taken there before he died. The calendar and clocks in the room have not been changed since then, and still show the exact time of his death: 6:20pm on 2 June 1882.

Caprera also has a famous sailing school, the Centro Velico Caprera (see p199).

Compendio Garibaldino

☎ 0789 72 71 62. ◷ 9am–1:30pm daily; 9am–6:30pm Jun–Sept. ● public hols. ✗ ▨ ▨ ⚐

Santo Stefano

Road map D1.
ℹ Azienda Autonoma Soggiorno La Maddalena (0789 73 63 21).
This small island lies halfway between Palau and the island of Maddalena and can be reached via the boats that depart at regular intervals from La Maddalena harbour. Dominating the scene is the Santo Stefano (or San Giorgio) fortress, also known as Napoleon's fort, built at the end of the 18th century.

There is a tourist village on the beach of Pesce, on the western coast.

Spargi

Road map D1. ⛴ from La Maddalena. ℹ Azienda Autonoma Soggiorno La Maddalena (0789 73 63 21).
Spargi is little more than 2 km (1 mile) in diameter and is completely uninhabited. The terrain is fairly barren and the coast steep and inaccessible, but there is a lovely beach for bathing, even though it has no facilities. An ancient Roman ship was found opposite the Cala Corsara cove on the southern coast; its cargo is now in the Museo Archeologico Navale "Nino Lamboglia" at La Maddalena.

Budelli

Road map D1.
ℹ Azienda Autonoma Soggiorno La Maddalena (0789 73 63 21).
This beautiful uninhabited island is remarkable for its unique beach of rose-coloured sand. Even though there are no facilities, Budelli is popular with visitors because of its beautifully unspoiled natural setting.

The clear, unpolluted water is also ideal for scuba diving, either to observe marine life or for underwater fishing.

SAILING IN NORTHERN SARDINIA

The Straits of Bonifacio are dotted with small islands and rocks with lighthouses which create natural buoys, making the area ideal for yacht and dinghy racing. The wind is pretty constant, and in summer the west wind blows steadily at 40 km per hour (24 mph).

The Costa Smeralda Yacht Club at Porto Cervo, founded by the Aga Khan, is the main sailing facility in this area. This world-famous club organizes several major sailing races and other competitions. The most well-known are the Sardinia Cup, an international deep-sea championship held in even-numbered years, and the Settimana delle Bocche, a summer race for speed-boats from all over Italy.

In the odd-numbered years the old harbour at Porto Cervo provides space for 50 or so vintage boats: from the *gozzo* with its characteristic lateen sail to 30-m (98-ft) schooners. This popular event, which has been held since 1982, is

usually followed by the world yacht championship for boats in the Maxi class.

Other important races, such as the European and world championships of various yacht categories, also take place here. The Costa Smeralda Yacht Club represented Italy in the 1983 America's Cup with the yacht *Azzurra* and in 1987 the club organized regattas to select the Italian representative in the America's Cup in Perth, Australia.

Yachts racing in the Straits of Bonifacio

San Trano, a 12th-century hermitage near Luogosanto

Luogosanto ⑨

Road map C1. 1,900. Pro Loco (079 65 22 73). first Sun in Aug: San Quirico's feast day.

THE VILLAGE of Luogosanto is surrounded by maquis, and is well known for the production of bitter honey, often served with *seadas (see p181)*. The village is typical of the Gallura region, backed by greenery and wind-eroded pinkish-grey rocks. Every seven years a colourful and solemn ceremony celebrates the opening of the Porta Santa (holy door) of the church of Nostra Signora di Luogosanto.

San Quirico's feast day ends with a dinner for all the villagers. The traditional dish *carr'e coggbju*, made with pork and cabbage, is served.

About 1 km (half a mile) to the east of Luogosanto is the **San Trano hermitage**, perched at 410 m (1,345 ft), dominating the landscape towards the north of the town. This small church was built in the 12th century in memory of the hermit saints San Nicola and San Trano, who, according to the legend, lived in the small cave to the rear of the altar.

Nearby is the Filetta spring, whose waters are famous throughout the island. In recent years, squares, steps and street lamps have been set around the spring.

Sant'Antonio di Gallura ⑩

Road map D1. 1,700. Town Hall (079 66 90 13). first Sun in Sep: Sant'Antonio's feast day.

THIS VILLAGE HAS always been an important farming and sheep-raising centre. In the heart of town, situated on a rocky spur, is a small, recently founded archaeological park, known for its intricate landscape of wind-sculpted rocks. This same site was inhabited in prehistoric times. During the first week of September, the feast days of Sant'Antonio, San Michele and Sant'Isidoro are celebrated with a procession. Decorated oxen and tractors follow the statues of the saints through the streets.

ENVIRONS: 2 km (1 mile) away is the artificial lake of Liscia, capable of holding 150,000,000 cubic m (5 billion cubic ft) of water.

Calangianus ⑪

Road map C2. 4,800. City Hall (079 66 00 00). third Sun in Sep: Sant'Isidoro's feast day.

IN THE FORESTS around the town of Calangianus you can see evidence of cork harvesting everywhere: the barked cork oaks have that characteristic reddish colour that will remain until the bark grows again, while the cork strips themselves are heaped up in large piles to dry.

Calangianus is the cork production centre of the Gallura region and there are numbers of workshops and factories for processing the material. There is also an important trade school whose curriculum focuses on the cultivation of cork oaks and

The artificial lake of Liscia near Calangianus

making the maximum use of cork bark. In September every year Calangianus hosts an exhibition and trade fair of cork oaks and their many by-products, both on an industrial and domestic scale.

In the centre of the old town, in a small, isolated square, is the small parish church of Santa Giusta, which was built in the 17th century.

Cork items produced in the Gallura region

ENVIRONS: Near the village of **Luras** (northwest of Calangianus), a series of prehistoric dolmens is open to visitors. To reach the site, go through the village in the direction of Luogosanto and then turn right just before the end of town. At the point where the paved road ends, take the dirt road on the right, which takes you to the **Ladas Dolmen**, the most impressive of them all. It has a rectangular plan, is roofed with two granite slabs, and is 6 m (19 ft) long and 2.20 m (7 ft) wide.

Tempio Pausania 🕛

Road map C2. 🏛 *14,000*. 🚉
ℹ️ *Pro Loco (079 63 12 73).*

THE CAPITAL OF Gallura, Tempio Pausania consists of a large number of modern buildings which tend to obscure the charming old town. Investigate further and discover two- and three-storey buildings with dark granite stone walls and characteristic balconies. A short walk from the central Piazza Gallura, site of the town hall and other public buildings, is the **Cathedral** – founded in the 15th century but rebuilt in the 1800s. Also nearby are the Oratorio del Rosario and the small **Santa Croce** church, all well worth visiting.

Not far from town are the **Rinaggiu springs**, whose mineral water is famous for its beneficial qualities. As well as the traditional festivals, an international folklore festival is held here in July (*see p27*).

Detail of Santa Croce

ENVIRONS: A short distance away, on state road SS133, is the turning for the **Maiori Nuraghe**, one of the best preserved megalithic structures in the area.

By heading south from the town on state road 392 for 17 km (10 miles) you will pass close to the summit of **Monte Limbara** (1,359 m, 4,459 ft), which can be reached in a few minutes on foot from the paved road.

Along the way you will see the Curadoreddu road house (about 6 km, 4 miles, from Tempio Pausania); here, a turning to the left will take you to an abandoned fish farm, from which you can admire an impressive view of mountain rock pools and waterfalls. Water flows from one great mass of rocks to the other, creating cascades and hollows. The spectacle is at its most striking during the winter months.

The bed of the mountain stream near Curadoreddu

CORK AND THE HANDICRAFTS OF GALLURA

Cork is obtained from the stripped bark of cork oak trees (*Quercus suber*) and has always been a fundamental part of the Gallura regional economy. The material is used for everyday purposes as well as local handicrafts. Among kitchen utensils in use are cork spoons and ladles (such as the *s'uppu*, a small ladle used to collect water), buckets and different containers for water and wine, and large serving dishes – called *agiones* in dialect – for roasts and other dishes. Today the Tempio Pausania region produces 90 per cent of the bottle stoppers used in Italy, although the cork is also used as a building and insulating material. Cork is very versatile, thanks to its lightness, resistance to air and water, its insulating properties and long life.

Strips of cork bark ready for processing

Cork cannot be stripped from the tree before it is at least 25–30 years old. The first layer stripped is porous and elastic and of scant commercial use. Only nine to ten years after this first barking process is the true – and profitable – new layer of cork obtained. The trees are then stripped every nine to ten years, and the layers thoroughly seasoned before use.

A barked cork oak tree

The Valle della Luna (Valley of the Moon) near Aggius

Aggius ⓭

Road map C1. 🏃 *1,200.* 🛈 *Town Hall (079 62 03 39).* 🎭 *first Sun in Oct: feast days of Santa Vittoria and Madonna del Rosario.*

NATURAL FEATURES have shaped this village and its surroundings. A granite outcrop dominates the landscape of Aggius, both in the high ground of the Parco Capitza, which towers over the town, and in the amazing labyrinth of rock formations in the nearby Valle della Luna.

Once the dominion of the Doria family from Genoa, and then ruled by the Aragonese, Aggius owes its present prosperity to the quarrying and processing of granite. Local handicrafts are also important to the economy – especially rug-making, every stage of which is carried out using traditional techniques.

The centre of Aggius is a pleasant place to walk thanks to the loving care with which the old stone houses have been preserved; they are among the most attractive in

the Gallura region. On the first Sunday in October traditional festivities are held, including the *di li 'agghiani*, for un-married men, at which the Gallura *suppa cuata* (bread and cheese soup) is served.

The road to Isola Rossa quickly brings you to the **Valle della Luna**, with its weird rock formations, the result of glaciation.

On a left-hand curve a dirt road veers right. Follow this almost up to the bridge, then continue along the small road on the right, which leads to the **Izzana Nuraghe** in the middle of the valley.

Rock formations above Aggius

Berchidda ⓮

Road map C2. 🏃 *3,400.* 🚉
🛈 *Town Hall (079 70 30 01).*

BUILT ON THE SOUTHERN slopes of Monte Limbara, in a hilly landscape which stretches as far as Monte Azzarina, Berchidda is a large village whose economy is based on sheep raising, dairy products, cork processing and viticulture. The leading local wine is Vermentino (one of the best known of Sardinian white wines), and the local pecorino cheese is also of excellent quality.

About 4 km (2 miles) from the centre of Berchidda, a steep climb will take you to the ruins of the **Castello di Montacuto**, which was the fortress of Adelasia di Torres and her husband Ubaldo Visconti before becoming the domain of the Doria and Malaspina families from the mainland. Monte Limbara, the geographical heart of the Gallura region, towers in the back-ground.

Cheese and white Vermentino wine, locally-made produce from Berchidda

Buddusò ⓯

Road map C2 & D2. 🏃 *6,500.*
🛈 *Pro Loco (079 71 40 70).*

THE TOWN OF Buddusò is fairly prosperous thanks to sheep farming, granite quarrying and the processing and sale of cork.

The stone-paved streets in the old part of town wind around buildings made of dark stone. In the Roman era the main road from Kàralis

(Cagliari) to Olbia crossed the town, then known as Caput Thirsi. The church of **Santa Anastasia** and the paintings in the sacristy are worth a visit. A tour through the **Monti di Alà** is another worthwhile excursion.

ENVIRONS: Nearby are the **Iselle Nuraghe** (towards Pattada) and **Loelle Nuraghe**, on the road to Mamone.

A *cuile*, or shepherd's hut

San Teodoro ⓖ

Road map D2. 🏠 *2,900.*
🛈 *Azienda Autonoma Soggiorno di Olbia (0784 865 767).*

To the south of the Capo Coda Cavallo headland, just opposite the rocky island of Tavolara, the village of San Teodoro has grown rapidly in recent years due to increasing numbers of tourists.

The village also makes an excellent starting point for excursions to the Cinta beach, a long strip of sandy terrain that separates the **Stagno di San Teodoro** from the sea. Fairly close to the Orientale Sarda road, this 200-hectare (494-acre) lake and marsh is one of the few remaining coastal marshes that once lay south of the Bay of Olbia. Mallards and coots are easily sighted on the water. When the birds glimpse a bird of prey or other danger, they gather in large groups and make a loud noise to defend themselves.

Grey and red heron as well as Kentish plovers can be seen in search of food, and another common sight is the hovering kestrel, one of Italy's smallest raptors.

THE ISLAND OF TAVOLARA

This island is a mountain of limestone rising from the sea to a height of 500 m (1,640 ft). The eastern side is an inaccessible military zone, but the low sandy area called Spalmatore di Terra has beaches, a small harbour, a couple of restaurants and a few houses. Together with the neighbouring islands of Molara and Molarotto, home to over 150 moufflons, Tavolara is a marine reserve. The granite cliffs are pierced by caves and crevices. Sea lilies grow in the Spalmatore di Terra area and the rock is covered with juniper, helichrysum, rosemary and lentiscus. According to tradition, Carlo Alberto, the king of Piedmont and Sardinia, landed on the island to find the legendary "goats with golden teeth" (a phenomenon caused by a grass they eat), and was so fascinated by the island that he officially dubbed its only inhabitant, Paolo Bertolini, "king of Tavolara". In the summer there is a regular boat service to the island from Olbia *(see p142).*

The unmistakable profile of the island of Tavolara

Granite outcrops are used as a resting place by ducks.

Kestrel

The clear, still water is rich in food for birds.

Grey heron

The shores are ideal for mud-dwelling creatures.

Lapwing

The Stagno di San Teodoro

The village of Alà dei Sardi

Alà dei Sardi ⑰

Road map D2. 🏘 2,000.
ℹ Buddusò Pro Loco
(079 71 40 70). 🎭 4 Oct: countryside feast day of San Francesco.

ROCKS AND MAQUIS, and forests of enormous cork oaks with the characteristic marks of recent stripping, make up the landscape of Alà dei Sardi and its plateau, the last tract of the rocky interior overlooking the Bay of Olbia.

The main street of the village is lined with the small granite stone houses characteristic of this region.

ENVIRONS: Not far from Alà dei Sardi, off the road which leads to Buddusò, is the **Ruju nuraghe**, with the remains of a prehistoric village almost buried in the scrub.

Following signs to the town of Monti, the route crosses a sizeable plateau studded with astonishingly varied rock formations. At a fork, the road deviates for the sanctuary of San Pietro l'Eremita, and passes through some stunning scenery, with gaps allowing occasional views of the sea and the unmistakable profile of the island of Tavolara (see p153) in the distance. The Romanesque church of San Pietro l'Eremita has been relatively recently restored. Every year in August at Ferragosto (Assumption Day), the church is crowded with pilgrims from the surrounding villages.

Pattada ⑱

Road map C2. 🏘 3,800.
ℹ Buddusò Pro Loco (079 71 40 70).
🎭 29 Aug: Santa Sabina.

SITUATED IN THE middle of a territory rich in prehistoric nuraghi and other vestiges of the past, Pattada is world-famous for the production of steel knives, which began here because of a rich vein of iron ore which has been worked for centuries. The village blacksmiths still carry on the tradition of making steel blades, and handles from animal horn, and dozens

The Sa Fraigada forest near Pattada

THE KNIVES OF PATTADA

The best-known style of shepherd's knife made in Pattada is the *resolza* (the word derives from the Latin *rasoria*, or razor). The *resolza* is a jack-knife with a steel blade that may be as much as 14 cm (5 inches) long. The blacksmiths of Pattada only use traditional materials. Steel is hammered into shape in a forge and on an anvil; the handle is made from wood, or from moufflon, sheep or deer horn. The production of Pattada knives dates from the mid-19th century, and the

Sheath

The handles are made of wood or horn.

The blade is made of hand-wrought steel.

best knives are still hand-made by skilled craftsmen.

Among the masters at work today some, like Salvatore Giagu and Maria Rosaria Deroma, draw inspiration from the oldest types of Pattada knives, such as the fixed-blade *corrina*, which dates back to the 18th century. It is not easy to find real Pattada knives on sale, and you should avoid imitations. Production is a slow and complicated affair, but it is possible to order a Pattada knife to be made for you, although this procedure will take about a year.

An assortment of Pattada knives

The artificial lake created by the Rio Mannu at Pattada

of imitations of these Sardinian knives can now be found on the Italian mainland.

ENVIRONS: In the vicinity of Pattada is the **Fiorentini** – an area of greenery resulting from reforestation – and the ruins of the medieval castle of Olomene.

Ozieri ⑲

Road map C2. 🏠 *12,000.* 🚇
ℹ️ *Pro Loco (079 77 00 77) or Comunità Montana del Monte Acuto (079 78 10 600).* 📅 *second Sun in May: Sant'Antioco di Bisarcio.*

O ZIERI LIES in a natural hollow and its situation is one of the most attractive sights in northeast Sardinia. Both the traditions and architecture here are interesting, and the town has a fascinating history that goes back millennia and has added to the knowledge of the remote pre-nuraghic cultures which developed here.

The fabric and layout of the town are quite varied and blend in well with the slopes of the hills. Among the tall houses the occasional covered roof terrace filled with flowers can be glimpsed.

The major sights in the old town are **Piazza Carlo Alberto** and **Piazza Fonte Grixoni**, centred around an ancient fountain. On the edge of the historic quarter is the Neo-Classical **Cathedral**, which contains a splendid 16th-century Sardinian polyptych by the painter

known as the Maestro di Ozieri. The painting depicts the famous miracle of the Sanctuary of the Madonna of Loreto, and reveals Spanish influences as well as traces of Flemish mannerism. The 17th-century San Francesco monastery houses the **Museo Archeologico**, with finds from the archaeological digs in the area. Most of this material belongs to the era of the Ozieri civilization, the predominant culture here from 3500 to

Earthenware found in the Grotta di San Michele

2700 BC. It is also known as San Michele, from the name of the cave in which major finds were discovered.

The territory surrounding Ozieri is also rich in historic and archaeological sites and ruins, such as the *domus de janas* at Butule, the San Pantaleo necropolis and the dolmen at Montiju Coronas.

The **Grotta di San Michele** is a cave that lies behind the Ozieri hospital, near the track and field stadium (in fact, during the construction of the latter, part of the cave was destroyed). Large quantities of decorated ceramics were found here, as well as human bones, a mother-goddess statuette and pieces of obsidian from Monte Arci.

All these finds support the theory that there was some continuity from the earlier Bonu Ighinu culture to the time of the Ozieri.

🏛 **Museo Archeologico di Ozieri**
Piazza Canonico Spano.
📞 *079 78 76 38.* 🕐 *8:30am–1pm, 4–7pm Tue–Sun; 8:30am–1pm Mon.*
Grotta di San Michele, Ozieri Hospital.
🎫 *combined ticket for both sites.*

Terraces of houses climbing the slopes of the town of Ozieri

Sights of the Logudoro ⑳

Detail, Sant'Antioco di Bisarcio

AFTER THE FALL of the Roman Empire, Sardinia did not return to a central role in the Mediterranean until after the year 1000, when Pisan and Genoese merchants, soldiers and preachers came into contact with the different regional cultures of the island. The Romanesque churches in the north of Sardinia are the result of these encounters. It is difficult to assess how much of each single monument was created by local artists and artisans and how much by those from Pisa and Genoa. Whatever the facts, east of Sassari there is a series of Romanesque churches that has few equals in the rest of mainland Italy.

Nostra Signora di Tergu ⑦
This church was built over the remains of a monastery founded by monks from Montecassino in Tuscany.

Santissima Trinità di Saccargia ①
The Santissima Trinità, built in striped layers of black and white stone, is the most significant example of Romanesque architecture in northern Sardinia. The apse is decorated with frescoes of Christ and the saints. The church was restored in the early 1900s *(see pp158–9).*

• *Castelsardo*
Valledoria

Sassari

Nuraghe di Camarzu

San Michele di Salvènero (Ploaghe) ②
In the 12th century the monks of Vallombrosa built this church near the village of Salvènero, which has since disappeared. The church now stands abandoned in the middle of a series of road interchanges. Restored in the 13th century and again in 1912, this splendid monument needs to attract greater care and respect to safeguard its future.

Santa Maria del Regno (Ardara) ③
Santa Maria was consecrated in 1107, and is different from the Pisan Romanesque churches. The façade faces south, perhaps to soften the severity of the dark stone and squat bell tower.

•*Ploaghe*

San Pietro di Simbranos (or delle Immagini) ⑥

The traditional name of this church derives from the bas-relief on the façade depicting an abbot and two monks (the *immagini* or "images"). San Pietro, in the Bulzi area, was first built in 1113 and rebuilt in its present form a century later. This isolated and tranquil monument has a particular fascination because of its desert setting among canyons and rocks.

Nostra Signora di Castro (Oschiri) ⑤

Dominating Lake Coghinas, this church blends Lombard and local architectural elements. It was built in the second half of the 12th century and is surrounded by the *cumbessias* enclosure of pilgrims' houses, built at a later date.

Sant'Antioco di Bisarcio (Ozieri) ④

Sant'Antioco is a combination of Pisan Romanesque and French influences. Sant'Antioco was built from the second half of the 11th century to the late 12th century and was initially the cathedral of the Bisarcio diocese. It differs from the other churches on this tour in its architectural complexity, shown in the unusual two-storey porch, small windows and the decorative detail on the façade.

KEY

▬ Motorway

▬ Major road

═ Other roads

— River

0 kilometres 5

0 miles 5

Coghinas
Lago di Castel Doria
Tempio Pausania
érfugas
Coghinas
Monte Sassu
Lago di Coghinas
Olbia
Oschiri
N132
N597
N597
Ozieri ④
Ardara

Santissima Trinità di Saccargia ㉑

Portico frieze

BOTH SIMPLE and impressive, Sardinia's most famous Romanesque church stands in the middle of a windswept valley. Its name probably derives from *sa acca argia*, "the dappled cow". According to legend, this animal used to kneel in prayer on the site, which is why there are carvings of the cow on four sides of one of the capitals in the portico. Another account relates how, around the year 1112, the ruler of the region, Constantine, donated the small church to the Camaldolesi monks, who then decided to enlarge it with the help of Tuscan architects, craftsmen and labourers. Initially they added the apse and the bell tower with its alternating layers of black trachyte and white limestone. At a later stage they built the porch, the only one on a Sardinian church. The austere interior, with a tall, narrow nave lit by small openings or slots in the side walls, is very atmospheric.

Animal frieze
The severity of the exterior of the church is lightened with sculptures of animals.

The campanile
is 41 m (134 ft) tall and each side is 8 m (26 ft) wide.

★ Façade
Two rows of blind arches adorn the façade, each level decorated with rose windows and multi-coloured diamonds. The central arch has an opening in the form of a cross.

★ Carved Cows
It may be that the church was named after the carved cows on this capital, even though the portico was built after the main church.

Double-lancet Windows
*These date from the late
12th century.*

**The black and white
stripes** reveal Pisan
influence.

Monastery Ruins
*Only a few black and white
stone archways are left
of the first and most
important
Camaldolese
monastery in
Sardinia.*

VISITORS' CHECKLIST

Road map C2. 079 43 53 75.
8am–8pm daily (Oct–Mar:
1pm). From Sassari, follow N131
for 10 km (6 miles), then turn off
on road 597 to Olbia.

**Fresco
of Christ**
*Christ is depicted holding a
book in the act of benediction.*

The aisleless nave
was built after the
apse, which dates
from 1116.

★ **The Apse Frescoes**
*Romanesque frescoes are rare
in Sardinia – these are
attributed to Pisan artists.*

Portico Capitals
*The portico is supported by
columns with carved
capitals. They carry the
classic Romanesque motifs
of plants and animals.*

STAR FEATURES

★ **Façade**

★ **Carved Cows**

★ **Apse Frescoes**

Sassari ㉒

Coat of arms of Sassari

Sardinia's second most important city commercially, politically and culturally, Sassari lies on a tableland that slopes down to the sea among olive groves and fertile and well cultivated valleys. The city has a long history of invasions, conquests and raids, but also boasts a tradition of stubborn rebellion and uprisings. Pisans, Genoese and Aragonese have all attempted to subdue the city, but the indomitable spirit of the Sassari citizens has always succeeded in asserting independence. The city's hero is a rebel named Carlo Maria Angioj, who headed a revolt in 1796 against the Savoyard government, which had sought to impose a feudal system. Two presidents of the Italian Republic, Antonio Segni and Francesco Cossiga, were born in Sassari, as was the prominent Italian Communist Party leader Enrico Berlinguer.

The *Li Candareri* festival in Sassari

Exploring Sassari
The old town, with its winding alleyways branching off from the main streets, was once surrounded by walls that ran along present-day Corso Vico, Corso Trinità, Via Brigata Sassari and Corso Margherita. Only a few parts of the city walls (such as the section at the beginning of Corso Trinità) have survived the effects of time, but the old centre has preserved its original layout, even though it is now somewhat dilapidated.

A morning should be enough for a walk around the old town. The main sights are the Duomo (cathedral), the Fontana del Rosello fountain, the churches of Sant'Antonio, Santa Maria di Betlem and San Pietro in Silki, and the Sanna museum.

🏛 Duomo
Piazza Duomo. (079 23 20 67.
○ 4–7pm daily. 📷 &
Sassari cathedral is dedicated to San Nicola (St Nicholas). Its impressive Baroque façade is in rather striking contrast to its size and to the small, simple and elegant 18th-century Piazza Duomo with its characteristic semicircular shape. The end result of successive enlargements and changes carried out over the centuries, the Duomo was originally built on the site of a Romanesque church. The base of the façade and bell tower are still intact.

At the end of the 15th century the original structure underwent radical transformation that not only changed its shape but created today's unusual proportions. The side walls were propped up by buttresses decorated with gargoyles of mythical and monstrous animals, while the interior was rebuilt in the Gothic style.

In the late 18th century the upper portion of the façade was radically changed with the addition of rather grand decoration: volutes, flowers, cherubs and fantastic figures. In the middle, the statue of San Nicola is surmounted by the figures of the three martyr saints, Gavino, Proto and Gianuario, set in three niches. At a later stage, an octagonal section decorated with multicoloured majolica tiles was superimposed on the original Lombard-style lower part of the campanile. The interior, which has been totally restored, has retained its simple Gothic lines despite the presence of lavishly decorated Baroque altars. The choir, the work of 18th-century Sardinian artists, is particularly striking.

The Museo del Duomo, reached through the Cappella Aragonese (Aragonese chapel) on the right, houses the processional standard, a panel painting by an anonymous 15th-century

Detail of the façade of Sassari Cathedral

The Fontana del Rosello, dating from the Renaissance

VISITORS' CHECKLIST

Road map B2. 120,000. Ente Provinciale Turismo, Viale Caprera 36 (079-29 95 44 or 29 95 46). last Sun of month: Antiques Show in Piazza Santa Caterina; Easter Week: Maggio Sassarese; penultimate Sun in May: Cavalcata Sarda; 14 Aug: Faradda de li Candareri.

artist. There is also a silver statue of San Gavino, embossed using a Mexican technique that was in fashion in the late 17th century.

🔲 Fontana del Rosello
Via Col di Lana.
On the right-hand side of the church of Santissima Trinità, in Piazza Mercato, a small stone stairway known as the Col di Lana will take you to the Fontana del Rosello, the fountain at the lower end of the Valverde gorge.

Unfortunately, very little remains of the steep valley and woods that were once the natural backdrop for this little jewel of late Renaissance art. However, this has not diminished the locals' love for their fountain.

This was once the haunt of the enlightened bourgeoisie and the place where the local water-carriers drew water from the eight lions' mouths sculpted at the base of the fountain. It has become one of the city's symbols.

The fountain was executed in the early 1600s by Genoese artists, who still had a marked preference for the classical styles of the Renaissance.

The base consists of two superimposed white and green marble boxes. The lions' mouths are surrounded by statues symbolizing the four seasons. The original statues were destroyed in the 1795–6 uprisings *(see p160)*.

In the middle, a bearded divinity, known as Giogli, is surrounded by small towers symbolizing the city. On the top of the fountain are two arches which protect the figure of San Gavino.

SASSARI

Corso Vittorio Emanuele ②
Duomo ①
Fontana del Rosello ③
Mostra Permanente dell'Artigianato ⑥
Museo Sanna ⑧
Piazza d'Italia ⑦
Sant'Antonio Abate ④
Santa Maria di Betlem ⑤

0 metres　　300
0 yards　　　300

KEY

🚉 Railway station

🅿 Parking

ℹ️ Tourist information

✝ Church

🏛 Sant'Antonio Abate

Piazza Sant'Antonio. 🟢 *079 26 00 24.*
🔵 *7–10am daily, 4:30–7:30pm Sat.*

Dating from the early 1700s, the stately Baroque façade of this church, with its simple elegance and harmonious proportions, dominates the tree-lined square at the end of Corso Trinità.

The upper part of the portal still bears the emblem of the brotherhood responsible for building the church. The Latin cross interior boasts one of the most elegant high altars in Sassari, which bears a carved and gilded wooden altar-piece. The panels were executed in the late 18th century by the Genoese painter Bartolomeo Augusto.

The church stands in Piazza Sant'Antonio, once the site of the old northern gate of the same name, and formerly the hub of the city's commercial and political life. The only vestiges of the past are a part of the medieval city walls, and a battlemented tower to the left of the church.

🏛 Santa Maria di Betlem

Piazza Santa Maria.
🔵 *7:30am–noon, 5–7pm daily.*

The church of Santa Maria di Betlem is situated in the square of the same name, at the northwestern entrance to the city. Built by Benedictine monks in 1106, it was later donated to the Franciscans. Unfortunately, the elegant original structure was the subject of frequent rebuilding in the 18th and 19th centuries, and the church has lost its early qualities of lightness and purity of form. The only intact part of the earlier church

The Romanesque church of San Pietro in Silki, Sassari

is the 13th-century façade, decorated with small columns and capitals and pierced by a lovely 15th-century rose window. The Gothic interior, once austere, has been spoiled by the heavy-handed Baroque decoration and altars; yet the original side chapels are intact, each dedicated to a craftsmen's guild as a reminder of the social role the church played in the community. To this day, on 14 August, the date of the *De li Candareri* festivities, the votive candles donated by the various guilds are carried here in procession from the Chiesa del Rosario.

Detail of an Art Nouveau-style house

The cloister is partly walled in but can still be visited. It contains the 14th-century granite stone Brigliadore fountain, once the source of most of Sassari's water supply.

🏛 San Pietro in Silki

Via delle Croci. 🟢 *079 21 60 67.*
🔵 *6:30am–noon, 3:30–6pm daily.*

The Romanesque church of San Pietro in Silki faces a lovely tree-lined square and

was most probably named after the medieval quarter built here in the 1100s. Its simple 17th-century façade has a large atrium leading to the Gothic nave with four side chapels. The first of these was dedicated to the Madonna delle Grazie in the second half of the 15th century. It is named for a statue of the Virgin Mary, found inside a column from the square in front of the church. The statue is one of the best examples of Catalan Gothic sculpture in Sardinia.

On the other side of the square, opposite San Pietro, is the Frati Minori monastery, which houses one of the island's richest libraries. The collections consist of over 14,000 volumes, removed from Franciscan monasteries after their closure.

🚏 Corso Vittorio Emanuele

The city's main street crosses the heart of the old town and connects Piazza Sant'Antonio and Piazza Cavallino. The Corso is lined with 19th-century houses and 16th-century Aragonese buildings, and you can often catch a glimpse of courtyards and interiors that testify to their former splendour. This is Sassari's main shopping street, with shops of all kinds, from clothing to ironmongery.

🏛 Mostra Permanente dell'Artigianato

Viale Mancini. 🟢 *079 23 01 01.*
🔵 *9am–1pm, 5–7:30pm Mon–Sat.*
📷 ♿

Facing the Emiciclo Garibaldi public gardens, a shop in a modern building houses the

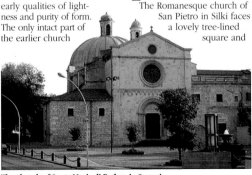

The church of Santa Maria di Betlem in Sassari

Permanent Exhibition of Sardinian Handicrafts, a collection of the best work from the island's various crafts cooperatives. The large rooms overlook an inner garden which allows light into the display cases housing the most precious objects. These include filigree necklaces and earrings, coral jewellery designed according to old drawings, and pottery and ceramics created using traditional techniques.

Hanging on the walls are traditional Sardinian rugs, which resemble abstract paintings with their geometric patterns. There is also fine bobbin lacework and – still interesting though not so valuable – baskets of dwarf palm wood, terracotta pots and other everyday objects whose design and techniques have been handed down over centuries of tradition.

🏛 Museo Archeologico Nazionale "GA Sanna"

Via Roma. 📞 079 27 22 03.
🕐 9am–8pm Tue–Sun.
📷 🍴 ♿

The Sassari archaeological museum was donated to the Italian state by the Sanna family, who built these premises in 1931 to house finds collected by Giovanni Antonio Sanna, an important figure in the island's history and director of the local mine.

Two entire storeys are given over to various periods of Sardinian civilizations, from the Neolithic to the Middle Ages. Arrowheads, nuraghic bronze statuettes, amphoras,

Entrance to the Museo Nazionale "GA Sanna" in Sassari

furnishings, weapons, tools, ceramics and jewels are on display in chronological order. On the ground floor, panels illustrate the evolution of Sardinia, and every room has time charts on display.

There are also architectural reconstructions of prehistoric buildings such as dwellings, *domus de janas* (rock-cut tombs) and giants' tombs. In the last hall, among floor plans, sarcophagi and statues there is a reconstructed mosaic floor from a patrician Roman villa in nearby Turris Libisonis (present-day Porto Torres). The mosaic shows lobsters, sea horses, and seals chasing one another in an eternal circle. The next room contains a small art gallery with works by Sardinian artists from the 14th to the 20th centuries.

There is also a traditional crafts section divided into four rooms with jewels, costumes, musical instruments and craftsmen's tools, almost all of which are still used in central-northern Sardinia.

🏛 Piazza d'Italia

This large square is laid out at the edge of the 19th-century quarter of Sassari. It is a well-proportioned public space, surrounded by elegant Neo-Classical buildings and with tall palm trees and well-kept flower beds, guarded by a statue of Vittorio Emanuele II.

One of the finest buildings is the Palazzo della Provincia (provincial government building), built in pure Neo-Classical style. The council chamber on the first floor is open to the public. On the walls are 19th-century paintings depicting important events in the city's political history, such as *The Procla- mation of the Sassari Statutes* and *Carlo Maria Angioj Entering Sassari (see p160)*. You can also see the adjacent royal apartments, built in 1884 on the occasion of the King of Sardinia's visit. In summer the courtyard is the venue for concerts and plays.

The lovely 19th-century Bargone and Crispi arcades on the northwestern side of Piazza d'Italia shelter the city's oldest bars and *pasticcerie* (pastry shops) and lead to Piazza Castello.

🏛 Santa Caterina

Via Santa Caterina. 📞 0781 23 16 92. 🕐 pm for mass.
This church was built at the end of the 16th century for the Jesuits and combines Sardinian Gothic style with Renaissance elements.

In the interior there are paintings by the artist Giovanni Bilevelt.

Sassari's Piazza d'Italia, framed by the Neo-Classical Palazzo della Provincia

The harbour at Castelsardo

Castelsardo ㉓

Road map C2. 🚶 *5,500.* ⓘ *Pro Loco (079 47 15 06).* 🎭 *Easter Monday: Lunissanti procession.*

PERCHED ON a volcanic headland, Castelsardo has known a number of name changes in its history. The town was founded in 1102 by the aristocratic Doria family from Genoa, and was originally known as Castelgenovese, a name it kept until 1448, when it became Castellaragonese, after the town's new conquerors. The present name of Castelsardo dates from 1776.

The town is dominated by the castle (**Castello**), which now houses a museum with exhibits of traditional basketweaving. Overlooking the sea is the cathedral of Sant'Antonio Abate.

Local basketwork

The alleyways of the centre of town are lined with small shops selling all kinds of local handicrafts. Fish-lovers will do well here, as the local cuisine is based on freshly caught fish and lobsters.

On Easter Monday, the traditional **Lunissanti** procession is held in Castelsardo. The streets are lit by flaming torches, and traditional hooded figures form a slow procession, to the sound of three songs, *Lu Stabat, Lu Jesu* and *Lu Miserere*. These songs are centuries old, and probably date from before Catalan rule. They have been handed down by word of mouth ever since. The solemn procession, one of the most well-known of Sardinia's Easter festivals, ends at the church of **Santa Maria**.

Castello and Museo dell'Intreccio

Via Marconi. ◯ *9am–1pm, 2–5pm (Apr–Oct: 9am–midnight) daily.* 🅿
This fortress was built in the 13th and 14th centuries. The place is now occupied by the **Museo dell'Intreccio** (museum of wickerwork). Local baskets are made from traditional materials such as palm, cane and asphodel. From the castle terraces there are lovely views of the Golfo dell'Asinara, and on clear days you can even see the hills on Corsica.

Sant'Antonio Abate in Castelsardo

⛪ Cattedrale di Sant'Antonio Abate

Via Seminario. ◯ *8am–6pm daily.*
Constructed in the 17th century on the site of an existing Romanesque church, the cathedral has a bell tower roofed with majolica tiles. From the tower there is a splendid view of the water below. The cathedral contains fine 16th-century, carved wooden furnishings.

The town of Castelsardo and the castle above

The Roccia dell'Elefante (Elephant Rock) near Castelsardo

🔒 Santa Maria

Via Vittorio Emanuele. ⬜ *ask priest for keys.*

In the heart of the old town, the upper part of Castelsardo, stands the church of Santa Maria. The building does not have a façade, and entry is gained through the side door. In the interior is a 14th-century crucifix known as the *Cristo Nero* (Black Christ). The church is the focus of the Lunissanti Easter procession, which starts and ends here.

🏞 La Roccia dell'Elefante

To one side of the road near Multeddu, not far from Castelsardo, stands the impressive Roccia dell'Elefante (Elephant Rock). This massive block of dark trachyte rock has been gradually sculpted by the wind into the shape of an elephant with its trunk raised. In ancient times the rock was used as a burial place. At the base you can still see small carved openings for several *domus de janas* (rock-cut tombs).

Isola Rossa ㉔

Road map C1.

THE HILLS of Gallura slope down towards the sea, forming a landscape characterized by rose-coloured crags, sculpted into strange shapes by wind erosion. The small fishing village of Isola Rossa lies on a headland, at the foot of an impressive 16th-century sentinel tower.

The fishing fleet at Isola Rossa

The village is not an island *(isola)*, but was given its name ("red island") after the small, reddish-coloured rock island out in the bay. Fishing boats are drawn up on the beach below the village after each day's catch is brought in.

The coastline either side of Isola Rossa is worth visiting, especially towards the east, where Monte Tinnari overlooks the sea. To the west, the coast gently slopes to meet the mouth of the Rio Coghina, a short distance from Castelsardo.

ENVIRONS: A short distance from Isola Rossa is the small agricultural town of **Trinità d'Agultu**, which developed in the late 19th century around the church of the same name. As is so often the case in Sardinia, the simple country church became a sanctuary and pilgrimage site. As a result, it is also an important trade and commercial centre during the associated religious festivities and pilgrimages.

THE FISHING INDUSTRY

The Sardinians are historically a nation of shepherds. Despite this, fishing is still an important activity, even though for centuries it has been carried out almost exclusively by non-Sardinian immigrants: people from the island of Ponza at Castelsardo, and Neapolitans, who founded the village of Isola Rossa in the early 20th century. Nowadays a major source of income in these two places is the cultivation of mussels and shellfish. Tuna fishing, once widespread off the northwest coast, no longer survives in Sardinia, the small trawlers having been unable to compete with deep-sea fishing, now practised on an industrial scale.

Craftsman at work making a lobster pot

TRAVELLERS'
NEEDS

WHERE TO STAY

THE LEGENDARY ALLURE of the beaches in Sardinia has resulted in a boom in tourist facilities, especially along the coast, and visitors can now choose from a wide range of hotels and holiday villages. The exclusive and world-famous hotels built on the Costa Smeralda in the early 1960s cater for the wealthy, but it is not difficult to find less expensive accommodation. You can find luxury hotels and resorts in the south, while the western coast offers reliable

Logo of ESIT, the Sardinian Tourist Board

family-run lodgings. On the eastern coast, comfortable and well-equipped tourist villages are easily found, many offering self-catering as an option. There are some excellent hotels in the interior, especially in the Gennargentu and Barbagia areas, where you can also take advantage of organized tours and hikes. For further information, listings and descriptions of hotels, farm holidays and tourist villages, turn to page 171 and pages 174–7.

The Hotel Torre Moresca at Cala Ginepro, Orosei (*see p175*)

GRADES OF HOTEL

HOTELS IN SARDINIA are graded on a star-rating system, from one star, which stands for minimum comfort and service, to five stars for luxury accommodation. The four-star category offers first-class service without the very high prices of five-star hotels. Three-star lodgings, especially family-run establishments, sometimes offer better value for your money, but this is generally the exception rather than the rule.

Most Sardinian hotels also have a restaurant which is usually open to non-residents as well. The majority of hotels, whatever their category, provide a range of facilities. Along the coast, for example, hotels are likely to offer beach equipment such as umbrellas and deckchairs.

HOLIDAY VILLAGES

THE HOLIDAY VILLAGES OF Sardinia, mostly situated on or near the coast, offer a variety of types of accommodation. The choice varies from vast establishments with hundreds of rooms and good facilities and service, to smaller sites, which may be elegant and expensive. The larger holiday villages offer more than one type of lodging within a single site. At Forte Village, for example, there are six different hotels, each in a different style, ranging from the 38-room Le Dune to the 152-room Castello. At some places you can choose between serviced apartments (*residence*) or a normal three- or four-star hotel, with a range of charges. Some tourist villages offer all-inclusive packages that even include drinks at the bar. Sardinian tourist villages often require guests to take half or full board, as do many hotels.

Logo of the Hotel Sporting at Porto Rotondo

In some resorts guests may choose to rent a self-catering apartment or bungalow and then decide whether or not to have the other services and facilities included in the package. These services usually include the use of sports facilities and entertainment, such as a disco or night club, baby-sitters for those travelling with small children, beach facilities, the swimming pool and use of the various bars and restaurants. Many villages offer an excellent range of equipment for water sports.

Renting an apartment in a tourist resort is a worthwhile alternative to renting a villa, especially if you plan to be on holiday for less than a month. It allows you to be independent while at the same time giving you access to a range of services and facilities should you find you need them.

For a listing of these resorts see page 171.

A café in the small square at Porto Cervo

The Hotel Victoria at Tortolì, near Arbatax (see p175)

PRICES

ITALIAN LAW REQUIRES every hotel to place the National Tourist Board price list, with the maximum prices for the current year, on the door of each room. The prices quoted should never be exceeded. Room prices shown on this list, or quoted by the hotel staff when you book, normally include taxes and service. However, it is advisable to check whether or not breakfast is included, to avoid any misunderstandings.

Hotels on the coast usually require guests to take half or full board. In low season you could try asking for a bed and breakfast rate, but this is unlikely to be possible in the high season. Winter rates are quite different from summer rates: in the summer prices may be as much as double. Hotel prices reach their peak in the two middle weeks of August. This is also true of the tourist villages (except that rates here are calculated on a weekly basis).

The location of your hotel will also affect the price. Hotels, villages and even pensions on the coast are always more expensive than lodgings in the interior.

You may be able to negotiate special rates for groups or for longer stays.

EXTRAS

GENERALLY SPEAKING, you will pay separately for drinks consumed with your meal, anything taken from the mini-bar in your room, room service and telephone calls. A word of warning: phone calls in particular can be subject to very high surcharges.

In some cases air conditioning may be charged as an extra. Glimpses of Sardinia's lovely coast may also be regarded as chargeable and you may pay extra for rooms with a sea view. It is always a good idea to check on extras like this when booking or choosing your room.

LOW SEASON

IF YOU PLAN TO GO to Sardinia in any season other than summer, it is a good idea to check beforehand on the availability of accommodation. Most hotels are run on a seasonal basis; and tend to open around Easter and close in the autumn. The end of the season may very well depend on unpredictable circumstances such as a sudden turn of bad weather.

BOOKING AND PAYING

IF YOU DECIDE to travel during the summer, especially in the Italian holiday months of July and August, and if you want to stay on the coast, you must book well in advance, since the island is overflowing with visitors in this period. If you are booking your hotel separately from your travel arrangements, it is quite likely that you will be asked to send some money as a deposit. This can be done by credit card or international money order. When you arrive at your hotel or village, the person at the reception desk will ask for your passport; this is to register travellers with the police, a legal requirement. You will be given a receipt on checking out, another legal formality.

CAMPING

TOGETHER WITH *agriturismo*, or farm holidays, camping is the most inexpensive way of staying on the island. Sardinia has a number of good camp sites, some of which are located in quiet areas with lovely views. Most of them are situated along the coast, often in eucalyptus or pine woods. There are far fewer sites in the interior.

Camping sites, like hotels, get extremely crowded in the summer. If you are travelling around and have not booked in advance, you need to start looking for a place to stay as early as noon.

Some camping sites also have a small number of bungalows with a bathroom and kitchen area, but the prices can be steep.

Most Sardinian camping sites are open from Easter to October. Some may be open for the Christmas period, offering bungalows or camper vans with heating.

Camping outside official sites is strictly forbidden, and camping on the beach is particularly frowned on. You need permission to camp on private property (from the owner), and in state forests.

The Hotel Hieracon, on the island of San Pietro (see p174)

The L'Agnata holiday farm at Tempio Pausania

FARM HOLIDAYS

A FARM HOLIDAY *(agriturismo)* is an excellent way of coming into direct contact with Sardinian customs and traditions. Unlike other regions in Italy, Umbria and Tuscany in particular, Sardinia can offer a genuinely rustic atmosphere. Very few rooms have private bathrooms, though many farm managers are now taking steps to remedy this situation. Farmhouses in Sardinia tend not to be placed in isolated countryside: true to tradition, at least half the farms are in villages. Local farmers and shepherds often live in villages and travel some distance to work the fields or take their sheep to pasture.

The highest concentration of farms offering holidays is found in the provinces of Sassari and Oristano, while there are very few in the Cagliari region. The only drawback – depending on your point of view – might be a certain lack of privacy: everybody eats at the same table, guests and host family alike. You will probably find yourself becoming almost a part of the family before you leave. Meals consist of produce grown on the farm – cheese, meat, vegetables and even honey – cooked according to local tradition. It is an excellent way of getting to know the specialities of the region. In general, farms offer accommodation by the week on a half- or full-board basis. Many of them also organize hikes, horseback riding and mountain bike and canoe excursions.

VILLA RENTAL

R ENTING A HOUSE for two weeks or a month is the most economical solution for a family or a group of friends who want to spend their entire holiday by the sea. This option is especially recommended for families with small children and babies. Note however that the charge for cleaning tends to be the same for a week as for a longer stay.

If you are looking for a house to rent you should contact the local Pro Loco and Azienda di Soggiorno information offices (given in the information for each town in this guide). Tourist offices sometimes offer a specialized service supplying lists of private homes available in the vicinity and their prices. Travel agents and holiday companies can also arrange this type of accommodation.

Prices for rental are usually quoted on a weekly basis, and a deposit is normally

A typical holiday house for rent in the Sulcis region of Sardinia

requested. When you rent a house or apartment it is advisable to ascertain the exact size of the house and number of bedrooms. In some houses the living room also functions as a bedroom. Before signing any contract, also check whether gas, water, electricity and telephone expenses are part of the rent or are considered "extras". Make a note of the readings on the meters on arrival if these items are extra.

USING THE LISTINGS

The hotels on pages 174–7 are listed according to area and price.

🏢	air-conditioning
🛁	all rooms with bath and/or shower
🍸	mini-bar in room
📺	television in all rooms
⬆	lift
🌳	garden or terrace
🧒	facilities for children
P	hotel parking available
♿	wheelchair access
🍴	restaurant in hotel
🏊	swimming pool
💳	credit cards accepted
AE	American Express
MC	MasterCard
DC	Diners Club
V	VISA

Price categories show the maximum per night for a double room with breakfast or, where shown, for half or full board per day, and per person.
€ under €50
€€ €50–100
€€€ €100–150
€€€€ €150–200
€€€€€ over €200.

DIRECTORY

TOURIST OFFICES

ESIT (Ente Sardo Industrie Turistiche)
Via Mameli 97, Cagliari.
070 602 31 or freephone 800 01 31 53.

HOLIDAY VILLAGES

Club Méditerranée
Caprera,
Isola La Maddalena.
Road map D1.
0789 72 70 78.
FAX 0789 72 74 14.

Club Méditerranée Santa Teresa
Località La Marmorata,
Santa Teresa di Gallura.
Road map C1.
0789 75 15 20.
FAX 0789 75 15 25.

Club Vacanze Cala Moresca
Località Bellavista,
Arbatax.
Road map D4.
0782 66 73 66.
FAX 0782 28 85 00.

Ventaclub Capo Boi
Località Piscadeddus,
Villasimius.
Road map D6.
070 79 80 15.
FAX 070 79 81 16.

Ventaclub Monte Turri
Località Bellavista,
Arbatax.
Road map D4.
0782 66 75 50.
FAX 0782 66 78 92.

Villaggio Valtur
Santo Stefano,
Isola La Maddalena.
Road map D1.
0789 70 98 12.
FAX 0789 70 85 73.

CAMPING

Arcobaleno
Località Porto Pozzo,
Santa Teresa di Gallura.
Road map C1.
0789 75 20 40.

Arzachena
Località Cannigione,
Arzachena.
Road map D1.
0789 881 01.
FAX 0789 881 01.

Baia Blu La Tortuga
Località Vignola Mare,
Aglientu (Sassari).
Road map C1.
079 60 20 60.

Baia Chia
Località Chia, Domus De Maria (Cagliari).
Road map C6.
070 923 01 85.

Cala Fiorita
Località Agrustos,
Budoni (Nuoro).
Road map D2.
0784 84 62 90.

Cala Gonone
Cala Gonone,
Dorgali (Nuoro).
Road map D3.
0784 931 65.

Camping Garden Cala Sinzias
Castiadas,
Cala Sinzias (Cagliari).
Road map D6.
0781 85 21 12.

Europa
Località Torre del Pozzo,
Cuglieri (Oristano).
Road map B3.
0785 380 58.

International Camping
Località Valledoria.
Road map D6.
079 58 40 70.

Is Arenas
Is Arenas (Oristano).
Road map B5.
0785 522 84.

Isola dei Gabbiani
Località Porto Pollo,
Palau (Olbia).
Road map D2.
0789 70 40 19.
FAX 0789 70 40 77.

La Caletta
Carloforte,
Località La Caletta.
Road map B6.
& FAX 0781 85 21 12.

Nurapolis
Narbolia (Oristano).
Road map B4.
0783 522 83.
FAX 0783 522 55.

Porto Pirastu
Località Capo Ferrato,
Muravera (Cagliari).
Road map D5.
070 99 14 37.
FAX 070 99 14 39.

Sennisceddu
Pau (Oristano).
Road map C4.
0783 93 92 81.

Sos Flores
Tortolì, Arbatax (Nuoro).
Road map D4.
0782 66 74 85.
FAX 0782 62 46 27.

Spiaggia del Riso
Località Campolongo,
Villasimius.
Road map D6.
070 79 10 52.
FAX 070 79 71 50.

Telis
Località Porto Frailis,
Tortolì (Nuoro).
Road map D4.
0782 66 71 40.

FARM HOLIDAY ASSOCIATIONS

Agriturist
Via Bottego 7,
Cagliari.
Road map C6.
070 30 34 86.

Consorzio Agriturismi di Sardegna
Via Duomo 17,
Oristano.
Road map B4.
0783 41 16 60.

Terranostra
Via Roma 231, Cagliari.
Road map C6.
070 28 05 37.

Turismo Verde
Via Libeccio 31, Cagliari.
Road map C6.
070 37 37 33
FAX 070 37 20 28.

FARM HOLIDAYS

L'Agnata
della famiglia De Andrè,
Valle di Baldu,
Tempio Pausania (Sassari).
Road map C2.
079 67 13 84.

Azienda di Gino Camboni
Località L'Annunziata,
Castiadas (Cagliari).
Road map D6.
070 99 49 152.

Azienda di Giovanna Minnia Addis
Riu Riu, Tergu (Sassari).
Road map C2.
079 47 61 24.

Azienda di Lucia Sotgiu
Via Amsicora 9,
Nurachi (Oristano).
Road map B4.
0783 41 02 96.

Fenu
Località Sa Tuerra,
Teulada (Cagliari).
Road map C6.
070 92 83 013.

Il Cavallino
Padru (Nuoro).
Road map D2.
0789 510 14.

Le Querce
Località Valli di Vatta,
Porto Cervo
(Sassari).
Road map D1.
0789 992 48.

Lu Striglioni
Murta Maris,
Olbis (Sassari).
Road map D2.
0789 405 24 or
360 61 68 67.

Sa Perda Marcada
Sa Perda Marcada,
Arbus (Cagliari).
Road map B5.
070 975 87 14.

Sos Rios
Sos Rios,
Torpe (Nuoro).
Road map D4.
0784 82 61 32.

Sardinia's Best: Hotels

T HE MAJORITY OF THE luxury hotels in Sardinia are to be found in the Gallura region and close to the beaches of the Costa Smeralda. However, there are increasing numbers of smaller hotels in other less famous and much less expensive areas of Sardinia. All the hotels on this map offer something special and are highly recommended for their particularly favourable position along the coast or in the mountains, for architecture that blends in with the landscape, and for excellent service. Book well in advance if you plan to stay in the high season and note that many hotels close for the winter.

Villa Las Tronas
This seaside villa at Alghero is now a comfortable hotel. All the rooms have views of the coast and the only "noise" is that of the sea (see p175).

THE WESTERN COAST

CAGLIARI AND THE SOUTH

Le Dune
Tucked away among the Piscinas dunes, this hotel occupies two old mine buildings which have been restored with great attention to detail (see p174).

Forte Village
At this seaside holiday village the hotels are surrounded by Mediterranean maquis. Facilities for relaxation are excellent, and include thalassotherapy pools (see p174).

THE NORTH AND THE COSTA SMERALDA

CENTRAL SARDINIA AND BARBAGIA

THE EASTERN COAST

Pitrizza
The most exclusive hotel on the Costa Smeralda is sited at Liscia di Vacca. The service and facilities are impeccable (see p176).

0 km   20

0 miles   20

Hotel Cala di Volpe
The first hotel to be built on the Costa Smeralda was designed by Jacques Couelle in the 1960s (see p177).

Su Gologone
At the foot of Supramonte di Oliena, this hotel offers decor and cuisine in the best tradition of the Barbagia region, as well as the chance to go horseback riding (see p175).

Tanka Village
Surrounded by woods, this resort near Villa- simius has the feel of a tropical village. Tanka is well-equipped for water sports (see p175).

CAGLIARI AND THE SOUTH

ARBUS – INGURTOSU

Le Dune

Road map B5. Località Piscinas.
📞 070 97 71 30. **FAX** 070 97 72 30.
Rooms: 25. 🖩 🛏 🍽 P 🔧 🍴
🏊 ⚡ AE, DC, MC, V. ◯ Jan–Dec.
€€€ half board.

A charming hotel in a recently restored mine building alongside the Piscinas dunes.

CAGLIARI

Calamosca

Road map C6. Viale Calamosca 50.
📞 070 37 02 52. **FAX** 070 37 03 46.
Rooms: 47. 🛏 📺 P 🔧 🍴
⚡ DC, MC, V. ◯ Jan–Dec. €€

The only hotel in Cagliari right by the beach, 1.5 km (1 mile) from the centre of town.

Hotel Mediterraneo

Road map C6. Lungomare Colombo 46. 📞 070 30 12 71. **FAX** 070 30 12 74. **Rooms:** 140. 🖩 🛏 🍽 📺 🏊 🔧 P 🍴 ⚡ AE, DC, MC, V. ◯ Jan–Dec. €€€

A modern building, just a few minutes' drive from the centre of Cagliari and the provincial roads leading to the coast.

Regina Margherita

Road map C6. Viale Regina Margherita 44. 📞 070 67 03 42. **FAX** 070 66 83 25. **Rooms:** 100. 🖩 🛏 🍽 📺 ⚡ 🔧 P ⚡ AE, DC, MC, V. ◯ Jan–Dec. €€€

Below the Saint Remy ramparts and the Castello quarter, an ideal hotel for those who want to stay near the historic centre of Cagliari.

DOMUS DE MARIA

Chia Laguna

Road map C6. Località Chia Laguna.
📞 070 923 91. **FAX** 070 92 30 141.
Rooms: 315. 🖩 🛏 🍽 📺 🔧 P 🔧 🍴 🏊 ⚡ AE, DC, MC, V. ◯ Jan–Dec. €€€ half board.

A large hotel complex very similar to a holiday village. The Chia Laguna is set in a scenic position overlooking the Chia bay, with one of the best beaches on the coast.

ISOLA DI SAN PIETRO

Hieracon

Road map B6. Località Carloforte, Corso Cavour 63. 📞 0781 85 40 28. **FAX** 0781 85 48 93. **Rooms:** 21; **apartments:** 7. 🖩 🛏 🍽 📺 🔧 🍴 ⚡ AE, DC, MC, V. ◯ Jan–Dec. €€

A villa with a good restaurant. The period rooms are prettier but noisier than those at the back.

ISOLA DI SANT'ANTIOCO

Maladroxia

Road map B6. Località Maladroxia.
📞 0781 800 00 87. **FAX** 0781 830 92.
Rooms: 21. 🛏 🔧 P 🍴 ⚡ AE, MC, V. ◯ Jun–Nov. €€

A big house on the seaside, with wooden furniture, large public rooms and true family hospitality.

PORTOSCUSO

La Ghinghetta

Road map B6. Località Sa Caletta, Via Cavour 28. 📞 0781 50 81 43. **FAX** 0781 50 81 44. **Rooms:** 8. 🖩 🛏 🍽 📺 🔧 🔧 P 🍴 ⚡ AE, DC, MC, V. ◯ May–Nov. €€

This hotel on the beach has charming rooms furnished in different styles and a well-known restaurant with a Michelin star.

SANTA MARGHERITA DI PULA

Flamingo & Mare Pineta

Road map C6. 📞 070 920 83 61. **FAX** 070 920 83 59. **Rooms:** 134; **apartments:** 60. 🖩 🛏 🍽 🔧 P 🔧 ⚡ AE. ◯ May–Oct. €€ half board.

Two hotels with four- and three-star ranking, in Mediterranean style and overlooking a lovely sandy beach.

Is Morus

Road map C6. 📞 070 92 11 71. **FAX** 070 92 15 96. **Rooms:** 85. 🖩 🛏 🍽 📺 🔧 P 🔧 🍴 🏊 ⚡ AE, DC, MC, V. ◯ May–Oct. €€€€ half board.

A luxury hotel on the coast with access to the 18-hole golf course at the nearby Is Molas Hotel, run by the same management.

Forte Village

Road map C6. 📞 070 921 71. **FAX** 070 92 12 46. **Rooms:** 759. 🖩 🛏 🍽 📺 🏊 🔧 P 🔧 🍴 🏊 ⚡ AE, DC, MC, V. ◯ Mar–Oct. €€€€€ half board.

A Hollywood setting and first-class service distinguish the six hotels in this extensive resort. Facilities include a wide range of water sports and a health spa.

TEULADA

Baia delle Ginestre

Road map C6. Località Portu Malu.
📞 070 927 30 05. **FAX** 070 927 30 09. **Rooms:** 100; **villas:** 45. 🖩 🛏 🍽 📺 🔧 P 🍴 🏊 ⚡ AE, DC, MC, V. ◯ Apr–Oct. €€€

A Mediterranean-style holiday village, with small villas and rooms right on the gravel beach of the splendid Teulada coastline.

THE EASTERN COAST

BAUNEI

Santa Maria

Road map D4. Località Santa Maria Navarrese. Via Plammas 30.
📞 0782 61 53 15. **FAX** 0782 61 53 96. **Rooms:** 37. 🛏 📺 ⚡ 🔧 P 🍴 ⚡ AE, DC, MC, V. ◯ Apr–Nov. €€

In the heart of town, only a five-minute walk from the sea, the Santa Maria hotel is also a good starting point for hikes in the Codula di Luna.

BARÌ SARDO

La Torre

Road map D4. Località Torre di Bar.
📞 0782 280 30. **FAX** 0782 295 77.
Rooms: 60. 🖩 🛏 🍽 📺 🔧 🍴 🏊 ⚡ AE, DC, MC, V. ◯ Apr–Oct. €€

A modern, elegant hotel set in a superb location, opposite a 16th-century tower and with the sea directly in front.

DORGALI

Costa Dorada

Road map D3. Località Cala Gonone, Lungomare Palmesera 45. **[** *0784 933 33.* **FAX** *0784 934 45.* **@** htlcosta dorada@tiscalinet.it **Rooms:** *30.* 目 🛏 🍸 📺 📶 🖨 🛎 *AE, MC, V.* ☐ *Apr–Oct.* €€€ *half board.*

A pleasant hotel, designed in a blend of Spanish and Sardinian styles, situated opposite the little beach of Cala Gonone.

MURAVERA

Free Beach Club

Road map D5. Località Costa Rei, Via Ichnusa 25. **[** *070 99 10 41.* **FAX** *070 99 10 54.* **@** gestitour@iol.it **Rooms:** *438.* 目 🛏 🏃 🅿 🍴 ⛱ 🛎 *AE, DC, MC, V.* ☐ *Jun–Nov.* €€ *full board.*

The Free Beach Club is right on the beach, and offers accommodation in charming stone bungalows. There are assorted sporting activities and a baby-sitting service. The hotel makes an extra charge for air-conditioning.

OROSEI

Torre Moresca

Road map D3. Località Cala Ginepro. **[** *0784 912 30.* **FAX** *0784 912 70.* **Rooms:** *210.* 目 🛏 🍸 📺 📶 🏃 🅿 🍴 ⛱ 🛎 *DC, MC.* ☐ *May–Oct.* €€€ *half board.*

Mediterranean-style architecture amid greenery, and only 100 m (330 ft) from the sea. The Club Med-style service offers an assortment of activities and enter-tainment programmes.

TORTOLÌ

Victoria

Road map D4. Via Mons. Virgilio 72. **[** *0782 62 34 57.* **FAX** *0782 62 41 16.* **Rooms:** *60.* 目 🛏 🍸 📺 📶 🏃 🅿 🛎 🍴 🛎 *AE, DC, MC, V.* ☐ *Jan–Dec.* €€

Recent renovation has upgraded this hotel considerably. It has spacious rooms, and an additional bonus is the large terrace where you can enjoy the marvellous views of the coast while having your breakfast.

VILLASIMIUS

Stella Maris

Road map D6. Località Campulongu. **[** *070 79 71 00.* **FAX** *070 79 73 67.* **@** stella.maris@stella.maris.com **Rooms:** *43.* 目 🛏 🍸 📺 📶 🏃 🅿 🛎 🍴 🛎 *AE, DC, MC, V.* ☐ *May–Oct.* €€€ *half board.*

This was once a holiday place for the Jesuits, only 50 m (160 ft) from the beach. The building is now an elegant, modern hotel.

Tanka Village

Road map D6. **[** *070 79 51.* **FAX** *070 79 70 08.* **Apartments:** *968.* 🛏 🏃 🅿 🍴 ⛱ 🛎 *AE, DC, MC, V.* ☐ *May–Oct.* €€€

Situated in a fine location in the midst of greenery, this resort offers the best in facilities. There are different types of accommodation: from independent lodging to the Domus with hotel-type service. Good sports facilities.

CENTRAL SARDINIA AND BARBAGIA

ARITZO

Sa Muvara

Road map C4. Via Funtana Rubia. **[** *0784 62 93 36.* **FAX** *0784 62 94 33.* **Rooms:** *65.* 🛏 📺 📶 🏃 🅿 🛎 🍴 ⛱ 🖨 *AE, MC, V.* ☐ *Apr–Nov.* €€

This is one of the most famous hotels in the Barbagia area, well placed for hikes up Mount Gennargentu and other sports activities such as canoeing and kayaking. There is also an excellent restaurant serving typical Sardinian food.

GAVOI

Gusana

Road map C3. Località Gusana. **[** *0784 530 00.* **FAX** *0784 521 78.* **Rooms:** *35.* 🛏 📺 📶 🏃 🅿 🛎 🍴 ⛱ 🛎 *AE, MC, DC, V.* ☐ *Jan–Dec.* €

This small hotel is situated in a splendid position on Lake Gusana, surrounded by the Barbagia hills, with family hospitality and a good restaurant. Hikes and horseback riding.

NUORO

Fratelli Sacchi

Road map D3. Località Monte Ortobene. **[** *0784 312 00.* **FAX** *0784 340 30.* **Rooms:** *20.* 📺 🏃 🅿 🛎 🍴 🛎 *AE, DC, MC, V.* ☐ *Jan–Dec.*

Only 7 km (4 miles) from Nuoro, the Fratelli Sacchi offers family hospitality. The well-known restaurant serves Barbagia cuisine.

OLIENA

Cooperativa Enis

Road map D3. Località Monte Maccione. **[** *0784 28 83 63.* **FAX** *0784 28 84 73.* **Rooms:** *17.* 🛏 🏃 🅿 🍴 🛎 🖨 ☐ *Jan–Dec.* €

A three-star hotel, terraces with panoramic views and a good restaurant with Barbagia cuisine. Tours of the Gennargentu National Park are also on offer.

Su Gologone

Road map D3. Località Su Gologone. **[** *0784 28 75 12.* **FAX** *0784 28 76 68.* **@** gologone@tin.it. **Rooms:** *70.* 🛏 🍸 📺 🏃 🅿 🍴 🖨 ⛱ 🛎 🛎 *AE, DC, MC, V.* ☐ *Mar–Oct.* €€€

A quiet location, characteristic architecture, fine cuisine and warm hospitality. This is an ideal starting point for a tour of the Supramonte di Oliena.

THE WESTERN COAST

ALGHERO

Porto Conte

Road map B2. Località Porto Conte. **[** *079 94 20 35.* **FAX** *079 94 20 45.* **Rooms:** *148.* 目 🛏 📺 🏃 🅿 🍴 ⛱ 🛎 *AE, DC, MC, V.* ☐ *Apr–Oct.* €€ *full board.* **w** www.hotelporto conte.com

A pleasant, modern hotel over-looking the bay, ideal for a seaside holiday.

Villa Las Tronas

Road map B2. Lungomare Valencia 1. **[** *079 98 18 18.* **FAX** *079 98 10 44.* **Rooms:** *29.* 目 🛏 📺 📶 🏃 🅿 🍴 ⛱ 🛎 *AE, DC, MC, V.* ☐ *Jan–Dec.* €€€

For key to symbols *see p170*

This beautifully restored late 19th-century Art Nouveau villa is in a unique position on a headland overlooking Capo Caccia.

ARBOREA

Ala Birdi

Road map B4. Strada a Mare 24.
[0783 80 10 83. FAX 0783 80 10 86.
@ alabirdi@tiscalinet.it **Rooms:** 58;
villas: 58. 🛏 🗐 📺 📺 📤 🅿
🔣 🔢 🎱 🎱 🎱 AE, DC, MC, V.
🔲 Jan–Dec. €€

A hotel and 58 pretty little villas in a lovely pine forest. The Ala Birdi is well known for its equestrian facilities. The hotel also organizes interesting guided tours.

BOSA

Turas

Road map B3. Località Turas.
[0785 359 23. **Rooms:** 38.
📤 🅿 🔢 🎱 🔲 Jun–Nov. €€

This small hotel with typical 1970s architecture and decor is worth seeking out because of its splendid position at the end of Bosa beach.

CUGLIERI – SANTA CATERINA

La Baja

Road map B3. Località Santa Caterina di Pittinuri 20. [0785 381 05.
FAX 0785 381 05. @ coopsinis@
tiscalinet.it **Rooms:** 35. 📤 📤 🅿
🔢 🎱 🎱 AE, DC, MC, V.
🔲 Jan–Dec. €€

Situated opposite the Torre Spagnola (Spanish tower), with rooms overlooking the bay. Horseback riding, hikes and mountain cycling organized.

ORISTANO

Mistral 2

Road map B4. Via XX Settembre.
[0783 21 03 89. FAX 0783 21 10 00.
Rooms: 132. 🗐 📤 🍽 📺 🎱 📤
🅿 🔣 🔢 🎱 🎱 AE, DC, MC, V.
🔲 Jan–Dec. €€

Only five minutes by car from the central square of Oristano, this well-appointed modern hotel has storeys for non-smokers, a swimming pool and a restaurant on the premises.

STINTINO

Geranio Rosso

Road map B2. Via XXI Aprile 4.
[079 52 32 92. FAX 079 52 32 93.
Rooms: 15. 📤 🗐 📺 🔢 🎱
AE, DC, MC, V. 🔲 Jan–Dec. €€

This tiny hotel with a restaurant attached is in the centre of town, a couple of kilometres from the white Pelosa beaches.

Rocca Ruja

Road map B2. Località Capo Falcone.
[079 52 92 00. FAX 079 52 97 78.
Rooms: 99. 🗐 📤 🍽 📺 🎱 📤
🔣 🔢 🎱 🎱 AE, MC, V.
🔲 May–Oct. €€€ full board.

This modern complex includes a hotel and residence hotel, in a lovely setting facing the rocky island of Asinara.

TRESNURAGHES

Piccolo Hotel

Road map B3. Località Porto Alabe.
[0785 35 90 56. FAX 0785 35 90 80.
Rooms: 20. 📤 🎱 🅿 🔢 🎱 AE,
DC, MC, V. 🔲 Jan–Dec. €€

The Piccolo is a family-run hotel in an enchanting position on the coast. Excellent fish is served.

THE NORTH AND THE COSTA SMERALDA

ARZACHENA

Residenza Capriccioli

Road map D1. Località Capriccioli.
[0789 960 16. FAX 0789 964 43.
Suites: 34. 🗐 📤 📤 🅿 🎱 🎱
AE, DC, MC, V. 🔲 May–Oct. €€

About 100 m (330 ft) from the beach of Capriccioli, one of the best in the Costa Smeralda, the Residenza offers good accommodation at reasonable prices.

Le Ginestre

Road map D1. Località Porto Cervo.
[0789 920 30. FAX 0789 940 87.
@ ginestre@tin.it **Rooms:** 80.
🗐 📤 🍽 📺 📤 🅿 🔢 🎱 🎱 🎱
🎱 AE, DC, MC, V. 🔲 May–Sep.
€€€ half board.

One of the most renowned hotels on the Costa Smeralda. Set in a fantastic position on the Golfo

del Pevero, on pine-clad hills, Le Ginestre offers four-star hospitality and service.

Valdiola

Road map D1. Località Cala di Volpe. [0789 962 15. FAX 0789
966 52. **Rooms:** 33. 🗐 📤 📺 📤
🔣 🅿 🔢 🎱 🎱 AE, DC, MC, V.
🔲 Jan–Dec. €€€

The Valdiola is a well-appointed, pleasant hotel which represents good value for money. An enchanting view, informal atmosphere and good service.

Villaggio Le Magnolie

Road map D1. Località Liscia di Vacca. [0789 95 10 00.
FAX 0789 95 15 15. **Rooms:** 61.
📤 📺 🎱 📤 🅿 🔢 🎱
🎱 AE, DC, MC, V. 🔲 Apr–Oct.
€€€ half board.

The Villaggio consists of three well-run residence hotels and a hotel situated between the scented maquis and the sea. Sports facilities and entertainment for everybody, children included.

La Bisaccia

Road map D1. Località Baia Sardinia. [0789 991 62.
FAX 0789 991 62. **Rooms:** 120.
🗐 📤 🍽 📺 🎱 📤 🅿 🔢 🎱
🎱 AE, DC, V. 🔲 May–Oct.
€€€€ half board.

The Bisaccia is surrounded by maquis vegetation and faces the sea; it includes a four-star hotel and a three-star annexe.

Pitrizza

Road map D1. Località Liscia di Vacca. [0789 93 01 11.
FAX 0789 93 06 11. **Rooms:** 50.
🗐 📤 🍽 📺 🎱 📤 🅿 🔢 🎱
🎱 AE, DC, MC, V. 🔲 May–Oct.
€€€€€ half board.

The most exclusive hotel in Sardinia deserves its worldwide fame. The style, service and simple elegance are worthy of a five-star luxury hotel.

Villaggio Forte Cappellini

Road map D1. Località Baia Sardinia.
[0789 990 57. FAX 0789 990 57.
Rooms: 59. 📤 📤 🔢 🎱 🎱
🎱 AE, DC, V. 🔲 May–Sep.
€€€€ full board.

This classic holiday village is beside the sea and features the usual range of sports activities and entertainments. Children under 15 are not allowed.

Cala di Volpe

Road map D1. Località Cala di Volpe. **☎** 0789 97 61 11.
FAX 0789 97 66 17. **Rooms:** 123.

🖥 🛏 ▼ TV 🏊 🔊 🛆 🅿 🍴
🚠 🅮 AE, DC, MC, V.
⭕ Feb–Oct. €€€€€
full board.

The spectacular architecture of one of the first and most exclusive hotels on the Costa Smeralda was the work of Jacques Couelle. Every luxury is provided.

Romazzino

Road map D1. Località Romazzino.
☎ 0789 97 71 11. **FAX** 0789 97 76 14.
Rooms: 99. 🖥 🛏 ▼ TV 🏊 🔊 🅿
🚠 🍴 🚠 🅮 🅰 AE, DC, MC, V.
⭕ May–Oct. €€€€€ full board.

One of the loveliest buildings in the Costa Smeralda, built in the Neo-Mediterranean style, with fascinating views towards the islands of Soffi and Mortorio.

CASTELSARDO

Hotel Villaggio Pedraladda

Road map C2. Via Zirulia 50.
☎ 079 47 03 83. **FAX** 079 47 04 99.
Rooms: 128. 🛏 🔊 🚠 🅿 🍴 🚠
🅮 DC, MC, V. ⭕ Apr–Oct.
€€ full board.

Only 600 m (0.5 mile) from Castel-sardo, the hotel and residence hotel both have terraces with sweeping views of the sea, tennis courts and a disco. Scuba and skin diving lessons provided.

LA MADDALENA

Cala Lunga

Road map D1. Località Porto Massimo. **☎** 0789 73 40 42.
FAX 0789 73 40 33. **Rooms:** 65.

🖥 🛏 TV 🏊 🚠 🔊 🅮 ▼ 🚠
🅮 AE, DC, MC, V. ⭕ May–Oct.
€€€ half board.

Cala Lunga is situated in a bay which is protected from the west and the mistral winds, and has private coves and a yacht harbour 6 km (4 miles) from the centre of La Maddalena.

Giuseppe Garibaldi

Road map D1. Via Lamarmora.
☎ 0789 73 73 14. **FAX** 0789 73 73 26. **Rooms:** 19. 🖥 🛏 ▼ TV 🔊
🔊 🚠 🅮 AE, DC, MC, V.
⭕ Jan–Dec. €€

This small hotel in the old section of La Maddalena is named after the 19th-century hero. The closest beach is 10 minutes on foot, the furthest half an hour by car.

OLBIA

Sporting

Road map D1 & D2. Località Porto Rotondo. **☎** 0789 340 05.
FAX 0789 343 83. **@** sporthot@tin.it
Rooms: 27. 🛏 ▼ TV 🚠 🅿
🍴 🚠 🅮 AE, DC, MC, V. ⭕ Apr–Oct. €€€€€ half board.
W www.tin.it/hotelsporting

The Sporting hotel has always been a favourite with Porto Rotondo VIPs. It is elegant but informal. All the rooms afford access to the beach.

PALAU

Capo d'Orso

Road map D1. Località Cala Capra. **☎** 0789 70 20 00.
FAX 0789 70 20 09. **Rooms:** 60.

🖥 🛏 ▼ TV 🚠 🅿 🍴 🚠
🅮 AE, DC, MC, V. ⭕ Apr–Oct.
€€€ half board.

A series of small terraced villas in the middle of luxuriant maquis undergrowth and offering a splendid panoramic view.

SAN TEODORO

Due Lune

Road map D2. Località Puntaldia.
☎ 0784 86 40 75. **FAX** 0784 912 70.
Rooms: 59. 🖥 🛏 ▼ TV 🚠 🅿
🅰 🍴 🚠 🅮 AE, DC, MC, V. ⭕
May–Oct. €€€€ half board.

A nine-hole golf course, and the island of Tavolara opposite. This charming complex consists of small villas of granite and stone.

SANTA TERESA DI GALLURA

Grand Hotel Corallaro

Road map C1. Località Rena Bianca.
☎ 0789 75 54 75. **FAX** 0789 75 54 31.
Rooms: 81. 🖥 🛏 ▼ TV 🏊 🔊
🚠 🍴 🚠 🅮 AE, DC, MC, V.
⭕ Apr–Oct. €€ half board.

A four-star hotel that is ideal for those who want a holiday by the sea. It is right in front of you, with Corsica on the horizon.

Hotel Miramare

Road map C1. Piazza della Libertà 6. **☎** 0789 75 41 03.
FAX 0789 75 41 03. **Rooms:** 25.

🖥 🛏 ▼ 🅮 AE, DC, MC, V.
⭕ Mar–mid Dec. €€ full board.

This small family-run hotel is situated only a few meters away from the Aragonese tower. Many of the rooms have a magnificent view, providing glimpses of Corsica on clear days.

Moresco

Road map C1. Via Imbriani 16.
☎ 0789 75 41 88. **FAX** 0789 75 50 85.
Rooms: 45. 🛏 TV 🅿 🍴 🅮
MC, V. ⭕ Apr–Oct. €€ half board.

The Moresco is a charming three-star hotel overlooking the Rena Bianca, the lovely white sandy beach of Santa Teresa, and quite near the central square.

SASSARI

Grazia Deledda

Road map B2. Viale Dante 47.
☎ 079 27 12 35. **FAX** 079 28 08 84.
Rooms: 127. 🖥 🛏 ▼ TV 🔊
🍴 🅿 🅮 🅰 AE, DC, MC, V.
⭕ Jan–Dec. €€

In the heart of town, a short stroll from the Emiciclo Garibaldi gardens, is this modern, comfort-able hotel named after Sardinia's Nobel-prize-winning novelist.

Leonardo da Vinci

Road map B2. Via Roma 79.
☎ 079 28 07 44. **FAX** 079 285 72 33.
@ e.davinci@ssnet.it **Rooms:** 117.

🖥 🛏 ▼ TV 🔊 🚠 🅿 🅮 AE, DC,
MC, V. ⭕ Jan–Dec. €€

A new, elegant bed and breakfast with spacious rooms near the central Piazza Italia, often described as Sassari's "living room". Discounts are offered for weekend stays.

TEMPIO PAUSANIA

Petit

Road map C2. Piazza Alcide de Gasperi 9/11. **☎** 079 63 11 34.
FAX 079 63 17 60. **@** petithotel@ tiscalinet.it **Rooms:** 59. 🖥 🛏 ▼ TV
🚠 🅮 🅰 🅿 🍴 🅮 AE, DC, MC, V.
⭕ Jan–Dec. €€

Modern and quiet, with a splendid view of the main square. The restaurant offers the best in Gallura regional cuisine.

For key to symbols see p170

WHERE TO EAT

THE RELATIVELY RECENT arrival of tourism in Sardinia means that it is an excellent place for appreciating regional variations in cuisine. Fish and seafood fill restaurant menus along the coast, while meat and stuffed pasta are commonly found in the interior. In fact, restaurants that do not serve typical regional dishes are a rarity. The rhythm for mealtimes is Mediterranean, with lunch being served from

Lucia Pennisi and home-made, fresh pasta, Sant'Antioco

1–3pm and the evening meal from 9–10:30pm. In many cases restaurants stay open until 10:30–11pm, especially in summer. Almost all restaurants and trattorias close one day a week and close for a month for annual holidays, so check business hours if you have chosen a particular destination. All the restaurants listed on pages 184–7 have been chosen as among the best in their category.

The Locanda Rosella at Giba, in the Cagliari region

TYPES OF RESTAURANTS

IN TERMS OF price, cuisine and atmosphere, there is not much difference between a restaurant (ristorante) and a trattoria in Sardinia. Even a fairly expensive restaurant may still be decorated in a functional, country style, with simple furniture. The pizzerias are rarely luxurious, but have the advantage of offering decent eating at lower prices. If you can, choose pizzerias with wood-burning ovens; the quality is better. In the summer, refreshment stalls on the beaches sell sandwiches and fish and pasta dishes for those spending the day at the seaside. In general, the bars here do not offer snacks and sandwiches for a quick meal.

PRICES AND PAYING

A THREE-COURSE meal will cost about €15–€30. In top restaurants the bill may add up to €35–€45 euros but

only rarely will it go above €50. In pizzerias you can have a two-course meal with a glass of beer or half-litre of wine for €15–20. The bill always includes a cover charge (coperto or pane e coperto), which varies from €1–€3, and service. It is customary to leave 12–15 per cent of your bill as a tip.

Restaurants are obliged by law to give customers a legal receipt (ricevuta fiscale) when they pay. This must have the name of the establishment and an official "fiscal number"; any other piece of paper is illegal and you are liable to a fine if you leave the restaurant without one, so you have every right to demand a genuine bill. Many restaurants accept major credit cards (such as VISA, MasterCard, American Express and Diners) but, just in case, be prepared to pay in cash, especially when you go to bars, cafés or smaller, family-run establishments.

FIXED-PRICE MENUS

MANY RESTAURANTS offer menus at fixed prices (menù a prezzo fisso or menù turistico). Some prepare a menu of Sardinian specialities once a week, giving you a chance to try regional dishes such as porceddu (suckling pig), which you would otherwise have to order in advance. Upmarket restaurants may offer a special menu called a menù degustazione or menù gastronomico, for a fixed price. This usually gives you the chance to taste five or six house specialities.

CLOSING DAYS

ALL RESTAURANTS close for one day each week, except during the high season (July and August). The closing days for each establishment

Dal Corsaro, one of Cagliari's top restaurants (see p184)

recommended in this guide are clearly shown in the listings on pp184–7. Most places also close for about one month for annual holidays, usually in the winter, except for the restaurants in Cagliari, which are closed in August.

VEGETARIAN FOOD

SARDINIA is not ideal for strict vegetarians. People who eat fish, but not meat, will not have problems along the coast. In the interior the choice may be limited to pasta and soup dishes with fresh bread and cheeses. (However, do not forget that some soup dishes may be prepared with meat stock.)

A thirst-quenching snack of fresh fruit eaten on the beach

RESERVATIONS

RESTAURANTS are often crowded, particularly in the evening and during the summer. Consequently it is advisable to book ahead even in the cheaper establishments, or else arrive fairly early to avoid a long wait.

THE MENU

RESTAURANTS do not always provide a written menu. Where this happens, the waiter will give you a list of the day's dishes at your table and help you to choose. You may wish to begin with an *antipasto*, or appetizer, such as sliced sausage, cured hams or vegetables in oil, artichoke hearts or olives perhaps.

Aperitif time in an Alghero bar

Coastal restaurants offer seafood appetizers (clams, mussels, cuttlefish, baby squid, sea anemones and assorted molluscs). This is followed by the first course *(primo)*, which may consist of soup, pasta, ravioli or, occasionally, a rice dish. The second course *(secondo)* will be meat or fish, and may include the famous *porceddu* (suckling pig). Some first courses, such as *pane frattau* (*carasau* bread in broth) or *fregula* pasta with clams, make substantial meals. The meal ends with cheese, fruit or dessert such as ice cream, with coffee and perhaps a Sardinian liqueur *(see p183)*.

WINE AND DRINKS

MOST RESTAURANTS, even those in the medium-price range, stock a good selection of regional wines and liqueurs *(see pp182–3)*. Some may offer non-Sardinian wines. Almost all restaurants provide house wine.

CHILDREN

CHILDREN are welcome in restaurants, especially family-run ones, where it is easier to prepare special dishes or half portions.

SMOKING

FEW RESTAURANTS in Sardinia take a very rigid line on smoking – non-smoking areas in restaurants are quite rare.

WHEELCHAIR ACCESS

ONLY A FEW restaurants in Sardinia are equipped to deal with the disabled (with ramps and toilet facilities). However, few restaurants have steps, and access is not normally a problem. It is a good idea to call the restaurant beforehand to ensure an easily accessible table and assistance when you arrive.

USING THE LISTINGS

Key to the symbols in the listings on pages 184–7.

🍴 fixed-price menu
🍷 good wine list
♿ wheelchair access
🚭 non-smoking area
🌂 outdoor tables
V vegetarian dishes
🚼 children's portions
🗐 air-conditioning
⚫ closed

🖪 credit cards accepted
AE American Express
MC MasterCard
DC Diners Club
V VISA

Average prices for a three-course meal for one, including half a bottle of wine, cover charge, taxes and service.

€ under €20
€€ €20–30
€€€ €30–40
€€€€ €40–50
€€€€€ over €50.

What to Eat in Sardinia

Sospiri pastries

Despite the fact that Sardinia is surrounded by water, the island's most famous dish is *porceddu*, suckling pig roasted over an open fire until it is tender and the skin crispy. It is often served on traditional cork trays strewn with myrtle leaves, on a layer of *carasau* bread. Meat roasted on the spit is still a classic dish for celebrations such as feast days, or religious festivals. Lamb and mutton also feature strongly in the island's cuisine, and Sardinia's best-known cheese is pecorino, made from sheep's milk. Pasta is often hand-made, and comes in a variety of forms, including the stuffed pasta called *culungiones* (ravioli). Fish and seafood are eaten along the coast, and Spanish influences are still evident in the cooking of the west, where lobster *alla catalana* can be found.

Malloreddus *are gnocchi (like dumplings), served with fresh tomato sauce and minced sausage, flavoured with saffron.*

Carasau bread

Coccoi bread

Savoy biscuits

Pan di sapa

Papassinos　　Almond pastries　　Pardulas　　Amarettus

BREAD AND PASTRIES

There are countless different types of bread in Sardinia, from fat loaves to thin crispy circles. Perhaps the most famous is *carasau*, baked in a very thin, round layer. Pastries and cakes are usually made with flour, honey and almonds, and vary from one village to the next.

Zuppa gallurese *is a soup made of dried durum wheat bread, stock and grated pecorino cheese, baked in the oven.*

Fregula *(or* fregola*) is a granular pasta, similar to couscous. It is served with clams, like pasta, or in broth as a soup.*

Succu *is* fregula *(like couscous) simmered in mutton stock and flavoured with saffron and pecorino cheese.*

Culungiones *are large ravioli stuffed with potato purée, egg yolk, mint, onion and a little cheese, served with tomatoes or meat sauce.*

Pane Frattau *is made with* carasau *bread rounds, softened in stock and flavoured with pecorino cheese, tomato sauce and eggs.*

Cordula *is a plait formed from lamb entrails, rolled onto a skewer and roasted on a spit.*

Porceddu *is traditionally roasted for celebrations. A young suckling pig weighing about 4 kilos (9 lbs) is spit-roasted over a fire and basted at intervals with melted lard.*

Stufato di capretto *is a rich casserole made with kid goat, wine, artichokes and saffron. Sometimes eggs are added to make a kind of fricassée.*

Buccinis *(a type of mollusc)* and arselle *(clams), are often served as antipasti (appetizers).*

Burrida *is cooked fish, marinaded in garlic, parsley, hazelnuts and vinegar for a day. There are many variations.*

Catalan lobster *is a typical speciality of Alghero. The lobster is served with a vinaigrette sauce made from lobster juices and egg, blended with a dash of olive oil and lemon.*

Seadas *(or* sebadas*) are fritters, stuffed with cheese and lemon peel, then fried. They are eaten with plenty of Sardinian honey.*

Pecorino

Ricotta

Fiore sardo

SARDINIAN CHEESES

Sardinian sheep or goat's cheese is either served newly made and fresh *(caprino, fiore sardo)* or mature (pecorino, *canestrato*). Ricotta (sheep's milk) is always soft and creamy.

Pardulas *(also known as* casadinas*) are fresh cheese pastries, flavoured with saffron, vanilla and lemon or orange peel.*

What to Drink in Sardinia

GRAPEVINES FIRST CAME to Sardinia from the eastern Mediterranean, where the Phoenicians had long cultivated vineyards. The warm climate tends to yield very ripe grapes, which are then turned into strong, deeply-coloured wines, often used for blending. Today the general quality of Sardinian wines is rising rapidly, with better viticultural practices, more careful selection in the vineyard and better hygiene in the winery. All types are made, from red *(rosso)*, white *(bianco)* and rosé *(rosato)* to rich dessert wines. Many qualify for the status of *denominazione di origine controllata* (DOC), with guaranteed provenance and quality standards. Sardinian wines are almost always made from a single grape variety. Perhaps the best-known is Vernaccia di Oristano, the first to gain DOC in Sardinia.

Old winemaking equipment

Vernaccia

Slightly sparkling Sinis

Grape harvesting

Nieddera rosé and Cannonau

RECOMMENDED WHITES

- **Cantina Sociale della Riforma Agraria, Alghero**
  Vermentino di Sardegna
  Aragosta
- **Cantina Sociale Gallura**
  Vermentino
- **Tenuta Sella & Mosca, Alghero**
  Terre Bianche

WHITE WINES

THE WHITE WINES of Sardinia go well with fish and seafood dishes, and some are sturdy enough to go with meat dishes such as pork. Nuragus is a widely planted white grape, producing rather neutral, soft and fruity wines. Vermentino is also widely grown and the wines have more complex flavours. Both Vermentino di Sardegna and Vermentino di Gallura, made mostly around Sassari and Nuoro province, tend to be fairly strong. There is also a sparkling version. DOC Vermentino from Cala Viola and Usini is very good. The Campidano area produces the fruity, dry white Semidano.

RED WINES

THE MOST WELL-KNOWN red wine is Cannonau, which is usually full-bodied and strong, although some lighter versions are made. Most Cannonau is produced in the province of Nuoro in eastern Sardinia. It goes well with roast meat and game. Another wine to drink with game and mature cheese is Monica di Sardegna, a dry red with intense perfume that should be drunk while still young. Less common but equally good DOC reds are the light, dry Mandrolisai, Campidano di Terralba and Carignano del Sulcis. Other reds, such as Tanca Farrà di Alghero and Terre Brune del Sulcis are blends of native Sardinian and imported grape varieties.

Cannonau grapes

RECOMMENDED REDS

- **Azienda Giuseppe Cabras, Nuoro**
  Cannonau
- **Tenuta Sella & Mosca, Alghero**
  Anghelu Ruju
- **Attilio Contini, Cabras**
  Nieddera

DESSERT WINES

SARDINIA produces a number of sweet dessert wines, both white and red. Besides mature white Vernaccia and sweet red Cannonau, there is Moscato di Sardegna, made from Muscat grapes and bottled at three years old. It is sweet but has good acidity, and an alcoholic content of 15°. Tempio Pausania Muscat tends to be lightly fizzy, while the Cagliari version is strong and sweet. The red Girò di Cagliari and amber-coloured Nasco are also strong and sweet. Two dessert wines made from semi-dried grapes come from the Alghero region: Torbato and Anghelu Ruju, both produced with Cannonau grapes. The Bosa and Cagliari Malvasia wines are similar to Vernaccia.

Sparkling Vernaccia

Malvasia di Bosa

Cantina Sociale della Vernaccia at Oristano

Vernaccia grapes

Malvasia grapes

Moscato grapes

Harvesting black grapes from Cannonau vines

RECOMMENDED DESSERT WINES

- *Centro Enologico Sardo, Villacidro*
  Malvasia
- *Centro Enologico Sardo, Villacidro*
  Moscato Dolce (Muscat)
- *Fratelli Serra, Zeddiani*
  Vernaccia
- *Meloni Vini, Selargius*
  Malvasia di Cagliari
  Cantina Sociale Dolianova
  Moscato di Cagliari

DIGESTIVI

THE BEST-KNOWN spirit in Sardinia is *abbardiente* (named from the Spanish *aguardiente*), a *grappa* or eau-de-vie. Among the best are made from the strong-tasting Cannonau and the more delicate Malvasia. Grappa here is also called *fil'e ferru* (wire), from the wire used to mark hiding places for illegally produced grappa. Grappa flavoured with wild fennel, juniper and thistle is a relatively new style. The most famous liqueur, however, is Mirto, both red and white, made with wild myrtle leaves and berries. The Sardinians' favourite is Zedda Piras.

Cork-covered bottles with characteristic decorative motifs

CAGLIARI AND THE SOUTH

ASSEMINI

Su Zaffaranu

Road map C5. Via Coghinas 1.
📞 070 94 11 46. 🔲 V 🔲 🔲 🔲
⬤ Mon, Christmas, 1 Jan.
💳 AE, MC, V. €€

On state road SS130 connecting Cagliari and Iglesias, 5 km (3 miles) from the airport and 10 km (6 miles) from the centre of Cagliari, this fish restaurant features mussels with spring vegetables, crayfish tails with rocket, pasta with artichokes and salted mullet roe, gilthead bream with Vernaccia or baked in salt, *seadas* and fresh cheeses.

BARUMINI

Su Nuraxi

Road map C4. Provincial road (SP).
📞 070 93 68 305. 🔲 🔲 🔲 V
🔲 🔲 🔲 ⬤ Tue in winter.
💳 DC, MC, V. €€

Handy because of its proximity to the *nuraghi* and the new mineral museum. Typical home-made dishes are on offer such as *porceddu, fregula* with sauce or clams. Parking for caravans.

CAGLIARI

Antica Hostaria

Road map C6. Via Cavour, 60.
📞 070 66 58 70. 🔲 V 🔲
⬤ Sun, Aug, Christmas, 1 Jan.
💳 AE, DC, MC, V. €€

This small, cosy place is on the ground floor of an old building. The specialities are seasonal: risotto with radicchio, pappardelle (wide noodles) with salmon and prawns, spaghetti with clams and *bottarga* (dried mullet roe), salad of porcini and ovoli mushrooms, game and fish.

Lillicu

Road map C6. Via Sardegna 78.
📞 070 65 29 70. 🔲 🔲 🔲 🔲
⬤ Sun, 10 Aug–1 Sep. 💳 AE, DC,
MC, V. €€

Lillicu, in the alley behind Via Roma, is furnished with white marble tables. The specialities are fish dishes: dogfish (marinated in garlic, nuts, vinegar and fish liver), fish soup and sea anemone.

Saint Remy

Road map C6. Via Torino 6.
📞 070 65 73 77. 🔲 V 🔲 🔲
⬤ Mon lunch and Sun, various other times. 💳 AE, DC, MC, V. €€

Occupying a 17th-century monastery, Saint Remy has a special atmosphere. Food is carefully prepared: ravioli with ricotta, saffron and orange, *fregula* with mussels, lamb with artichokes or mushrooms, squid with herbs and potatoes, fish with Vernaccia.

Dal Corsaro

Road map C6. Viale Regina Margherita 28. 📞 070 66 43 18.
🔲 🔲 V 🔲 🔲 🔲 ⬤ Sun, Aug,
Christmas. 💳 AE, DC, MC, V.
€€€

Dal Corsaro is one of the best restaurants in Sardinia. The menu features squid salad with French beans and balsamic vinegar, fish-stuffed ravioli with fresh tomatoes, clams and prawns, fillet of sea bass with saffron and potatoes.

CALASETTA

Da Pasqualino

Road map B6. Via Roma 99.
📞 0781 884 73. 🔲 🔲 🔲
⬤ after 10pm, Tue in winter, Nov.
💳 AE, MC, V. €€

Fish is the speciality here: fish soup with gurnard, scorpion fish, moray eel, squid, shellfish, as well as mixed fish, grilled or pan-fried.

CARLOFORTE

Al Tonno di Corsa

Road map B6. Via G Marconi 47.
📞 0781 85 51 06. 🔲 V 🔲 🔲
⬤ Mon, 23 Dec–23 Jan.
💳 AE, MC, V. €€

In the old part of town, on the hill behind the seafront, Al Tonno offers such typical local fare as couscous, *musciame* (sun-dried dolphin) and above all a varied selection of tuna *(tonno)* dishes.

Da Nicola

Road map B6. Via Dante 46 (winter) Corso Cavour 32 (summer). 📞 0781 85 40 48. 🔲 🔲 🔲 🔲 🔲
⬤ Mon in winter, Dec–Jan.
💳 AE, DC, MC, V. €€

Da Nicola moves to the seafront in summer. The cooking is a blend of Arab and Ligurian: couscous with vegetables, veal and beef, lobster, tuna, swordfish and crayfish.

IGLESIAS

Villa di Chiesa

Road map B5. Piazza Municipio 9/10.
📞 0781 231 24. 🔲 🔲 🔲
⬤ Mon, except in Aug. 💳 V. €€

This fish restaurant in a medieval square offers delectable dishes such as spaghetti with salted mullet roe and clams, and also many meat and game specialities.

THE EASTERN COAST

ARBATAX

Del Porto

Road map D4. Via Bellavista 14.
📞 0782 66 72 26. 🔲 🔲 🔲 V 🔲
⬤ Dec–Mar. 💳 DC, MC, V. €€

On the quay, 100 m (330 ft) from the seafront, Del Porto focuses on fresh fish and features fish risotto, *culungiones* and *burrida* (marinated skate).

BAUNEI

Golgo

Road map D4. Località San Pietro.
📞 0337 81 18 28. 🔲 🔲 🔲 🔲
🔲 🔲 ⬤ Oct–Easter. €€

A typical stone construction in the open country serving characteristic Sardinian dishes: from *pane frattau* with suckling pig to macaroons with almond paste.

DORGALI

Colibrì

Road map D3. Via A Gramsci 15.
📞 0784 960 54. 🔲 🔲 🔲
⬤ Oct–Easter. €€

This modern restaurant offers typical Barbagia cuisine such as *pane frattau, maccarones furriaos* (baked macaroni), roast suckling pig, mutton with herbs.

OROSEI

Su Barchile

Road map D3. Via Mannu 5.
📞 0784 988 79. @ subarchile@
tiscalinet.net 🔲 🔲 🔲 V 🔲 🔲
💳 AE, DC, MC, V. €€€

In the old town. In the summer you can eat in the terrace garden: home-made bucatini pasta with shellfish, fish ravioli and seafood risotto as well as meat dishes.

POSADA

Sa Rocca

Road map D2. Piazza Eleonora d'Arborea 30. 0784 85 41 66. ⛪ V ⬚ ● *Mon in winter, Easter, Nov.* AE. €€

This restaurant lies below the castle with a view of the sea (only 1 km away). Classic Sardinian fare such as ravioli, gnocchi with clams, mixed grilled fish, grilled veal chops and, if you ring in advance, suckling pig and lobster.

TORTOLÌ

Da Lenin

Road map D4. Via San Gemiliano 19. 0782 62 44 22. ⬚ ● *after 10pm, Sun, 20 Dec–20 Jan.* AE, DC, MC, V. €€

Excellent fish specialities as well as classic meat dishes. Ravioli with *bottarga*, black tagliatelle with salmon, grilled fish and, in the autumn, gilthead bream baked in foil with porcini mushrooms.

VILLASIMIUS

Carbonara

Road map D6. Via Umberto I 60. 070 79 12 70. ⬚ V ⬚ ● *variable, Wed in winter.* AE, DC, MC, V. €

Risotto *alla corsara* with shellfish, spaghetti with clams and *bottarga*, and ravioli with Vernaccia are the house specialities at Carbonara.

CENTRAL SARDINIA AND BARBAGIA

ARITZO

Sa Muvara

Road map C4. Via Fontana Rubia 35. 0784 62 93 36. **FAX** 0784 42 94 23. 🍴 ⛪ ⬚ V ⬚ ● *10pm, Dec–Easter.* AE, DC, MC, V. €€

Good basic Barbagia food: risotto with chestnuts, pasticcio *all' aritzese* (strudel with potatoes,

mushrooms, ham and fresh tomatoes), aromatic herb soups, sausages made on the premises and roast meat dishes.

FONNI

Miramontes

Road map D3. Via Pruncuspina. 0784 573 11. 🍴 ⛪ V ⬚ ● *Wed, Oct.*

One km (half a mile) from Fonni, on the road to Montespada, this country restaurant offers typical fare: ravioli, *malloreddus, pane frattau*, barbecued suckling pig and lamb, and their own sausages, made on the premises.

GAVOI

Gusana

Road map C3. Gusana. 0784 53 000. ⛪ ⬚ ▤ ● *Mon.* AE, DC, MC, V. €

A true selection of Barbagia cuisine, based on the staple of *purpuzza* (sausage meat): home-made gnocchi and ravioli with meat sauce, plus eel and trout.

NUORO

Canne al Vento

Road map D3. Viale Repubblica 66. 0784 20 17 62. V ⬚ ▤ ● *Sun, 10 days in Aug, Christmas.* AE, DC, MC, V. €€

This restaurant in the centre features Barbagia dishes: *mallor-eddus*, boar, mutton, horse meat and suckling pig, as well as grilled, salted or wine-marinated fish.

Da Giovanni

Road map D3. Via IV Novembre 9. 0784 305 62. 🍴 ⬚ V ⬚ ● *Sun.* AE, MC, V. €

Da Giovanni is in the heart of town and offers the typical Nuoro soup, *filindeu* (plaited pasta simmered in mutton stock), fettuccine ribbon noodles with a sauce of wild boar meat, stewed wild boar and baked fish.

OLIENA

Su Gologone

Road map D3. Località Su Gologone. 0784 28 75 12. @ gologone@tin.it 🍴 ⛪ ⬚ V ⬚ ▤ ● *Nov.* AE, DC, MC, V. €€€

Su Gologone is 12 km (7 miles) from Nuoro, surrounded by greenery, and is known for its typical meat dishes: roast suckling pig, lamb and goat, as well as *pane frattau*, ravioli, *malloreddus* and *seadas* with honey.

ORGOSOLO

Ai Monti del Gennargentu

Road map D3. Settiles. 0784 40 23 74. 🍴 ⛪ V ⬚ €€

This restaurant in the countryside, 6 km (4 miles) from Orgosolo, has its own organic fruit orchard and kitchen garden. Among the many typical dishes are vegetable and ham soup and home-made pasta and tangy sheep's milk cheese.

THE WESTERN COAST

ALGHERO

Al Tuguri

Road map B2. Via Maiorca 113. 079 97 67 72. 🍴 ⬚ V ⬚ ▤ ● *Sun, 20 Dec–20 Jan.* MC, V. €€

This restaurant occupies three floors in a charming, rebuilt 15th-century building. The menu is seasonal: mussels and broad beans, fresh pasta with sea urchins, Majorca-style fish, onion soup with eggs.

Rafel

Road map B2. Via Lido 20. 079 95 03 85. @ rafel@tiscalinet.it ⬚ ⬚ ▤ ● *Thu in winter, 20 Dec–20 Jan.* AE, DC, MC, V. €€

At Rafel's first courses are cooked while you wait: fresh sauces flavoured with clams, sea urchin roe (in winter), and crab meat. Fish soup upon request. The fish on the menu varies according to the day's catch. House desserts include the special sorbets with fruit-of-the-season flavours, from lemon to strawberry and peach.

La Lepanto

Road map B2. Via Carlo Alberto 135. 079 97 91 16. ⬚ ⛪ ⬚ V ⬚ ○ *until late.* ● *Mon in winter.* AE, DC, MC, V. €€€

This restaurant is in the old town, with verandas overlooking the sea. The menu is mainly fish, often traditionally presented: lobster, spaghetti Alghero-style, pasta with aubergines and crayfish.

BOSA

Tatore

Road map B3. Via IV Novembre.
📞 0785 37 31 04. 🍴 🛇 🔽 👥
🍽 🛇 Wed. €€€

Tatore offers mostly fish dishes: spaghetti *allo scoglio* with shellfish, risotto with seafood, fish soup, mixed grilled or fried fish.

CABRAS

Sa Funtà

Road map B4. Via Garibaldi 25.
📞 0783 29 06 85. 🛇 🛇 ▼ 👥
🛇 Sun, Jan, Feb. €€€

A small, elegant establishment in Oristano tradition: soup with herbs (in winter), *bottarga* (dried mullet roe) as a first course, *burrida* (fish in spicy sauce), or fresh mullet.

CUGLIERI

Meridiana

Road map B3. Via Littorio 1.
📞 0785 394 00. 🍴 🛇 🛇 👥
📄 🛇 Mon, Thu, Jan. 💳 AE, DC, MC, V. €€€

A range of fish specials: crayfish and mushroom salad, fried squid with courgettes, sea urchins on toasted bread, *bottarga* and figs, swordfish risotto, clam and mussel soup. Booking is advised.

GHILARZA

Al Marchi

Road map C3. Via Concezione 4.
📞 0785 522 80. 🛇 🛇 🛇 ▼ 👥
📄 🛇 Mon, two weeks in Jan.
💳 AE, DC, MC, V. €€€

In the heart of town. Traditional island appetizers, followed by raviolini with a light tomato sauce, porcini mushrooms, mutton baked in foil, grilled meat in wine sauce.

ORISTANO

Da Gino

Road map B4. Via Tirso 13.
📞 0783 714 28. 🛇 👥 📄
🛇 Sun, from mid-Aug to early Sep.
💳 MC, V. €€

In a characteristic building in the heart of Oristano, which has been completely restored, you can enjoy pasta with sea urchins or sea anemones, Gino's special lobster, and various game dishes.

Da Giovanni

Road map B4. Via Colombo 8.
📞 0783 220 51. 🍴 🛇 🛇 🔽
👥 🛇 Mon. 💳 DC, MC, V. €€

The owner exhorts people to enjoy "fish, fish and more fish". It comes straight off the boat, and quickly arrives on the table. Seafood sauce, spaghetti with sea urchins and *bottarga*, barbecued squid, bass with Vernaccia, stewed cuttlefish with peas, gilthead, bream, dentex and lobster.

Il Faro

Road map B4. Via Bellini 25.
📞 0783 30 08 61. 🍴 🛇 ▼ 🛇
🔽 👥 📄 🛇 after 10pm, Sun eve (all day in summer), 20 Dec –10 Jan, 2 weeks in Jul. 💳 AE, DC, V. €€€

Il Faro is well-known for its traditional cuisine and seasonal fish: mullet, sea bass, gilthead bream, as well as ravioli with ricotta cheese and asparagus tips and Sardinian desserts.

PORTO TORRES

Li Lioni

Road map B2. SS131, Località Li Lioni. 📞 079 50 22 86. @ lilioni@tiscalinet.it 🛇 🔽 🛇 ▼ 👥 🅿
🛇 after 10pm, Wed, Nov.
💳 AE, DC, MC, V. €€

In the countryside, 3 km (2 miles) from Porto Torres, Li Lioni is in a rustic setting with a large garden. All the meat dishes are cooked over an open fire in the fireplace. Try the macaroni with wild boar or mutton sauce, *culungiones*, and barbecued veal kebabs.

STINTINO

Silvestrino

Road map B2. Via Sassari 12.
📞 079 52 30 07. @ albergo-silvestrino@tin.it 🍴 🛇 🛇 🔽 ▼
👥 🛇 after 10pm in winter; Thu, Nov–Apr. 💳 AE, MC, V. €€

In the centre of Stintino, on the ground floor of a hotel, Silvestrino boasts a family atmosphere and more than 50 years of customer appreciation for its special lobster soup, grilled fish and prize-winning *baci alla Silvestrino*: oven-baked cheese croquettes topped with bechamel and tomatoes.

THE NORTH AND THE COSTA SMERALDA

ARZACHENA

Grazia Deledda

Road map D1. Road to Baia Sardinia.
📞 0789 989 90. FAX 0789 989 88.
🛇 ▼ 🍴 👥 📄 🛇 🛇 Nov–Apr. 💳 AE, DC, MC, V. €€€€€

Overlooking the beautiful bay of Cannigione, this restaurant is furnished with rare examples of Sardinian handicrafts. The cooking is sophisticated and includes soup of ovoli and porcini mushrooms, and *moscardini* (octopus) with Vermentino. Highish prices but the seafood is always super fresh.

Tiana

Road map D1. Località Tiana, road to Palau. 📞 0789 821 95. 🛇 🔽 🛇 🛇
👥 📄 💳 AE, DC, MC, V. €€

Varied seafood appetizers, spaghetti with lobster, mixed grilled and fried fish, baked dentex with shellfish, but above all specialities of the Gallura region. Tiana is only 2 km (1 mile) from the Costa Smeralda crowds.

CASTELSARDO

Fofò

Road map C2. Lungomare Anglona 1.
📞 079 47 01 43. @ hfofo@tin.it
🍴 🛇 🛇 🛇 👥 🛇 Wed.
💳 AE, DC, MC, V. €€

Lobsters from the nearby fish farm are prepared according to various recipes, such as Aragonese lobster soup. An alternative is risotto *alla corsara* with shellfish. If you order beforehand you can also have suckling pig or lamb.

LOIRI–PORTO SAN PAOLO

Cala Junco

Road map D2. Viale Pietro Nenni 8/10. 📞 0789 402 60. 🍴 🛇 🛇
▼ 👥 📄 🛇 Tue in winter, 15 days in Jan. 💳 AE, DC, MC, V. €€

Cala Junca is by the sea, only 20 minutes from Olbia, and offers fish as well as many other traditional dishes. Among the first courses are soups such as *zuppa gallurese* and *minestra della nonna* with chard, and home-made pasta such as tagliatelle with mushrooms and mushroom sauce. Other choices include *mazzamurro* (a kind of flan made with bread soaked in milk, pecorino cheese and tomatoes), *fregula* with mussels, *pane frattau* and lobster.

OLBIA

Bacchus 2

Road map D2. Via G D'Annunzio (Centro Martini). 0789 216 12. V Sun during winter, Nov. AE, DC, MC, V. €€

Bacchus has antipasti with original combinations of vegetables and fish, *culurgiones* stuffed with cheese and mint, rolled parcels of fillet of beef with smoked ham, stuffed squid and a selection of special desserts.

Gallura

Road map D2. Corso Umberto 145. 0789 246 48. V 20 Dec–6 Jan. AE, DC, MC, V. €€€€€

Creativity is the key word here, beginning with the pasta (with sage, carrot or saffron) and the delectable sauces (courgette flowers and mussels). Main courses include all sorts of meat and fish dishes, and the desserts are delicious.

PALAU

Il Porticciolo

Road map D1. Piazza del Comune. 0789 70 85 98. Mon. MC, V. €€

This is a small, family-run trattoria, with a daily-changing menu, and choices dependent on the local market. Simple, good cooking, with both fish and meat on offer. The *astice alla catalana* (Catalan-style lobster) in particular is recommended. From the desserts, try the excellent tiramisù.

Zio Nicola

Road map D1. Porticciolo Turistico. 0789 70 85 20. V Wed in winter. AE, DC, MC, V. €€

Located in the port, this restaurant is run with great professionalism. The menu includes a range of meat and fish, grilled or panfried, prepared simply and with great care. There are plenty of tables outside in a large, tree-shaded garden. Rapid, good service.

La Gritta

Road map D1. I Faraglioni di Porto Faro. 0789 70 80 45. 15 Oct–15 Mar. AE, DC, MC, V. €€€€

One of Sardinia's top restaurants, with a large covered terrace overlooking the bay of Porto Rafael. Among many delicacies are stuffed squid with saffron sauce, linguine with delicate fish sauce and fish with potatoes and olives. Excellent wine list, including the grappas.

PORTO CERVO

Gianni Pedrinelli

Road map D1. Località Piccolo Pevero. 0789 924 36. V lunchtime except Sat and Sun, Nov. AE, DC, MC, V. €€

Fregula with mussels, fresh tomatoes and clams, pasta with lobster, home-made gnocchi, fish in salt, and grilled suckling pig are the specials at Pedrinelli.

PORTO ROTONDO

Il Baretto

Road map D1. Piazzetta Rudalza. 0789 340 18. Oct–Easter. AE, DC, MC, V. €€€

As this is a summer restaurant, most tables are outside, but there is also an air-conditioned room. Specials are first courses such as fresh fish or ricotta ravioli and seafood risotto, followed by fish cooked in foil and suckling pig.

SASSARI

L'Assassino

Road map B2. Vicolo Ospizio Cappuccini 1B. 079 23 50 41. Sun. AE, DC, MC, V. €

A typical Sassarese restaurant offering all kinds of meat dishes (including lamb, pork and horse) and, in the winter, lamb's feet with herbs or various sauces.

Gianni e Amedeo

Road map B2. Via Alghero 69. 079 27 45 98. V Sun, 15 days in Aug, 15 days at Christmas. AE, DC, MC, V. €€€

Furnished in rustic style, but the cooking is high quality in the best

tradition of fish and seafood cookery. Classic dishes like *gnocchetti* or Sardinian ravioli with *pecorino*, mint and potato. To round off a delicious meal, try the *seadas* with a glass or two of Mirto (myrtle) liqueur.

SAN TEODORO

La Columbella

Road map D2. Piazzetta di Puntaldia. 0784 86 41 76. V Sun eve, Mon in winter. AE, DC, MC, V. €€€€

This restaurant has a terrace overlooking the sea, and offers elegant cuisine and atmosphere, featuring 50 dishes, mostly fish, from roast skate with raisins to seafood pesto sauce for the home-made pasta.

SANTA TERESA DI GALLURA

Canne al Vento

Road map C1. Via Nazionale 23. 0789 75 42 19. lunch, after 10pm, Mon, 30 Sep–1 Apr. MC, V. €€

A family-run restaurant serving characteristic Sardinian dishes such as *zuppa cuata* soup with bread, cheeses and mutton stock, lemon-flavoured ravioli and mutton with herbs.

Riva

Road map C1. Via del Porto 29. 0789 75 43 92. AE, DC, MC, V. €€€

Only 200 m (650 ft) from the port, Riva was destined to be a fish restaurant, but in the summer it also has suckling pig, *pane frattau* and *malloreddus*. The specialities are seafood risotto, razor-clam and mussel soup, fish ravioli, spaghetti with crab, and gilthead bream with Vermentino or Torbato wine.

TEMPIO PAUSANIA

Il Pizzicotto

Road map C2. Via Gramsci, 37. 079 67 04 77. V Fri. €

Simple rustic cuisine: *zuppa gallurese* made with durum wheat bread, cheeses and meat stock, home-made gnocchi, *seadas* and a range of different kinds of pizza and flat bread.

Shops and Markets

Sardinia produces a great variety of handicrafts that are hard to find in other regions of Italy. Among these are hand-woven rugs, linen napkins, *pibbiones* (embroidered fabrics) and baskets. Traditional materials and techniques are used for all these products, and while some are still made in the traditional style, others have been adapted to more modern tastes. Crafted goods are often made to a very

Local olives

high standard of design and workmanship, and include coral and filigree pins and brooches, pottery and crockery, and items made from cork and wrought iron.

In the larger towns and tourist resorts, traditional souvenirs are sold, such as ashtrays in the shape of nuraghi, costumed dolls and seashell pictures. Specialities such as pecorino cheese, salted mullet roe, sweets and wine are also worth trying.

OPENING HOURS

Shops in sardinia generally open in the morning at 9am and close at 1pm for lunch. Afternoon hours are 4–8pm (4:30–8:30pm in the summer). In the cities most shops close for two or three weeks in August while, on the coast, they tend to open on a seasonal basis, from June to September.

A potter at the wheel

HOW TO PAY

The majority of the larger shops and department stores accept credit cards, but it is advisable to check in advance. The smaller shops and artisan's workshops will generally prefer payment in cash. You must get a receipt (*ricevuta fiscale*) when you pay; it is required by law and you may be asked to produce it as you leave the shop. It will also be needed should you want to change purchased articles later on.

DEPARTMENT STORES

The main department store in Cagliari is **La Rinascente** in Via Roma. Other large stores are **Upim** and **Standa**, which you will also find in other Sardinian towns and cities. Recently, large shopping centres have grown up on the outskirts of towns, with a wide selection of goods on offer, from shoe shops and clothing stores to supermarkets and fast food restaurants.

HANDICRAFTS

Local handicrafts are on sale all over Sardinia. In the villages, women display their wares, such as baskets, rugs or ceramics, outside their homes.

Shops that belong to the *Istituto Sardo Organizzazione Lavoro Artigianale* (**ISOLA**), Sardinian Institute of Handicrafts, offer quality products from the local craftsmen's cooperatives, including rugs, tablecloths, leather, jewellery, baskets, pottery, carved wood

Local handicrafts for sale in a certified ISOLA shop

and wrought-iron objects. All ISOLA products carry a seal of quality guaranteeing their origin and authenticity.

You can find good bargains at the *Fiera del Tappeto* (Carpet Fair), held at Mogoro in late July–August. Handicrafts can also be purchased at holiday farms. Other useful addresses can be found in the Esit publication *Sardegna – Un Mare di Tradizioni*.

A fish stall in Cagliari's covered market, San Benedetto

REGIONAL SPECIALITIES

Gastronomic specialities in Sardinia are sold in the food section of supermarkets as well as in delicatessens and specialist shops or directly from the producers.

The **Mercato Coperto di San Benedetto**, an indoor market in Cagliari, offers an excellent choice of regional delicacies. *Bottarga* (mullet roe) can be bought at **Vaghi**, on Via Bayle, which also sells sea urchin pâté. Salted *bottarga* can be bought directly from the manufacturer at **Fratelli**

San Francesco's feast day celebrated at Lula with barbecued *porceddu*

A dish of typical Sardinian honey

Manca in Cabras. Smoked fish is on sale at **Sarda Affumicati** in Buggerru.

Cakes and sweets are also a Sardinian speciality and a fine selection is on offer in several shops, including **Sorelle Piccioni** in Quartu Sant'Elena, **Colomba Codias** in Olbia and **Acciari** at Porto Torres.

A visit to a winery *(cantina)* to taste the wines before buying can prove both interesting and good value. It is sometimes possible to taste wines in a wine shop *(enoteca)*.

Other useful addresses of shops and workshops are listed in the publication by Esit, *Sardegna – Un Mare di Delizie.*

DIRECTORY

HANDICRAFTS

Alghero
Centro Forme
Via Lamarmora 64.
079 97 53 52.

Cagliari
ISOLA
Via Bacaredda 176–8.
070 40 07 07.

Nuoro
ISOLA
Via Monsignor Bua 10.
0784 335 81.

Olbia
Sardartis srl
SS125, km 313.
0789 669 33.

Cerasarda
Road for Palau, km 2,800.
0789 500 32.

Oristano
Cooperativa
Sutrobasciu
Via Gramsci 1.
0783 99 05 81.

Porto Cervo
ISOLA
Sottopiazza.
0789 994 28.

Sant' Antioco
Cooperativa Sant'
Antioco Martire
Lungo Mare Vespucci 30.
0781 820 85.

Sassari
ISOLA
Viale Mancini.
079 23 01 01.

REGIONAL SPECIALITIES

Alghero
Sella & Mosca
I Piani. 079 99 77 00.

Buggerru
Sarda Affumicati
Portixeddu.
0781 549 14.

Cabras
Fratelli Manca
Via Cima 5.
0783 29 08 48.

Cagliari
Cantina Sociale
Villa Cidro.
070 931 12 10.

Mercato San Benedetto
Via San Benedetto.

Olbia
Colomba Codias
Via Australia 12.
0789 682 26.

Ozieri
Pasticceria Pietro
Pinna
Via Pastorino 35.
079 78 74 51.

Porto Torres
Acciari
Corso Vittorio
Emanuele 38.
079 51 46 05.

Quartu Sant'Elena
Sorelle Piccioni
Via Marconi 312.
070 81 01 12.

Sassari
Fratelli Rau
Via Gorizia 7.
079 29 22 64.

Tonara
Salvatore Pruneddu
Via Porru 7.
0784 638 05.

WINE

Cabras
Azienda Attilio
Contini
Via Genova 48.
0783 29 08 06.

Cagliari
Enoteca Cagliaritana
Scalette Santa Chiara.
070 65 56 11.

Jerzu
Società Cooperativa
Vitivinicola di Jerzu
Via Umberto I 1.
0782 700 28.

Olbia
Trattoria Sperrittu
Via Delle Ferme.
0789 215 99.

Oristano
Cantina Sociale della
Vernaccia
Stabilimento Rimedio.
0783 331 55.

**Quartu Sant'
Elena**
Cantina Sociale
Via Marconi 489.
070 82 60 33.

Sant'Antioco
Cantina Sociale
Via Rinascita 46.
0781 830 55.

Sassari
Cantina Fratelli
Dettori
Via Manunta 2.
079 816 77.

Serdiana
Cantina Argiolas
Via Roma 56.
070 816 77.

What to Buy in Sardinia

SARDINIA OFFERS A GREAT VARIETY of traditional island products and local handicrafts, ranging from hand-woven rugs, bedspreads and pillowcases to baskets woven in asphodel, reed or raffia. Some of the finest baskets are made in Flussio and Castelsardo. Other household articles, such as kitchenware and tableware, are made of cork or ceramics, materials which are also used to make large plates, statues and bas-reliefs. Filigree jewellery production is widespread and worn by the women for festivals and weddings; the best is made in Alghero and Bosa.

Filigree pendant

Gold buttons

Pin and earrings

JEWELLERY

Traditional Sardinian jewellery, such as earrings, brooches and buttons, often worn with local dress, is made of filigree and coral. Goldsmiths also make bracelets and necklaces in modern designs, including elegant coral spirals.

Cork ice bucket

At Calangianus, in the Gallura region of the Costa Smeralda, cork is used to make numerous household articles such as boxes, umbrella stands, bowls and ice buckets.

Circular amphora

Flower vase

Vases and jugs made to a modern design

POTTERY

Sardinian pottery is hand-thrown and glazed with natural colours. The most common articles are vases, plates and jugs and the designs are simple and fluid. Some potters have modified traditional designs to suit modern tastes.

Basket-weaving is an ancient craft that is still widely practised. Baskets are made of straw, raffia, dwarf palm, asphodel, corn sheaves or wicker in delicate, natural colours.

Rug made in Nule

Tapestry from Mogoro

A *pibbiones* rug

RUGS AND TAPESTRIES

Among the typical hand-woven articles are woollen rugs, linen bedspreads and napkins, and tapestries. The rugs are made from coloured wool with lively geometric or floral designs. The *pibbiones* rugs consist of an embroidered raised pattern knitted with small needles on neutral coloured fabric.

***Wood carving** is an ancient Sardinian tradition. The most common articles produced are chests, kitchen implements, chopping boards and ceremonial masks.*

***Lace-making** is a rare craft that requires great skill. At Oliena you can find delicate shawls made of black silk embroidered with bright colours. At Bosa you can still see women making filet lace.*

Carved mask

Lacework from Dorgali

GASTRONOMIC DELICACIES

Typical Sardinian products include cakes and cheeses which vary from region to region. Other specialities include jam, wine and liqueurs, such as myrtle and lemon, salted mullet roe and vegetables in oil.

Typical Sardinian cakes

Salted mullet roe   **Myrtle liqueur**   **Typical Sardinian delicacies**

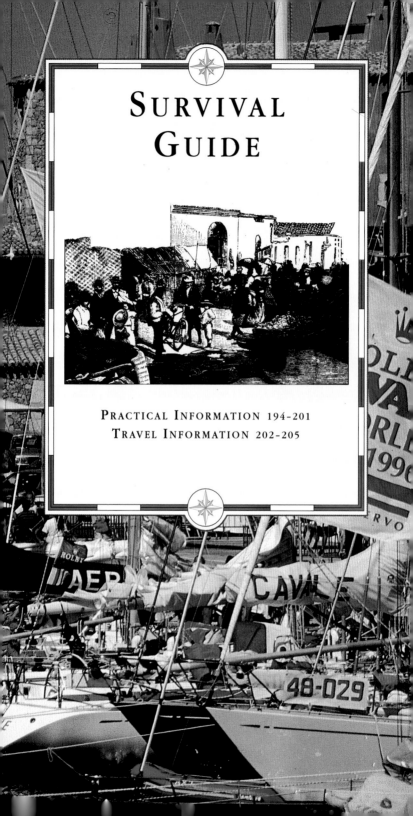

SURVIVAL GUIDE

PRACTICAL INFORMATION

BEACHES AND CLEAN BLUE sea are the principal attractions for visitors to Sardinia, and the coastline, especially in the northeast, gets very crowded from early July to late August. Visiting the island out of season can have its advantages, apart from avoiding the bustling crowds. The weather can be very hot in midsummer and visits to the towns and countryside, rich in history, ancient culture, old traditions and spellbinding scenery, are all the more easily appreciated in spring, early summer and autumn.

Tourist information sign

Tourism is a relatively new phenomenon in Sardinia, and the familiar problems of funding and staffing for monuments and museums occur here as on the mainland. Do not be surprised to see signs such as *chiuso per restauro* (closed for restoration). Provision of information for travellers is far from perfect but is improving; there are now more tourist offices, opening at regular hours, able to provide maps and guides to help you plan your time. Attempts to speak Italian, however halting, are always appreciated.

Cooling off in midsummer

WHEN TO VISIT

IN JULY AND AUGUST practically the whole of Italy goes on holiday and everywhere is overcrowded, in particular the ferries to and from Olbia and Cagliari, and the seaside hotels and resorts. Prices are much higher and you need to plan your visit ahead to make

sure of accommodation. The most crowded areas are the Costa Smeralda, the beaches near the Golfo di Cagliari and the area around Stintino.

The best months to visit the beautiful interior are May, June and September. Spring is particularly delightful, when flowers are in bloom.

In winter the cold can be quite intense, especially at higher altitudes.

TOURIST INFORMATION

THERE ARE SEVERAL different categories of tourist office, depending on the size and status of each town. Each provincial capital has an **Ente Provinciale per il Turismo** (EPT), a provincial tourist office where information and literature are available. Some of the more famous sites have an **Azienda Autonoma di Soggiorno e Turismo** (AAST), or local tourist office. In small

towns and villages the Pro Loco, or local Town Hall, takes over the tourist information role. Information on tours and trips is issued at the EPT or the **Ente Sardo Industrie Turistiche** (ESIT), the Sardinian tourist board.

The local newspapers, *La Nuova Sardegna* and *L'Unione Sarda*, are also valuable sources of information, with complete day-by-day listings.

For those with access to the Internet, there is a useful website at www.sardinia.net where you can find information on farm holidays and so on as well as details of exhibitions and events.

IMMIGRATION AND CUSTOMS

EUROPEAN UNION (EU) residents and visitors from the United States, Canada, New Zealand, Australia, Japan, need no visa for up to three months but must have one for a longer stay. Non-European Union citizens must carry a valid passport with them, while for EU citizens an ID with photo will suffice. It is however, adviseable to check the requirements before travelling. Non-EU citizens can bring in either 400 cigarettes or 100 cigars or 500 grams of tobacco, 1 litre of spirits, 2 litres of wine and 50 grams of perfume. Valuable goods may be imported only for strictly personal use.

Snowy scene in the interior, not unusual in midwinter

Shops, Banks and Post Offices

THIS GUIDE provides the opening hours for the island's museums and archaeological sites. Shops are open from 8 or 9am to 1pm and from 3:30 or 4pm (in winter) or 5pm (in summer) to 7 or 8pm from Monday to Saturday, with one early closing day during the week. Banks are open from Monday to Friday from 8:30am to 1:30pm and 2:30pm to 3:30pm. Small post offices are open from 8:30am to 1:30pm while larger offices open until 6pm (12:30pm on Saturday). The Italian national

An elegant shop offering Sardinian handicrafts

telephone company, Telecom Italia, runs both coin-operated and card *(scheda telefonica)* public phones in all towns.

Museums and Monuments

NORMALLY museums and archaeological zones are open every morning except Monday, but many sites are also open in the afternoon and, in summer, opening hours are extended.

Museum entrance fees vary from €1 to €4 and, in line with EU rules, there are discounts or free entry for children, young people under 18 and senior citizens.

Churches in the interior are usually closed in the middle of the day and may only be open for mass. If a church is closed, the parish priest *(parroco)* or sexton may open it for you as a special favour for a short visit. A small contribution to church funds will always be welcome in return for assistance.

Festivals

SARDINIA'S FESTIVALS HAVE a very long history and are colourful and unusual affairs. The busiest times of year for

Traditional rituals, still part of the community year in Sardinia

seeing traditional festivals are Carnival and Easter. Tourist offices provide information on feast days and festivals, and dates are also given in the information for each town in this guide.

Disabled Travellers

UNFORTUNATELY, special facilities for the disabled are rare, even in the larger towns, and touring can be quite a frustrating experience for wheelchair users.

For further information on advice and assistance for the disabled, contact the ESIT offices in Cagliari.

Personal Security and Health

O**N THE WHOLE,** SARDINIA is a safe place for visitors and only a few precautions are needed for a pleasant stay. There is some petty crime, so take extra care of money and belongings in the busy passenger terminals of the ports and in cities. Do not leave valuables in your car if the parking place is unsupervised. On the whole, rural areas are generally safer than cities. During the summer, forest fires are a very serious problem, so be sure to follow the instructions of the local police or firemen should an emergency arise. If you fall ill, the nearest pharmacy *(farmacia)* is a good first stop.

CREDIT CARDS AND LOST PROPERTY

I**T IS NEVER A GOOD IDEA** to carry a lot of cash with you. The major credit cards (Visa, MasterCard, American Express and Diners Club) are accepted by the majority of shops, restaurants and hotels on the island. It is reasonably easy to find automatic cash dispensers *(bancomat)* in all the large cities, but interest will be charged on currency exchange withdrawals, so you may prefer to carry travellers' cheques as well.

Generally speaking, it is safe to park where you like, as car theft is not common, especially in small towns. However, if anything is stolen, go immediately to the local police or carabinieri to report the theft; you will need the report for the insurance claim.

FIRE HAZARDS

U**NFORTUNATELY,** forest fires are a real problem in Sardinia, especially in the summer. Except for rare cases

Fire, a constant danger

of accidental fire that may be caused by a thrown-away cigarette, most fires on the island are started deliberately. In some instances forest and brush are destroyed to make way for more grazing land but, more often than not, the motive is to clear space for new buildings. In an attempt to halt the practice, a law has been passed prohibiting construction in areas destroyed by fire, but even this has not stopped arsonists. In the dry heat of summer, fire spreads rapidly in the undergrowth of

the maquis, and the main enemy of the firemen is the wind, which is capable of carrying the fire a long way in a very short time. Fire-fighting is carried out by the local fire brigades as well as the state forest rangers, volunteers and specially equipped fire-fighting planes positioned in key areas of the island.

MEDICAL TREATMENT

S**HOULD YOU NEED** medical assistance during your stay, Sardinia has a network of hospitals and casualty departments *(pronto soccorso)*, as well as pharmacies which can dispense advice as well as medicines. European Union nationals are entitled to Italian medical care, but you need to carry an E111 form.

In all the tourist resorts there is a *Guardia Medica* (emergency treatment centre) equipped to give medical attention to summer visitors. These seasonal surgeries are often closed in the winter and, in an emergency in low season, you will have to go to one of the main hospitals.

Pharmacies in Sardinia are open from Monday to Friday, 9am–1pm and 4–7pm and Saturday morning. Lists of the night and holiday opening rotas for the local area are carried on the chemist's door.

FIRE PREVENTION RULES

1. Always take care to extinguish cigarettes before discarding them.
2. Never light a fire except in areas where this is explicitly permitted.
3. If you see a fire, you must report it to the local firemen.
4. Do not stop or park your car to watch a fire; you may block the roads and interfere with fire-fighting operations.
5. Pay attention to the wind direction: it is highly dangerous to be down-wind of a fire, as it may spread quite rapidly and catch you unawares.

Policemen on horseback at the Poetto beach near Cagliari

COUNTRYSIDE CODES

D URING YOUR STAY you are likely to spend a good deal of time exploring outdoors, so be prepared for any problems that may occur.

In the summer, whether you are on the beach or in the interior, be wary of too much sun, as it may cause serious burns and sunstroke. If it is windy, you may not be aware you are burning.

If a storm breaks and you need to take shelter, do not head for isolated trees or rocky peaks, which may attract lightning.

Although you cannot simply camp wherever you like, you can make private arrangements with landowners to pitch your tent away from official camping sites. Make sure you take away all your rubbish and do not light fires.

Bear in mind that grazing in the open countryside is still quite common in Sardinia: pigs, sheep, cows and horses may well decide to see whether campers have anything good to eat in their tents. In hilly areas sheepdogs

Camping on the beach, forbidden in Sardinia, but private arrangements can be made on farmland with landowners

should be avoided, since they are trained to chase away any potential intruders.

While walking or trekking in the countryside you may come across gates or fences barring your way. It is always a good idea, if possible, to ask whether you can go through. Having done so, remember to close the gate so that animals are unable to escape. If you plan a lengthy hike, make sure you carry enough water with you, as villages may be few and far between. Lastly, despite the wildness, there are no poisonous snakes.

CURRENCY

Twelve countries have replaced their traditional currencies with the euro. Austria, Belgium, Finland, France, Germany, Greece, Ireland, Italy, Luxembourg, Netherlands, Portugal and Spain chose to join the new currency; the UK, Denmark and Sweden stayed out, with an option to review their situation.

The euro was introduced on 1 January 1999, but only for banking purposes. Notes and coins came into circulation on 1 January 2002. All euro notes and coins can be used anywhere inside the participating member states.

Euro bank notes have seven denominations. The €5 note (grey in colour) is the smallest, followed by the €10 note (pink), €20 note (blue), €50 note (orange), €100 note (green), €200 note (yellow) and €500 note (purple). The euro has eight coin denominations: €1 and €2; 50 cents, 20 cents, 10 cents, 5 cents, 2 cents and 1 cent. The €2 and €1 coins are silver and gold in colour. The 50-, 20- and 10-cent coins are gold. The 5-, 2- and 1-cent coins are bronze.

Visitors will find automatic exchange machines at the airports. However, it is always a good idea to have some euros at hand for any immediate expenses.

Euro notes

EMERGENCY TELEPHONE NUMBERS

General Emergencies
📞 113.

Police (Carabinieri Pronto Intervento)
📞 112.

Fire (Vigili del Fuoco)
📞 115.

Road Emergencies (Soccorso Stradale)
📞 116.

Medical Emergencies
📞 118.

Directory Enquiries
📞 12.

Nautical Information
📞 196.

Mountain Emergencies (Soccorso Alpino)
📞 070 72 81 63 or 070 28 62 00 or 0784 310 70.

USING BANKS

B ANK OPENING HOURS are usually 8:30am–1:30pm and 3–4:30pm from Monday to Friday. All banks close at weekends and on public holidays. Credit cards, once regarded with suspicion in Sardinia, are now accepted without question by hotels, restaurants and shops, especially those in the tourist areas. All the major credit cards are accepted, the most popular cards being Visa and MasterCard (Access). You will not have difficulty in finding an automatic cash dispenser *(bancomat)* in larger towns.

Water Sports

Diving in the crystal-clear waters of Sardinia

Despite the impressive beauty of its interior, Sardinia's fame is more strongly associated with the sea. The development of the tourist industry means that the island now offers a good range of facilities for water sports, in particular sailing, windsurfing and scuba diving. There are diving centres and sailing schools in almost all the coastal resorts, and many of the holiday villages are well-equipped for water sports. Canoeing is a different matter, since the lack of navigable rivers limits your choice in the interior, and sea canoeing is only practised in a few places along the coast.

Sailing along the coast

SAILING

With its marvellous sea and coastline, Sardinia is regarded as a paradise for boating of all kinds, whether your preferred style is a billion-dollar luxury yacht on the Costa Smeralda or a simple dinghy for hire from one of the more affordable centres. The conditions vary considerably and even experienced sailors find the Sardinian coast a challenge because of the strong and variable winds. A good source of useful information for a sailing holiday is volume 1A of *Portolano del Mediterraneo* (Mediterranean Pilot's Book), which is published by the Istituto Idrografico della Marina Militare. Another useful publication is the pamphlet *I Porti Turistici della Sardegna* (Sardinian Yacht Harbours), available from all tourist information offices. You need permission from the harbour master to moor in most of Sardinia's harbours.

SCUBA DIVING

The coastline offers plenty of opportunities for experienced divers. Among the most famous spots for diving are the coasts of Asinara and Gallura, Capo Caccia, Carloforte, the Golfo di Orosei and the area around the island of Tavolara. Many diving centres – often based at sports shops – organize diving trips. You can also buy or rent diving equipment and get advice on diving sites.

WINDSURFING

Windsurfing equipment is available for hire at almost all the tourist beaches. Some of the sailing centres also offer boards for hire and can organize lessons.

Windsurfing in the open sea

WINDSURFING BEACHES

The following beaches are the best on the island for windsurfing *(see pp18–19)*:

Bosa Marina
Poetto – Cagliari
*Calagrande – Isola di
   Sant'Antioco*
Saline – Isola di Sant'Antioco
Monti d'a Rena – La Maddalena
Porto Massimo – La Maddalena
*Porto Taverna – Porto San Paolo
   Lotzorai*
Marinella – Olbia
Porto Istana – Olbia
Torre Grande – Oristano
Porto Pollo – Palau
Capo Testa – Santa Teresa di Gallura
La Cinta – San Teodoro
Putzu Idu – San Vero Milis
Platamona - Sorso
La Pelosa – Stintino

The Centro Velico Caprera sailing school

The safety rules for sailing also apply to this sport: the winds can be very strong and fickle (especially the mistral), so do not go too far out.

CANOEING

ALTHOUGH there are very few navigable rivers for canoeing in the interior – and the variable weather makes practising the sport even more difficult – you can canoe in the lakes or along certain stretches of the coast.

OTHER SPORTS

THERE ARE NUMEROUS COVES along the Sardinian coasts where you can explore the rocks and the water and observe the varied marine life. Snorkelling is perhaps best left to the experienced: strong winds and currents can easily create difficult and dangerous conditions.

Subaqua fishing with a harpoon and aqualung is not permitted but freshwater fishing is possible in the lakes and reservoirs. You will need a permit to fish in the rivers.

In some holiday villages water-based tours are offered to guests, and some also provide dinghies in which to explore the coastline.

Canoeing in the fabulous Cala Sisine cove

DIRECTORY

SAILING AND WINDSURFING CENTRES

Yacht Club Cagliari
Marina Piccola.
070 37 03 50.

Windsurfing Club Cagliari
Marina Piccola.
070 37 26 94.

Carloforte Yacht Club
0781 85 64 57.

Windsurfing Vela Club Portoscuso
Portoscuso, Cagliari.
0781 50 95 38.

Centro Velico Caprera – La Maddalena
Porto Palma.
0789 73 85 29.

Club Nautico La Maddalena
Via G Cesare 20.
0789 72 79 85.

Circolo Nautico Arbatax
0782 66 75 66.

Circolo Nautico Olbia
Via Genova 69.
0789 261 87.

Yacht Club Porto Rotondo
0789 340 10.

Yacht Club Alghero
079 95 20 74.

Yacht Club Costa Smeralda – Porto Cervo
Porto Cervo.
0789 90 22 00.

Circolo Nautico Oristano
Torregrande.
0783 21 01 72.

DIVING CENTRES

Area Mare Diving
Cannigione.
0789 884 28.

D.C. Porto Massimo
La Maddalena.
0789 73 40 42 or
329 433 45 82.

Nautilus
Palau.
333 21 09 75.

Oyster Sub Diving Center
Palau.
0789 70 20 70.

Orso Diving Club – Poltu Quato
0789 990 01.

Nautica – Portisco
0789 335 12.

Centro Sub Isuledda Compagnia dell'Avventura
Cannigione, Arzachena.
0789 862 53.

Centro Sub Tavolara
Porto San Paolo.
0789 403 60.

Scuola Sub Aquarius
Coda Cavalio.
0784 83 41 24.

Aqua Diving Center Puntaldia
Puntaldia,
San Teodoro.
0784 86 43 90.

Tanka Village Diving Center – Villasimius
070 795 64.

Air Sub Service – Villasimius
070 79 20 33.

Isla Diving
Carloforte.
0781 85 56 34 or
335 46 25 02

Centro Sub Caribù
c/o Villaggio Capo Caccia.
079 94 66 66.

L'Argonauta Diving Center
Cala Gonone.
0784 930 46.

CANOEING

Federazione Italiana Canoa
070 65 27 48.

Associazione Italiana Kayak da Mare – Cagliari
070 66 04 89.

Canoa Club Acque Selvagge – Cagliari
070 72 58 25.

Canoa Club Oristano
0783 21 03 35.

Outdoor Sports

NEGLECTED FOR YEARS because attention was focused on tourist development along the coast, the interior landscape of Sardinia offers plenty of opportunity to practise outdoor sports. The countryside can be explored on foot or on horseback – riding centres have made great advances in recent years and are in great demand. Facilities for hiking and rock climbing are good and increasing numbers of mountain climbing routes are in the process of being marked out.

The Su Rei riding centre in Sulcis

HORSE RIDING

SARDINIA IS IDEALLY suited for trekking and horse riding. Horses have long been an integral part of the island's culture, as the animal has been part of local life since Phoenician times: many of the religious feast days and festivities include breakneck rides and horse races.

The many isolated minor roads, mule tracks and paths, far away from traffic and noise, particularly in the interior, are ideal for pleasant rides, and many are not too difficult for beginners.

There are nearly 100 Sardinian equestrian clubs and centres, large and small, offering facilities for this sport. Most are equipped to organize lessons and rides for beginners as well as extended treks for experienced riders.

Most of the stables and clubs are located near Cagliari, Nuoro and Oristano, but there has been an increase in the number of holiday farms *(see p170)* offering horse riding and riding excursions for their guests, whatever their ability.

Supramonte, Giara di Gesturi and the Valle della Luna are three of the most interesting and popular destinations for those who love long treks in the Sardinian countryside.

ROCK CLIMBING

IN THE 1960s THE Italian mountaineer Alessandro Gogna published *Mezzogiorno di Pietra* (Midday Stone), which opened up the possibilities for rock climbing in Sardinia. Since those days enthusiasm for the sport has grown considerably, and the island's most challenging

Cliffs at the seaside with facilities for rock climbing

rocks and cliffs are tackled by climbers from all over Italy and Europe. Among the most popular climbing areas are Supramonte (Surtana, l'Aguglia), the cliffs at Iglesiente (Domusnovas), where hand- and foot-holds have recently been placed, and the Isili area in Nuoro province.

Essential reading for rock climbers who decide to come here is *Pietra di Luna* (Moon Stone) by Maurizio Oviglia, the most up-to-date guide to rock climbing in Sardinia.

Additional information can be obtained at the **Sezione di Cagliari del Club Alpino Italiano**. Climbing lessons and programmes are organized by a number of companies, including **Pietra di Luna** (070-29 18 28), **Barbagia Insolita**, the **Associazione La Montagna**, and **Marcello Cominetti** (3398 13 43 03).

WALKING AND TREKKING

WILD MOUNTAINS, hills dotted with prehistoric ruins, forests and maquis vegetation make up most of the terrain in the interior of Sardinia. The countryside is rugged but unspoilt and ideal for walking, hiking and more strenuous treks. However, facilities are few and far between, clearly signposted footpaths are rare and there are very few refuges or stopping places. It is always advisable to carry an up-to-date map and to take plenty of water when walking

The most rewarding and popular areas are Supramonte, the Gennargentu massif and the Sulcis area (which offers an unusual blend of hiking and industrial archaeology). Some stretches of the steep coastline are more suited to those with climbing experience.

In the Supramonte area experienced mountaineers can even tackle the wild and precipitous Su Gorroppu gorges. The trek takes a couple of days and special rock climbers' equipment is needed in order to make it down the vertical walls of the falls. This particular excursion is, therefore, not suitable for beginners.

THE SELVAGGIO BLU ROUTE

Its very name – Wild Blue – is the best possible description of this difficult route along the Golfo di Orosei, starting from Santa Maria Navarrese and ending at Cala Luna. The Selvaggio Blu was conceived a few years ago by Mario Verin and Peppino Cicalò. The course requires excellent

physical condition and preparation (since part of it consists of stretches of rock climbing, some of the descents are achieved by abseiling and you have to walk with a heavy load because of the distance between water supply sources) but the rewards are some of the most spectacular views of the Sardinian coast. The town of Baunei publishes a guide to Selvaggio Blu; for information, or if you are interested in buying the book, call 0782 61 08 23.

A stretch of the Selvaggio Blu trail

Whether walking or climbing, or a combination of both, make sure you have the best map possible to hand (a good map is published by IGM). You should also carefully calculate the time the tour will take and how much food and water will be needed, as it is possible to walk for kilometres without stumbling across a village.

SPELEOLOGY

THE MOUNTAINS OF Sardinia are riddled with dozens of fascinating caves to be explored, some of which have tourist facilities. The temperature inside is likely to be relatively high, more or less the yearly average of the surrounding area. Bear in mind that some of the difficult caves, such as the Golgo abyss (at Su Sterru), the Grotta Verde at Capo Caccia or the Su Palu cave near Orosei, are only open to experienced speleologists.

GOLF COURSES

SARDINIA has some famous golf courses, including the one at the **Pevero Golf Club** in Porto Cervo, designed by the architect Robert Trent Jones. This 18-hole golf course is internationally known for its tournaments.

OTHER SPORTS

THE ISLAND'S sports activites are not confined to the mountains and caves in its interior. More traditional sports such as tennis, football, swimming and five-a-side football can be pursued in the many sports grounds and courts throughout the island.

The golf course at Pevero

DIRECTORY	WALKING TOURS		SPELEOLOGY
HORSE RIDING	**Club Alpino Italiano** Cagliari. 070 66 78 77.	**Keya** Quartu Sant'Elena. 070 82 71 93.	**Federazione Speleologica Sarda** Via De Magistris, Cagliari. 070 27 23 31.
Equiturismo c/o Centro Vacanze Ala Birdi, Strada a Mare 24, Arborea. 0783 80 10 843.	**Compagnia dell'Avventura** Cannigione. 0789 862 53.	**Scoprisardegna** Porto Torres. 079 51 22 09. **Cooperativa Ghivine** Dorgali. 0784 967 21.	**Società Speleologica Italiana** Via Zamboni 61, Bologna. 051 25 00 49.
FISE (Federazione Italiana Sport Equestri) Via Cagliari 242, Oristano. 0783 30 29 32.	**Tramontana** Olbia. 0789 266 60.	**Barbagia Insolita** Oliena. 0784 28 60 05.	**GOLF COURSES** **Villaggio Arbatax Golf Club** 0782 66 70 65.
III (Istituto Incremento Ippico della Sardegna) Piazza Borgia 4, Ozieri. 079 78 78 52.	**Artrek Sardegna** Cagliari. 070 66 66 80. **L'Asfodelo** Cagliari. 070 65 73 85.	**Cooperativa Monte Maccione** Oliena. 0784 28 83 63.	**Is Molas Golf Club** Santa Margherita di Pula. 070 924 10 13.
Oasi Lipu Penisola Simis. 0783 52 81 00.	**Segnavia** Cagliari. 070 916 51 38.	**Associazione La Montagna** Roma. 063 21 68 04.	**Pevero Golf Club** Porto Cervo. 0789 95 80 20.

TRAVEL INFORMATION

SARDINIA IS SERVED by Europe's major air-lines, including the Sardinian Meridiana and the Italian carrier, Alitalia. In addition, there are many charter flights operating in the summer, often with low cost fares or as part of a package deal. The number of flights varies according to the season, with many more direct and charter flights during the busy summer months. If no direct flights or suitable connections are available, Alitalia and Meridiana provide regular domestic flights from

A Meridiana airlines plane

Italy's mainland cities throughout the year.
The island is also served by an excellent net-work of car and passenger ferries from ports on the Italian mainland. Slower ferries offer a long crossing, with berths for overnight trips, whereas the faster and more expensive ferry lines can almost halve the travelling time. During the peak summer season of July and August it is not easy to find places on passenger and, in particular, car ferries, so make sure to book your place well in advance.

ARRIVING BY AIR

THE MAIN AIRPORTS in Sardinia are Cagliari's **Elmas** airport, Alghero's **Fertilia** airport and the **Olbia-Costa Smeralda** airport. These are not very far from their respective city centres and offer public transport into town as well as taxi services. In the summer there is also a coach service from Olbia airport to the towns on the Costa Smeralda.
Alitalia and the Sardinian air-line **Meridiana** serve Cagliari and Olbia from a number of mainland Italian cities, provid-ing links to major European capitals. Meridiana also flies daily from Gatwick to Cagliari

via Florence, and low-cost air-line **Ryanair** serves Alghero direct from London Stansted. For charter flights in summer, see your travel agent or specialist tour operator.
Long-haul passengers will almost inevitably have to change in an Italian mainland or other European city. If you are travelling from the United States, American, United Air-lines and Delta offer direct flights to Rome or Milan where you can get a connection to one of the island's airports. Canadian Airlines flies from Canada and Qantas flies from Australia. Alitalia also has a regular service between these countries and Rome.

A Sardinia Ferries car ferry

TICKETS AND FARES

IF YOU ARE BASED in the UK it is worth scouring the small ads of newspapers for cut-price charters and discounted scheduled flights. Fares vary greatly during the year, but

Olbia's airport serving the east and the Costa Smeralda

A Tirrenia line car ferry

the most expensive periods are summer, Christmas and Easter holidays. Meridiana offers low-season economy flights.

For intercontinental flights the most economical option is to take a budget flight to London, Frankfurt or Amsterdam and get a Meridiana flight from there to the island.

FERRY SERVICES

SARDINIA IS EASILY reached by ferry from Italy's mainland ports. The crossing can be rather long (up to 16 hours from Naples to Cagliari, 7 hours between Civitavecchia and Olbia), although the more expensive ferry lines offer a much faster service. For overnight crossings, passengers can book a cabin.

Ferry services leave from Civitavecchia, Naples, Genoa, Livorno, Palermo, Trapani and Tunis in Tunisia. They dock at Sardinia's major tourist ports of Cagliari, Olbia, Golfo Aranci, Palau and Porto Torres. **Sardinia Ferries**' fast service connects Civitavecchia and Livorno with Golfo Aranci in just over four hours. **Tirrenia** offers a similar service from La Spezia and Civitavecchia to Olbia (a four- to five-hour trip). There are also ferries from Bonifacio in Corsica, bound for Santa Teresa di Gallura and between Palau and Porto Vecchio in Corsica during the high season.

PACKAGE HOLIDAYS

MOST TRAVEL AGENCIES, both in Italy and abroad, offer holidays to Sardinia. Obviously, the sea and coast are the greatest attraction, but there are also many options for holidays in the interior. Many holiday villages provide a wide range of entertainment and sports facilities for their guests, including diving and windsurfing, sailing lessons and horseback riding.

A Moby Lines ferry

DIRECTORY

AIRLINES

Meridiana
Cagliari
For information
070 65 13 81.
For reservations
199 111 333.
Elmas Airport, Cagliari
070 24 01 69.
Olbia
For information
078 95 29 99.
For reservations
199 111 333.
Costa Smeralda Airport,
Olbia
078 956 34 44.
Rome
800 40 11 60.

For reservations
199 111 333.
Milan
025 841 71.
For reservations
199 111 333.
w www.meridiana.it
UK
15 Charles II Street, London.
020 7839 2222.

Alitalia
Elmas airport, Cagliari
070 24 00 79.
Alghero, Fertilia airport
079 935 03 3/7.
Rome
Alitalia domestic flights
848 86 56 41.
Alitalia international flights
848 86 56 42.
w www.alitalia.it

Ryanair
0870 333 12 53 (UK).
199 114 114 (Italy).
w www.ryanair.com

FERRY COMPANIES

Tirrenia
Cagliari
For information
070 65 46 64.
Olbia
078 92 85 33.
Porto Torres
079 514 10 7/8.

Moby Lines
Milan
028 652 31.
Olbia
078 92 79 27.

Cagliari
070 65 53 59.
Rome
064 20 11 533.
w www.mobylines.it

Ferrovie dello Stato
848 88 80 88.

Sardinia Ferries
Information/reservations
019 21 55 11.
Olbia
078 92 52 00.
Milan
02 72 00 09 70 or
02 70 00 996.
Livorno
058 68 813 80.
w www.sardiniaferries.com

Getting Around Sardinia

MANY OF SARDINIA'S ROADS are characterized by an interminable number of curves and tight bends: annoying if you are in a hurry, but pleasant if you're on holiday and can take time to enjoy the scenery. With the exception of a few major roads, such as the N131 which connects the four corners of the island, the roads wind their way over hills and across plains so that, even though the traffic outside the towns is light, always calculate plenty of time when planning a tour. The empty roads, on the other hand, are perfect for cyclists.

A flock of sheep blocking a country road

Avis 📞 800 86 30 63.
Europcar 📞 070 24 01 26.
Hertz 📞 199 11 22 11.
Maggiore 📞 848 86 70 67.

ROAD RULES

THE SPEED LIMITS are the same as in the rest of Italy: 50 km/h (30 mph) in town, 90 km/h (55 mph) on normal roads, 130 km/h (80 mph) on motorways. Motorists are required to wear seat belts and motor cyclists and moped riders and passengers must wear helmets. Traffic is usually heavy in cities and towns.

BOAT HIRE

IN MANY PORTS it is possible to charter yachts, from one day to one week. The prices may include a crew or simply the use of the boat. Hiring a boat enables you to see the island away from the busy resorts. For information, make enquiries with the harbour authorities or boat owners.

BICYCLES AND MOUNTAIN BIKES

THE QUIET ROADS along the coast or the stunning countryside in the interior are ideal for outings or long trips by bicycle. If you prefer more arduous exercise, the steeper mountain roads are suitable for mountain bikes. Tourist offices will have suggestions for local bicycle routes and several associations exist with information about off-road tours by mountain bike.

TRAVELLING BY CAR

GIVEN THE INEFFICIENT public transport system, and the spectacular natural scenery, travelling by car is the best way to become acquainted with the island.

It is important, however, to be aware of the problems that may occur. Minor roads will often be blocked by flocks of sheep, adding to your travel time. Road signs are not always clear and may be missing just when you need them most. Should this occur, the best thing to do is to ask someone on the way, as Sardinians are courteous and will happily help. Another potential problem is petrol, as there are not many filling stations in the interior. Lastly, you will often find yourself forced to take difficult dirt roads – which Sardinians poetically call "roads with natural paving" – particularly when looking for an out-of-the-way church or archaeological site.

One way to be prepared for these potential hindrances is to carry a good, up-to-date road map. One of the best is published by the Touring Club Italiano, to a scale of 1:200.000.

RENTING A CAR

THE MAJORITY of international car rental companies are represented in Sardinia, with offices in the main port towns (Olbia, Cagliari, Porto Torres) and in the airports of Cagliari Elmas, Olbia-Costa Smeralda and Alghero Fertilia. Hertz offers discounts for those who fly with Meridiana.

A number of holiday companies offer fly-drive deals which allow you to fly to the most convenient airport and pick up a rented car on arrival.

Car rental, a convenient and comfortable way to see the island

A bicycle tour among the olive groves near Sassari

TOURING SARDINIA BY MOUNTAIN BIKE

Team Mountain Bike Orosei
℡ 078 49 13 30.

Società Ciclistica Mountain Bike
Dèsulo.
℡ 078 4619 792.

Pool Bike Serramanna
℡ 070 913 84 34.

Mountain Bike Club Taxus Baccata
Gonnasfanadiga.
℡ 070 979 98 64.

Mountain Bike Team Sardegna
Sinnai.
℡ 070 76 70 20.

Team Spakkaruote Sud Est Sardinia
Carbonia.
℡ 078 16 40 84.

Club Mountain Bike Città di Sassari
℡ 079 27 37 47.

TRAVELLING BY TRAIN

SARDINIAN TRAINS are narrow-gauge, making them more a tourist attraction than a true means of transport. The slow progress and inconvenient train times mean that trips to explore the island must be combined with the more efficient coach service run by the Azienda Regionale Sarda Trasporti (ARST) company.

A train ride in true late-19th-century style, such as on the Cagliari–Sòrgono route *(see p109)*, is an enjoyable and relaxing way to see the island's stunning scenery that has fascinated travellers and photographers from all over the world for many centuries.

In spring, the **Ferrovie della Sardegna** (Sardinian Railway) organizes train rides from Cagliari to Mandas and Seui on the Trenino Verde *(see pp92–3)*. "Vintage" wagons from 1913 are pulled by steam locomotives from the 1930s.

Ferrovie della Sardegna
Via Cugia 1, Cagliari. ℡ 070 58 02 46 or 070 34 23 41.

TRAVELLING BY COACH

THE AZIENDA REGIONALE Sarda Trasporti (ARST) coach company network covers almost all of the towns, cities and resorts throughout Sardinia. In order to meet the needs of the ever-growing number of visitors to the island, ARST has issued a special tourist pass *(biglietto turistico)*, which provides an ideal way of getting around the island. However, this is available to non-residents only, between 15 June and 15 September. The pass allows you to travel on all ARST coaches, and can be purchased for a period of 7, 14, 21 or 28 days, beginning with the first day you use it.

ARST INFORMATION OFFICES

Cagliari ℡ 070 409 81.
or 070 409 83 24.
Gùspini ℡ 070 97 02 36.
Lanusei ℡ 078 24 02 92.
Nuoro ℡ 078 429 50 38.
Olbia ℡ 078 955 30 00.
Oristano ℡ 078 37 17 76.
Sassari ℡ 079 263 92 00.

The narrow-gauge train known as the Trenino Verde

General Index

Phrase Book

IN AN EMERGENCY

Help!	**Aiuto!**	eye-**yoo**-toh
Stop!	**Fermate!**	fair-**mah**-teh
Call a doctor.	**Chiama un medico**	kee-**ah**-mah oon **meh**-dee-koh
Call an ambulance.	**Chiama un' ambulanza**	kee-**ah**-mah oon am-boo-**lan**-tsa
Call the police.	**Chiama la polizia**	kee-**ah**-mah lah pol-ee-**tsee**-ah
Call the fire brigade.	**Chiama i pompieri**	kee-**ah**-mah ee pom-pee-**air**-ee
Where is the telephone?	**Dov'è il telefono?**	dov-**eh** eel teh-**leh**-foh-noh?
The nearest hospital?	**L'ospedale più vicino?**	loss-peh-**dah**-leh pee-**oo** vee-**chee**-noh?

COMMUNICATION ESSENTIALS

Yes/No	**Sì/No**	see/ noh
Please	**Per favore**	pair fah-**vor**-eh
Thank you	**Grazie**	**grah**-tsee-eh
Excuse me	**Mi scusi**	mee **skoo**-zee
Hello	**Buon giorno**	bwon **jor**-noh
Goodbye	**Arrivederci**	ah-ree-veh-**dair**-chee
Good evening	**Buona sera**	**bwon**-ah **sair**-ah
morning	**la mattina**	lah mah-**tee**-nah
afternoon	**il pomeriggio**	eel poh-meh-**ree**-joh
evening	**la sera**	lah **sair**-ah
yesterday	**ieri**	ee-**air**-ee
today	**oggi**	**oh**-jee
tomorrow	**domani**	doh-**mah**-nee
here	**qui**	kwee
there	**la**	lah
What?	**Quale?**	**kwah**-leh?
When?	**Quando?**	**kwan**-doh?
Why?	**Perchè?**	pair-**keh**?
Where?	**Dove?**	**doh**-veh?

USEFUL PHRASES

How are you?	**Come sta?**	**koh**-meh stah?
Very well, thank you.	**Molto bene, grazie.**	**moll**-toh **beh**-neh **grah**-tsee-eh
Pleased to meet you.	**Piacere di conoscerla.**	pee-ah-**chair**-eh deh coh-**noh**-shair-lah
See you later.	**A più tardi.**	ah pee-**oo** tar-dee
That's fine.	**Va bene.**	va **beh**-neh
Where is/are ...?	**Dov'è/Dove sono ...?**	dov-**eh**/dov-eh soh noh?
How long does it take to get to ...?	**Quanto tempo ci vuole per andare a ...?**	**kwan**-toh **tem**-poh chee voo-**oh**-leh pair an-**dar**-eh ah ...?
How do I get to ...?	**Come faccio per arrivare a ...?**	koh-meh **fah**-choh pair arri-**var**-eh ah...?
Do you speak English?	**Parla inglese?**	**par**-lah een-**gleh**-zeh?
I don't understand.	**Non capisco.**	non ka-**pee**-skoh
Could you speak more slowly, please?	**Può parlare più lentamente, per favore?**	pwoh par-**lah**-reh pee-**oo** len-ta-**men**-teh pair fah-**vor**-eh?
I'm sorry.	**Mi dispiace.**	mee-dee-spee-**ah**-cheh

USEFUL WORDS

big	**grande**	**gran**-deh
small	**piccolo**	**pee**-koh-loh
hot	**caldo**	**kal**-doh
cold	**freddo**	**fred**-doh
good	**buono**	**bwoh**-noh
bad	**cattivo**	kat-**tee**-voh
enough	**basta**	**bas**-tah
well	**bene**	**beh**-neh
open	**aperto**	ah-**pair**-toh
closed	**chiuso**	kee-**oo**-zoh
left	**a sinistra**	ah see-**nee**-strah
right	**a destra**	ah **dess**-trah
straight on	**sempre dritto**	**sem**-preh **dree**-toh
near	**vicino**	vee-**chee**-noh
far	**lontano**	lon-**tah**-noh
up	**su**	soo
down	**giù**	joo
early	**presto**	**press**-toh
late	**tardi**	tar-dee
entrance	**entrata**	en-**trah**-tah
exit	**uscita**	oo-**shee**-ta
toilet	**il gabinetto**	eel gah-bee-**net**-toh
free, unoccupied	**libero**	**lee**-bair-oh
free, no charge	**gratuito**	grah-**too**-ee-toh

MAKING A TELEPHONE CALL

I'd like to place a long-distance call.	**Vorrei fare una interurbana.**	vor-**ray** far-eh oona in-tair-oor-**bah**-nah
I'd like to make a reverse-charge call.	**Vorrei fare una telefonata a carico del destinatario.**	vor-**ray** far-eh oona teh-leh-fon-**ah**-tah ah **kar**-ee-koh dell dess-tee-nah-**tar**-ree-oh
I'll try again later.	**Ritelefono più tardi.**	ree-teh-**leh**-foh-noh pee-oo **tar**-dee
Can I leave a message?	**Posso lasciare un messaggio?**	**poss**-oh lash-**ah**-reh oon mess-**sah**-joh?
Hold on.	**Un attimo, per favore**	oon **ah**-tee-moh, pair fah-**vor**-eh
Could you speak up a little please?	**Può parlare più forte, per favore?**	pwoh par-**lah**-reh pee-**oo** for-teh, pair fah-**vor**-eh?
local call	**telefonata locale**	te-leh-fon-**ah**-tah loh-cah-leh

SHOPPING

How much does this cost?	**Quant'è, per favore?**	kwan-**teh** pair fah-**vor**-eh?
I would like ...	**Vorrei ...**	vor-**ray**
Do you have ...?	**Avete ...?**	ah-**veh**-teh... ?
I'm just looking.	**Sto soltanto guardando.**	stoh sol-**tan**-toh gwar-**dan**-doh
Do you take credit cards?	**Accettate carte di credito?**	ah-chet-**tah**-teh **kar**-teh dee **creh**-dee-toh?
What time do you open/close?	**A che ora apre/ chiude?**	ah keh or-ah **ah**-preh/kee-**oo**-deh?
this one	**questo**	**kweh**-stoh
that one	**quello**	**kwell**-oh
expensive	**caro**	**kar**-oh
cheap	**a buon prezzo**	ah bwon **pret**-soh
size, clothes	**la taglia**	lah **tah**-lee-ah
size, shoes	**il numero**	eel **noo**-mair-oh
white	**bianco**	bee-**ang**-koh
black	**nero**	**neh**-roh
red	**rosso**	**ross**-oh
yellow	**giallo**	**jal**-loh
green	**verde**	**vair**-deh
blue	**blu**	bloo

TYPES OF SHOP

antique dealer	**l'antiquario**	lan-tee-**kwah**-ree-oh
bakery	**il forno /il panificio**	eel **forn**-oh /eel pan-ee-**fee**-choh
bank	**la banca**	lah **bang**-kah
bookshop	**la libreria**	lah lee-breh-**ree**-ah
butcher	**la macelleria**	lah mah-chell-eh-**ree**-ah
cake shop	**la pasticceria**	lah pas-tee-chair-**ee**-ah
chemist	**la farmacia**	lah far-mah-**chee**-ah
delicatessen	**la salumeria**	lah sah-loo-meh-**ree**-ah
department store	**il grande magazzino**	eel **gran**-deh mag-gad-**zee**-noh
fishmonger	**il pescivendolo**	eel pesh-ee-**ven**-doh-loh
florist	**il fioraio**	eel fee-or-**eye**-oh
greengrocer	**il fruttivendolo**	eel froo-tee-**ven**-doh-loh
grocery	**alimentari**	ah-lee-men-**tah**-ree
hairdresser	**il parrucchiere**	eel par-oo-kee-**air**-eh
ice cream parlour	**la gelateria**	lah jel-lah-tair-**ree**-ah
market	**il mercato**	eel mair-**kah**-toh
newsstand	**l'edicola**	leh-**dee**-koh-lah
post office	**l'ufficio postale**	loo-**fee**-choh pos-**tah**-leh
shoe shop	**il negozio di scarpe**	eel neh-**goh**-tsioh dee **skar**-peh
supermarket	**il supermercato**	eel su-pair-mair-**kah**-toh
tobacconist	**il tabaccaio**	eel tah-bak-**eye**-oh
travel agency	**l'agenzia di viaggi**	lah-jen-**tsee**-ah dee vee-**ad**-jee

SIGHTSEEING

art gallery	**la pinacoteca**	lah peena-koh-**teh**-kah
bus stop	**la fermata dell'autobus**	lah fair-**mah**-tah dell **ow**-toh-booss
church	**la chiesa**	lah kee-**eh**-zah
	la basilica	lah bah-**seel**-i-kah
closed for holidays	**chiuso per le ferie**	kee-oo-zoh pair leh **fair**-ee-eh
garden	**il giardino**	eel jar-dee-noh
library	**la biblioteca**	lah beeb-lee-oh-**teh**-kah
museum	**il museo**	eel moo-**zeh**-oh
railway station	**la stazione**	lah stah-tsee-**oh**-neh
tourist information	**l'ufficio di turismo**	loo-**fee**-choh dee too-**ree**-smoh

NUMBERS

1	uno	**oo**-noh
2	due	**doo**-eh
3	tre	treh
4	quattro	**kwat**-roh
5	cinque	**ching**-kweh
6	sei	**say**-ee
7	sette	**set**-teh
8	otto	**ot**-toh
9	nove	**noh**-veh
10	dieci	dee-**eh**-chee
11	undici	**oon**-dee-chee
12	dodici	**doh**-dee-chee
13	tredici	**tray**-dee-chee
14	quattordici	kwat-**tor**-dee-chee
15	quindici	**kwin**-dee-chee
16	sedici	**say**-dee-chee
17	diciassette	dee-chah-**set**-teh
18	diciotto	dee-**chot**-toh
19	diciannove	dee-chah-**noh**-veh
20	venti	**ven**-tee
30	trenta	**tren**-tah
40	quaranta	kwah-**ran**-tah
50	cinquanta	ching-**kwan**-tah
60	sessanta	sess-**an**-tah
70	settanta	set-**tan**-tah
80	ottanta	ot-**tan**-tah
90	novanta	noh-**van**-tah
100	cento	**chen**-toh
1,000	mille	**mee**-leh
2,000	duemila	**doo**-eh **mee**-lah
5,000	cinquemila	**ching**-kweh **mee**-lah
1,000,000	un milione	oon meel-**yoh**-neh

TIME, DAYS, MONTHS, SEASONS

one minute	un minuto	oon mee-**noo**-toh
one hour	un'ora	oon **or**-ah
half an hour	mezz'ora	medz-**or**-ah
a day	un giorno	oon **jor**-noh
a week	una settimana	oona set-tee-**mah**-nah
Monday	lunedì	loo-neh-**dee**
Tuesday	martedì	mar-teh-**dee**
Wednesday	mercoledì	mair-koh-leh-**dee**
Thursday	giovedì	joh-veh-**dee**
Friday	venerdì	ven-air-**dee**
Saturday	sabato	**sah**-bah-toh
Sunday	domenica	doh-**meh**-nee-kah
January	gennaio	jen-**nah**-yo
February	febbraio	feb-**bra**-yo
March	marzo	**mar**-tzo
April	aprile	a-**pree**-leh
May	maggio	**mah**-jo
June	giugno	**joo**-nyo
July	luglio	**loo**-lyo
August	agosto	ag-**os**-toh
September	settembre	set-**tem**-bre
October	ottobre	ot-**toh**-bre
November	novembre	no-**vem**-bre
December	dicembre	dee-**chem**-bre
Spring	primavera	pree-mah-**veh**-ra
Summer	estate	es-**tah**-te
Autumn	autunno	ow-**toon**-noh
Winter	inverno	een-**vair**-no
Christmas	Natale	nah-**tah**-le
Christmas Eve	la Vigilia di Natale	vee-**jee**-lya dee nah-**tah**-le
Good Friday	Venerdì Santo	ven-air-**dee** san-toh
Easter	Pasqua	**pas**-kwa
New Year	Capodanno	kah-poh-**dan**-noh
New Year's Eve	San Silvestro	san seel-**ves**-tro
Whitsun	Pentecoste	pente-**kos**-te

TRAVELLING

adult	l'adulto	ad-**ool**-toh
airport	l'aeroporto	a-air-oh-**por**-toh
baggage claim	il ritiro bagagli	ree-**tee**-roh bah-**gal**-yee
boarding card	la carta d'imbarco	**kar**-tah deem-**bar**-koh
boat	la barca	**bar**-kah
booking office	la biglietteria	beel-yet-teh-**ree**-ah
bus	l'autobus	**ow**-toh-booss
bus stop	la fermata dell'autobus	fer-**mah**-tah del-**ow**-toh-booss
check-in desk	l'accettazione	achet-ah-**tzyoh**-neh
luggage	i bagagli	bah-**gal**-yee
child (male)	il bambino	bam-**bee**-noh
child (female)	la bambina	bam-**bee**-nah
coach (bus)	la corriera	kor-ee-**air**-ah
connection	la coincidenza	ko-een-chee-**den**-tza

couchette	la cuccetta	koo-**chet**-tah
customs	la dogana	doh-**gah**-nah
delay	ritardo	ree-**tar**-doh
domestic	nazionale	natz-yoh-**nah**-leh
exit gate	l'uscita	oo-**shee**-tah
fare	la tariffa	tah-**reef**-fah
ferry	il traghetto	trah-**get**-toh
first class	prima classe	**pree**-mah **klas**-seh
flight	il volo	**voh**-loh
left luggage	il deposito bagagli	deh-**poh**-zee-toh bah-**gal**-yee
lost property	l'ufficio oggetti smarriti	oof-**fee**-cho **ojet**-tee zmar-**ree**-tee
luggage trolley	il carrello	kar-**rel**-loh
non-smoking	non fumatori	**noh**-n foo-mah-**toh**-ree
passport	il passaporto	pas-sah-**por**-toh
platform	il binario	bee-**nah**-ree-o
railway	la ferrovia	fer-roh-**vee**-a
reservation	la prenotazione	pre-noh-**tatz**-yoh-neh
return ticket	andata e ritorno	an-**dah**-tah ay ree-**tor**-no
seat	il posto	**poss**-toh
second class	seconda classe	sek-**on**-dah **klas**-seh
single ticket	solo andata	**soh**-loh an-**dah**-tah
smoking	fumatori	foo-mah-**toh**-ree
station	la stazione	statz-**yoh**-neh
supplement	il supplemento	soop-leh-**men**-toh
taxi	il taxi	**tak**-si
ticket	il biglietto	beel-**yet**-to
timetable	l'orario	oh-**rah**-ry-oh
train	il treno	**treh**-noh
underground	la metropolitana	met-roh-poh-lee-**tah**-nah

MOTORING

Fill her up	il pieno	eel **pyeh**-noh
Do you do repairs?	Effettua riparazioni?	ef-**fet**-tua ree-paratz-**yoh**-nee?
I'd like to hire a car	Vorrei noleggiare una macchina	vor-**ray** noh-ledg-**ah**-re oona **mah**-keena
automatic	con il cambio automatico	kon eel **kam**-bee-oh ow-toh-**mah**-tee-koh
boot	il portabagagli	porta-bah-**gal**-yee
car	l'automobile, la macchina	ow-toh-**moh**-bee-leh **mah**-kee-nah
car ferry	il traghetto	trah-**geh**-toh
diesel oil	gasolio	gaz-**oh**-lyo
garage (repairs)	il meccanico	mek-**ah**-neeko
four-star petrol	benzina super	ben-**dzee**-na **soo**-per
licence	la patente	pah-**ten**-teh
motorbike	la motocicletta	moh-toh-chee-**kleh**-ta
motorway	l'autostrada	ow-toh-**strah**-da
petrol	la benzina	ben-**dzeena**
petrol station	la stazione di servizio	statz-**yoh**-neh dee sair-**veetz**-yo
ring road	raccordo anulare	rak-**or**-do an-oo-**lah**-re
road	la strada	**strah**-da
traffic lights	il semaforo	sem-**ah**-foh-roh
unleaded petrol	benzina senza piombo	ben-**dzeena** sen-dza peeom-**boh**

SIGNS YOU MAY SEE ON THE ROAD

accendere i fari	headlights on
caduta massi	falling rocks
divieto di accesso	no entry
divieto di sosta	no stopping
dogana	customs
escluso residenti	residents only
ghiaccio	ice
lavori in corso	roadworks
nebbia	fog
parcheggio a pagamento	paying car park
parcheggio custodito	car park with attendant
pedaggio	toll
pericolo	danger
rallentare	reduce speed
senso unico	one way
uscita camion	works exit
zona pedonale	pedestrian area

(pronunciations for signs:)
ach-**en**-deh-reh / ee **fah**-ree / kah-**doo**-tah **mah**-see / dee-**vyeh**-toh dee ach-**eh**-so / dee-**vyeh**-toh dee **sos**-tah / dog-**ah**-nah / es-**kloo**-so reh-zi-**den**-ti / **gyah**-cho / lah-**voh**-ree een kor-so / **neb**-bya / par-**kej**-yo / a pah-gah-**men**-toh / par-**kej**-yo koo-sto-**dee**-toh / peh-**daj**-oh / peh-**ree**-koh-loh / rah-lehn-tah-reh / **sen**-tzo oo-nee-ko / oo-**shee**-tah **kah**-myon / **dzoh**-na peh-doh-**nah**-leh

STAYING IN A HOTEL

Do you have any vacant rooms?	**Avete camere libere?**	ah-**veh**-teh **kah**-mair-eh **lee**-bair-eh?
double room	**una camera doppia**	oona **kah**-mair-ah **doh**-pee-ah
with double bed	**con letto matrimoniale**	kon **let**-toh mah-tree-moh-nee-**ah**-leh
twin room	**una camera con due letti**	oona **kah**-mair-ah kon **doo**-eh **let**-tee
single room	**una camera singola**	oona **kah**-mair-ah **sing**-goh-lah
room with a bath, shower	**una camera con bagno, con doccia**	oona **kah**-mair-ah kon **ban**-yoh, kon **dot**-chah
I have a reservation.	**Ho fatto una prenotazione.**	oh **fat**-toh oona preh-noh-tah-tsee-**oh**-neh
balcony	**balcone**	bal-**coh**-neh
breakfast	**prima colazione**	**pree**-ma coh-lah-**tzyoh**-neh
key	**la chiave**	lah kee-**ah**-veh
porter	**il facchino**	eel fah-**kee**-noh
room service	**servizio in camera**	ser-**vitz**-yoh een **cah**-meh-rah

EATING OUT

Have you got a table for ...?	**Avete una tavola per ... ?**	ah-**veh**-teh oona **tah**-voh-lah pair ...?
I'd like to reserve a table.	**Vorrei riservare una tavola.**	vor-**ray** ree-sair-**vah**-reh oona **tah**-voh-lah
the bill, please.	**il conto, per favore.**	**kon**-toh pair fah-**vor**-eh
I am a vegetarian.	**Sono vegetariano/a.**	**soh**-noh **veh**-jeh-tar-ee-**ah**-noh/nah
beer	**la birra**	**bee**-rah
bread	**il pane**	**pah**-neh
bottle	**la bottiglia**	bot-**teel**-yah
breakfast	**la prima colazione**	pree-mah koh-lah-tsee-**oh**-neh
butter	**il burro**	**boor**-roh
carafe	**la caraffa**	kah-rah-**fah**
child's portion	**una porzione per bambini**	portz-**yoh**-neh pair bam-**bee**-nee
coffee	**il caffè**	kaf-**feh**
cover charge	**il coperto**	koh-**pair**-toh
cup	**la tazza**	**tat**-zah
dessert	**il dessert**	des-**ser**
dinner	**la cena**	**cheh**-nah
dish of the day	**il piatto del giorno**	pee-**ah**-toh dell **jor**-no
first course	**il primo**	**pree**-moh
fixed price menu	**il menù a prezzo fisso**	meh-**noo** ah **pret**-soh **fee**-soh
fork	**la forchetta**	for-**ket**-tah
glass	**il bicchiere**	bee-kee-**air**-eh
half-litre	**da mezzo litro**	da **met**-zoh **lee**-troh
knife	**il coltello**	kol-**tel**-loh
litre	**un litro**	**lee**-troh
lunch	**il pranzo**	**pran**-tsoh
main course	**il secondo**	seh-**kon**-doh
medium *(meat)*	**al punto**	al **poon**-toh
menu	**il menù**	meh-**noo**
milk	**il latte**	**lat**-teh
pepper	**il pepe**	**peh**-peh
plate	**il piatto**	p-**yat**-toh
rare *(meat)*	**al sangue**	al **sang**-gweh
receipt *(in bars)*	**lo scontrino**	skon-**tree**-noh
(in restaurants)	**la ricevuta**	ree-cheh-**voo**-tah
restaurant	**il ristorante**	rees-toh-**ran**-teh
salad	**l'insalata**	een-sah-**lah**-tah
salt	**il sale**	**sah**-leh
sandwich	**il panino**	pan-**ee**-noh
serviette	**il tovagliolo**	toh-val-**yoh**-loh
snack	**lo spuntino**	spoon-**tee**-noh
soup	**la minestra**	mee-**nes**-trah
spoon	**il cucchiaio**	koo-kee-**eye**-oh
starter	**l'antipasto**	an-tee-**pas**-toh
sugar	**lo zucchero**	dzoo-keh-roh
tea	**il tè**	teh
teaspoon	**il cucchiaino**	kook-yah-**ee**-noh
tip	**la mancia**	**man**-cha
vegetables	**il contorno**	eel kon-**tor**-noh
waitress	**la cameriera**	kah-mair-ee-**air**-ah
waiter	**il cameriere**	kah-mair-ee-**air**-eh
water	**l'acqua**	**ak**-wah
fizzy/still	**gassata/naturale**	gah-**zah**-tah/ nah-too-**rah**-leh
well done *(meat)*	**ben cotto**	ben **kot**-toh
wine	**il vino**	**vee**-noh
wine list	**la lista dei vini**	**lee**-stah day **vee**-nee

MENU DECODER

abbacchio	ab-**ak**-yoh	spring lamb
acciughe	ach-**oo**-geh	anchovies
aceto	ach-**eh**-toh	vinegar
acqua minerale	**ah**-kwah mee-nair-	mineral water
gassata/naturale	**ah**-leh gah-**zah**-tah/ nah-too-**rah**-leh	fizzy/still
aglio	**al**-ee-oh	garlic
agnello	ah-**niell**-oh	lamb
al forno	al **for**-noh	baked
alla griglia	ah-lah **greel**-yah	grilled
albicocche	al-bee-**kok**-eh	apricots
ananas	**an**-an-ass	pineapple
anatra	**an**-at-rah	duck
anguria	an-**goo**-rya	water melon
antipasti	ahn-ti-**pas**-ti	starters
aperitivo	apeh-ree-**tee**-voh	aperitif
aragosta	ara-**goss**-tah	lobster
arancia	ah-**ran**-cha	orange
aringa	ah-**reen**-gah	herring
arrosto	ar-**ross**-toh	roast
asparagi	as-**pah**-rah-ji	asparagus
baccalà	bak-al-**la**	dried cod
basilico	bas-**ee**-lee-ko	basil
besciamella	besh-ah-**mel**-ah	white sauce
birra	**beer**-rah	beer
bistecca	bees-**tek**-ka	steak
bottarga	bot-**ahr**-gah	salted mullet roe
branzino	bran-**zee**-no	sea bass
brasato	bra-**sah**-toh	braised beef
bresaola	breh-**sah**-oh-lah	slices of cold, wind-dried beef with oil and lemon
brioche	bri-**osh**	type of croissant
brodo	**broh**-doh	clear broth
budino	boo-**dee**-no	pudding
burro	**boor**-oh	butter
caffè	kah-**feh**	espresso coffee
caffè corretto	kah-**feh** koh-**reh**-toh	espresso coffee with a dash of liqueur
caffè lungo	kah-**feh** loon-goh	weak espresso coffee
caffè macchiato	kah-**feh** mak-**yah**-toh	espresso coffee with a dash of milk
caffè ristretto	kah-**feh** ree-**streh**-toh	strong espresso coffee
caffelatte	kah-**feh**-**lah**-teh	half coffee, half milk
calamari	kah-lah-**mah**-ree	squid
calzone	kal-**zoh**-neh	folded pizza filled with tomato and mozzarella
camomilla	kah-moh-**mee**-lah	camomile tea
cannella	kan-**el**-ah	cinnamon
cannelloni	kan-eh-**loh**-nee	stuffed pasta tubes
cappuccino	kap-oo-**chee**-noh	coffee with foaming milk
carciofi	kar-**choh**-fee	artichokes
carne	**kar**-neh	meat
carote	kar-**roh**-teh	carrots
castagne	kas-**tan**-yeh	chestnuts
cavolfiore	kavol-**fyoh**-reh	cauliflower
cavolo	**kah**-voh-loh	cabbage
cefalo	**che**-fah-loh	grey mullet
cernia	**cher**-nya	grouper *(fish)*
ciambella	cham-**bella**	ring-shaped cake
cicoria	chih-**kor**-ya	chicory
ciliege	chil-**yej**-eh	cherries
cioccolata	choc-oh-**lah**-tah	chocolate
cipolle	chip-**oh**-leh	onions
coniglio	kon-**ee**-lyo	rabbit
contorni	kon-**tor**-nee	vegetables
coperto	kop-**er**-toh	cover charge
coppa	**koh**-pah	cured pork, sliced finely and eaten cold
cordula	**kor**-doo-lah	Sardinian spit-roasted plaited lamb entrails
cotoletta	kot-oh-**let**-ta	pork or lamb chop
cozze	**kot**-zeh	mussels
crema	**kreh**-mah	custard dessert
crespella	**kres**-pel-lah	savoury pancake
crostata di frutta	kros-**tah**-tah dee **froo**-tah	fruit tart
datteri	**dat**-eh-ree	dates
digestivo	dee-jes-**tee**-voh	digestive liqueur
dolci	**dol**-chi	desserts, cakes
espresso	es-**pres**-soh	strong black coffee
fagiano	fah-**jah**-noh	pheasant
fagioli	fah-**joh**-lee	beans
fagiolini	fah-joh-**lee**-nee	long, green beans
fegato	**feh**-gah-toh	liver
fettuccine	feh-too-**chee**-neh	ribbon-shaped pasta
fichi	**fee**-kee	figs

Italian	Pronunciation	Meaning
filetto	fee-**leh**-toh	fillet (of beef)
finocchio	fee-**noh**-kyo	fennel
formaggio	for-**maj**-yo	cheese
fragole	**frah**-goh-leh	strawberries
frappé	frap-**eh**	whisked fruit or milk drink with ice
fregula	**freh**-goo-lah	small, granular pasta
frittata	free-**tah**-tah	type of omelette
fritto	**free**-toh	deep fried
fritto misto	**free**-toh mees-toh	seafood in batter
frittura di pesce	free-**too**-rah dee **pesh**-eh	variety of fried fish
frutta	**froo**-tah	fruit
frutta secca	**froo**-tah sek-kah	dried fruit
frutti di mare	**froo**-tee dee mah-reh	seafood
funghi	**foon**-g-ee	mushrooms
gamberetti	gam-beh-**reh**-tee	shrimps
gamberi	**gam**-beh-ree	prawns
gamberoni	gam-beh-**roh**-nee	king prawns
gelato	gel-**ah**-toh	ice cream
gnocchi	**nyok**-ee	small flour and potato dumplings
gorgonzola	gor-gon-**zoh**-lah	strong, soft blue cheese
granchio	**gran**-kyo	crab
granita	gra-**nee**-tah	drink with crushed ice
grissini	gree-**see**-nee	thin, crisp breadsticks
insalata	een-sah-**lah**-tah	salad
involtini	een-vol-**tee**-nee	meat rolls stuffed with ham and herbs
lamponi	lam-**poh**-nee	raspberries
latte	**lah**-teh	milk
lattuga	lah-**too**-gah	lettuce
leggero	leh-**jeh**-roh	light
legumi	leh-**goo**-mee	pulses
lenticchie	len-**teek**-yeh	lentils
lesso	**less**-oh	boiled
lepre	**leh**-preh	hare
limone	lee-**moh**-neh	lemon
lingua	**leen**-gwa	tongue
macedonia di frutta	mach-eh-**doh**-nya dee froo-tah	fruit salad
maiale	mah-**yah**-leh	pork
mandarino	man-dah-**ree**-noh	mandarin
mandorla	**man**-dor-lah	almond
manzo	**man**-dzo	beef
mascarpone	mah-skar-**poh**-neh	soft, sweet cheese
mela	**meh**-lah	apple
melanzane	meh-lan-**zah**-neh	aubergines
melone	meh-**loh**-neh	melon
menta	**men**-tah	mint
merluzzo	mer-**loo**-tzoh	cod
minestrone	mee-nes-**troh**-neh	thick vegetable soup
mirtilli	meer-**tee**-lee	bilberries
more	**mor**-eh	blackberries
nasello	nah-**seh**-loh	hake
nocciole	noch-**oh**-leh	hazelnuts
noce moscata	**noh**-che mos-**kah**-tah	nutmeg
noci	**noh**-chi	walnuts
olio	**oh**-lyo	oil
orata	oh-**rah**-tah	gilthead bream
origano	oh-**ree**-gah-noh	oregano
ossobuco	os-oh-**boo**-ko	stewed shin of veal
ostriche	**os**-tree-keh	oysters
pane carasau	**pah**-neh cah-rah-**sahw**	bread crisp, circular bread
panino	pah-**nee**-noh	filled roll
panna	**pah**-nah	cream
parmigiana di melanzane	par-mee-**jah**-nah de meh-lan-zah-neh	aubergine, tomato, mozarella and parmesan bake
parmigiano	par-mee-**jah**-noh	parmesan cheese
pasticcio	pas-**tich**-oh	pasta and meat bake
patate	pah-**tah**-teh	potatoes
pecorino	peh-coh-**ree**-noh	strong, hard ewe's milk cheese
penne	peh-**neh**	pasta quills
pepe	**peh**-peh	pepper (spice)
peperoncino	peh-peh-**ron**-chee-noh	cayenne pepper
peperoni	peh-peh-**roh**-nee	peppers
pera	**peh**-rah	pear
pesca	**pes**-kah	peach
pesce	**pesh**-eh	fish
piselli	pee-**seh**-lee	peas
polenta	poh-**len**-tah	boiled cornmeal with meat or vegetables
pollo	**poh**-loh	chicken
polpette	pol-**peh**-teh	meatballs
polpettone	pol-**peh**-toh-neh	meatloaf
pomodori	poh-moh-**doh**-ree	tomatoes
pompelmo	pom-**pel**-moh	grapefruit
porceddu	por-**ched**-doo	roast suckling pig
porri	**poh**-ree	leeks
prezzemolo	pretz-**eh**-moh-loh	parsley
primi piatti	**pree**-mee **pyah**-tee	first courses
prosciutto cotto/crudo	pro-**shoo**-toh **kot**-toh/**kroo**-doh	ham cooked/cured
prugne	**proo**-nyeh	plums
radicchio	rah-**deek**-yo	red chicory
ragù	rah-**goo**	mince and tomato sauce
ravanelli	rah-vah-**neh**-lee	radishes
ravioli	rah-vee-**oh**-lee	square-shaped egg pasta filled with meat
razza	**rah**-tzah	skate
ricotta	ree-**kot**-tah	white, soft cheese
ripieno	**ree**-pyeh-noh	stuffed
riso	**ree**-soh	rice
risotto	ree-**soh**-toh	rice cooked in stock
rognone	ron-**yoh**-neh	kidney
rosato	roh-**sah**-toh	rosé wine
rosolato	roh-soh-**lah**-toh	fried
rosmarino	ros-mah-**ree**-noh	rosemary
salame	sah-**lah**-meh	salami
sale	**sah**-leh	salt
salsa	**sal**-sah	sauce
salsiccia	sal-**see**-cha	sausage
salvia	**sal**-vya	sage
scaloppine	skah-loh-**pee**-neh	veal escalopes
seadas	say-**ah**-dahs	sweet cheese and lemon fritters
secco	**seh**-koh	dry
secondi piatti	seh-**kon**-dee pyat-ee	main courses
sedano	**seh**-dah-noh	celery
selvaggina	sel-vah-**jee**-nah	game
semifreddo	**seh**-mee-**freh**-doh	ice cream and sponge dessert
senape	**seh**-nah-peh	mustard
seppie	**sep**-pee-eh	cuttlefish
servizio compreso	ser-**vitz**-yo com-**preh**-soh	service charge included
servizio escluso	ser-**vitz**-yo es-**cloo**-so	service charge not included
sogliola	**sol**-yoh-lah	sole
sorbetto	sor-**bet**-oh	sorbet
speck	sp-**ek**	cured, smoked ham
spezzatino	spetz-ah-**tee**-noh	stew
spiedini	spyeh-**dee**-nee	meat or fish on a spit
spinaci	spee-**nah**-chee	spinach
spremuta	spreh-**moo**-tah	freshly squeezed juice
spumante	spoo-**man**-teh	sparkling wine
stufato	stoo-**fah**-toh	casserole
tacchino	tak-**ee**-noh	turkey
tagliatelle	tah-lyah-**teh**-leh	flat strips of egg pasta
tartine	tar-**tee**-neh	small sandwiches
tartufo	tar-**too**-foh	ice cream covered in cocoa
tè	teh	tea
tiramisù	tee-rah-mee-**soo**	dessert of coffee-soaked sponge, Marsala and mascarpone
tisana	tee-**zah**-nah	herbal tea
tonno	toh-**noh**	tuna
torta	tor-**tah**	tart, cake
torta salata	**tor**-tah sah-**lah**-tah	savoury flan
tortellini	tor-teh-**lee**-nee	stuffed pasta shapes
triglia	**tree**-lya	red mullet
trippa	tree-**pah**	tripe
trota	**troh**-tah	trout
uova	oo-**wo**-va	eggs
uova sode	oo-**wo**-va **soh**-deh	hard-boiled eggs
uva	**oo**-va	grapes
verdura	ver-**doo**-rah	vegetables
vino	**vee**-noh	wine
vino bianco	**vee**-noh **byan**-ko	white wine
vino da dessert	**vee**-noh dah deh-**ser**	dessert wine
vino da pasto	**vee**-noh dah **pas**-toh	table wine
vino da tavola	**vee**-noh dah **tah**-voh-lah	table wine
vino rosso	**vee**-noh **ros**-soh	red wine
vitello	vee-**tel**-loh	veal
vongole	**von**-goh-leh	clams
zafferano	zah-fair-**ah**-noh	saffron
zucca	**dzoo**-kah	pumpkin
zucchero	**dzoo**-kair-oh	sugar
zucchine	dzoo-**kee**-neh	courgettes
zuppa	dzoo-**pah**	soup
zuppa inglese	dzoo-**pah** een-**gleh**-seh	trifle

Acknowledgments

DORLING KINDERSLEY would like to thank the following organizations and people whose contributions have made the preparation of this book possible:

SPECIAL ASSISTANCE

Agriturismo di Lucia Sotgiu, Agriturismo Sa Perda Marcada, Hertz, Claire Littlejohn, Hotel Mediterraneo, Greca Mattan, Meridiana, Anna Chiara Montefusco, Filomena Rosato, Anna Sacripanti, Terranostra Sardegna.

DESIGN AND EDITORIAL ASSISTANCE

Gillian Allen, Samantha Borland, Antonugo Cerletti, Michelle Clark, Cooling Brown, Felicity Crowe, Vivien Crump, Fay Franklin, Annette Jacobs, Georgina Matthews, Lee Redmond, Ingrid Vienings, Tiziana Tuveri.

PICTURE CREDITS

Key: t=top; tl=top left; tlc=top left centre; tc= top centre; trc=top right centre; tr=top right; cla=centre left above; ca=centre above; cra=centre right above; cl=centre left; c=centre; cr=centre right; clb=centre left below; crb=centre right below; cb=centre below; bl=bottom left; br=bottom right; b=bottom; bc=bottom centre; bcl=bottom centre left; bcr=bottom centre right.

All the photographs were taken by the photographic agency OVERSEAS S.r.l., except for the following:

FABRIZIO ARDITO, Rome: 22tr, 22br, 23cr, 32cr, 33bl, 33br, 37t, 59b, 82b, 83b, 85b, 85c, 96b, 99c, 99cr, 102b, 103cl, 104t, 104bl, 105t, 106tl, 106cr, 106b, 108c, 111tl, 111cr, 116tr, 116cl, 119cl, 120t, 121t, 124l, 124c, 124b, 125t, 150t, 150b, 151tl, 151cr, 151br, 151cl, 152tl, 153tl, 155cr, 156tl, 156tr, 156c, 156b, 157tl, 157tr, 157c, 157b, 158tr, 158c, 158l, 159tl, 159tr, 159b, 164cr, 165t, 165c, 170b.

ANTONIO MANNU, Sassari: 24tl, 24cl, 24bl, 25tl, 25tr, 26tr, 28tc, 32bl, 41br, 43cr, 48tr, 52cl, 72tl, 95b, 102bcl, 103tl, 113b, 117tl, 117cra, 117bcr, 118cl, 118bl, 119cl, 121tl, 126tr, 126cr, 126bl, 127cr, 128tl, 129cr, 129b, 134cl, 134br, 135tl, 136t, 136bl, 154br, 154bl, 157cr, 157br, 160tl, 160cl, 160br, 162tr, 162bl, 163tc, 163b, 189tr.

RACCOLTA DELLE STAMPE ACHILLE BERTARELLI, Milan: 30b, 36, 37c, 37bl, 38c, 38b.

FABIO BRAIBANTI, Milan: 139, 147tr, 179c, 188cl, 191bl, 191tr, 191crb.

FABIO DE ANGELIS, Milan: 32tr, 32cra, 143bl, 190c, 191cr.

EUROPEAN COMMISSION, 197b

CRISTINA GAMBARO, Milan: 23b, 70cl, 70c, 91c, 108t, 109cl, 140b.

ILISSO EDIZIONI, Nuoro: 159cra, 159crb.

IMAGE BANK, Milan: 51bc, 127, 130t, 138.

ALFIO ELIO QUATTROCCHI, Cagliari: 20tr, 39t, 42cl, 53t, 62b, 70tr, 106tr, 109cr, 145t, 149t, 165b, 190bl, 191br.

FRANCINE RECULEZ, Milan: 180, 181, 191bc.

JACKET
Front - CORBIS: Archivo Iconografico S. A. c; Hubert Stadler bc; ROBERT HARDING PICTURE LIBRARY: S. Terry cl; THE IMAGE BANK/GETTY IMAGES: Paolo Curto main image.
Back - CORBIS: Patrick Ward t; ROBERT HARDING PICTURE LIBRARY: John Miller b.
Spine - THE IMAGE BANK/GETTY IMAGES: Paolo Curto.

Road Map of Sardinia